NEW DIRECTIONS IN MACHINE TRANSLATION

Distributed Language Translation

The goal of these series is to publish texts which are related to computational linguistics and machine translation in general, and the DLT (Distributed Language Translation) research project in particular.

Series editor
Toon Witkam
B.S.O./Research
P.O. Box 8348, NL-3503 RH Utrecht
The Netherlands

Other books in this series:

1. B.C. Papegaaij, V. Sadler and A.P.M. Witkam (eds.)
   Word Expert Semantics
2. Klaus Schubert
   Metataxis
3. Bart Papegaaij and Klaus Schubert
   Text Coherence in Translation

Dan Maxwell
Klaus Schubert
Toon Witkam (eds.)

NEW DIRECTIONS IN MACHINE TRANSLATION

Conference Proceedings,
Budapest 18-19 August, 1988

1988
FORIS PUBLICATIONS
Dordrecht - Holland/Providence RI - U.S.A.

Published by:
Foris Publications Holland
P.O. Box 509
3300 AM Dordrecht, The Netherlands

Distributor for the U.S.A. and Canada:
Foris Publications USA, Inc.
P.O. Box 5904
Providence RI 02903
U.S.A.

Sole distributor for Japan:
Toppan Company, Ltd.
Sufunotomo Bldg.
1-6, Kanda Surugadai
Chiyoda-ku
Tokyo 101, Japan

CIP-DATA

In co-operation with BSO, Utrecht
and John von Neumann Society, Budapest

ISBN 90 6765 377 2 (Bound)
ISBN 90 6765 378 0 (Paper)

Printed in the Netherlands by ICG Printing, Dordrecht.

Preface

Machine Translation has now become so intensive a field of activity, especially over the last few years, that it is hardly possible to give a complete cross-section of it at one single conference. It is significant that at the bi-annual COLING conferences, the largest gatherings of computational linguists, MT has become the biggest section. And an increasing number of specialized conference series, each one with a somewhat different 'footing' cover MT annually or bi-annually: MT Summit (Hakone, München), ASLIB (London), International Conference on Theoretical and Methodological Issues in MT (Colgate/Carnegie Mellon), etc.

In contrast to this seemingly established field, "New Directions in Machine Translation" attempts to highlight some new approaches and viewpoints, against the background of an up-to-date worldwide overview. The focus of attention is shifted towards the revived issue of interlingual vs. transfer architectures and new developments such as knowledge-based terminology.

The 'internationality ratio' was 104 conference participants from 26 different countries. The advantages of a 'compact' conference (16 papers in 2 days, no parallel sessions) worked out well, and it seems that the intangible but critical mass of keen interest and community sense was attained. Because of a relatively large percentage (20%) of participants versatile in Esperanto, we decided to include summaries in this language at the end of each paper.

We thank all involved in making this conference a success. To keep it "small and beautiful" we unfortunately had to turn down a few spontaneous last-minute requests for delivery of a paper. We are particularly grateful to Prof. Dr. Sgall, for his Summing-up Talk, and to our Budapest co-organizers.

Utrecht, October 1988 Toon Witkam

NEW DIRECTIONS IN MACHINE TRANSLATION

International Conference

Budapest 18-19 August 1988

Programme Committee

Dr. Dan Maxwell
Dr. Klaus Schubert
A. P. M. Witkam

Honorary Committee

Prof. Dr. Bálint Dömölki (Budapest)
Prof. Brian Harris (Ottawa)
Prof. Alan K. Melby (Provo)
Prof. Frank E. Knowles (Birmingham)
Prof. Dr. István Szerdahelyi † (Budapest)
Prof. Dr. Tibor Vámos (Budapest)

Organizing Committee

Mária Tóth
Gizella Hetthéssy
Dr. Péter Broczkó
Ilona Koutny
Birgitta van Loon
Toon Witkam

Contents

Recent Developments in Machine Translation
A Review of the Last Five Years

W. John Hutchins

University of East Anglia
The Library
Norwich NR4 7TJ
Great Britain

I. General overview

Ten years ago MT was still emerging from the decade of neglect which succeeded the ALPAC report. The revival of MT can be attributed to a number of events in the mid 1970's: the decision in 1976 by the Commission of the European Communities (CEC) to purchase the Systran system for development of translation systems for languages of the Community; the first public MT system (METEO) for translating weather reports from English into French; the beginnings of AI-oriented research on natural language processing including MT; and, in particular, the appearance of the first commercial systems ALPS and Weidner, followed shortly by Logos. It was perhaps these systems, however crude in terms of linguistic quality, which more than anything else alerted the translation profession to the possibilities of exploiting the increasing sophistication of computers in the service of translation. By the early 1980's there were again research projects in the United States, Japan and Europe.

Yet the greatest expansion of MT activity has occurred in the last five years; the level of global MT activity has probably reached, if not exceeded the highest levels during the mid 1960's at the time of the ALPAC report. Interest has grown steadily in Europe and again in the United States, but undoubtedly the greatest surge has occurred in Japan. "A rough guess would indicate that 800-900 people are presently engaged in research and development of MT systems in Japan" (Sigurdson/Greatrex 1987). The largest groups in Europe and the United States (those connected with Systran, the projects at Grenoble (GETA), Saarbrücken (SUSY, ASCOF), Utrecht (DLT) and Eindhoven (Rosetta), and the CEC (Eurotra project) probably involve in total about 250-300 persons. Non-Japanese commercial systems may account for another 150-200, and all other projects worldwide may well involve no more than a further 400. In numerical terms the dominance of Japan is clear.

The largest growth area has been in the marketing and sale of commercial MT systems, many for personal computers, and in the provision of MT-based services. The picture in MT research has also changed: in the early 1980's it was still concentrated largely in well-established projects at universities (Grenoble, Saarbrücken, Montreal, Texas, Kyoto, and the Eurotra project) and in connection with systems such as Systran, Logos, ALPS and Weidner; although these centres continue (except for the TAUM project in Montreal), most growth in the past five years has been in MT research supported by commercial companies (generally in the area of computer manufacture and software development), and in small-scale projects by individuals and small groups (often microcomputer-based AI-oriented experimental models).

This paper is an attempt to survey the field in this period and to provide, in effect, an updating of the historical review completed in late 1984 and early 1985 (Hutchins 1986). The aim is to give a general picture of the recent developments of systems and projects already established at that time and to document the emergence of new systems and projects worldwide. Descriptions of individual systems are given in section II. This part outlines the main issues and lines of development at the present time. There is no claim of completeness, but it is hoped that all significant activities have been noticed.

Together with the increased activity there has been a marked growth in publication in recent years. Monographs devoted exclusively to MT topics were rare in the 1970's; since the mid 1980's they have become frequent (e.g. Blatt et al.1985, Bennett et al. 1986, Hutchins 1986, Papegaaij 1986, Luckhardt 1987, Schubert 1987, Goshawke et al. 1987, Lehrberger/Bourbeau 1988). In addition there has been growth in the publication of proceedings of conferences devoted exclusively or partially to MT and MT-related topics (e.g. Coling 84, Picken 1985, Coling 86, Bátori/Weber 1986, Picken 1986, King 1987, Nirenburg 1987, Wilss/Schmitz 1987, Picken 1987, Slocum 1988). Other collections of articles have appeared edited by Bátori/Weber (1986) and by Slocum (1988); the latter of papers which had previously appeared in *Computational Linguistics*, the foremost journal in its field. The recent successful foundation of a journal devoted to MT (*Computers and Translation*, since 1986) and the regular appearance of MT items in journals such as *Lebende Sprachen*, *Meta*, *Sprache und Datenverarbeitung*, *Language Monthly* and the recently founded *Language Technology*, all are evidence of vigour and widespread interest. Apart from the monographs mentioned above, recent general surveys of the current scene and future prospects are Slocum (1985/1988), Lewis (1985), Tsujii (1986), and Tucker (1987).

1. Classification of MT system types

The first main distinction is in terms of overall strategy: whether translation from source language (SL) to target language (TL) takes place in a single stage ('direct translation'), in two stages (via an 'interlingua') or in three stages (the 'transfer' approach).

Most of the earliest systems were based on the 'direct translation' approach: systems were designed specifically for a particular language pair, analysis of the source language was limited to problems arising specifically in the translation into a particular target language, so that lexical items and structural features which were considered directly equivalent were not subjected to any syntactic or semantic treatment; where structural transformations (reordering of word sequences) were necessary or where multiple choices of lexical items occurred, the most common approach was to augment the relevant SL dictionary entries with contextual information or with directions for structure changes. SL analysis in the direct approach was thus strictly TL-oriented and dictionary-driven. Direct translation systems suffered from monolithic programs inextricably confusing analysis and generation processes, linguistic data, grammatical rules and programming instructions, and above all from the lack of explicit theoretical foundations.

The interlingua approach largely grew out of dissatisfaction with the perceived inadequacies of the 'direct' approach; but not entirely, for it had long been argued that MT of good quality would only come from translation of the 'meaning' of texts and this implied translation via a (universal) conceptual representation. An additional argument had also been that multilingual MT would be most effective (and most economic) if all languages in the system were translated into and from a single intermediary representation. Various suggestions for interlinguas have been put forward, from the creation of 'logical languages' to the adoption of existing natural languages or artificial languages, and these different approaches continue to the present.

The transfer approach arose primarily in the light of experience with research on interlingua systems. A number of problems had been encountered. Firstly there was the difficulty of establishing interlingual elements, even where only two languages were involved. There was some success with basic syntactic equivalences (by analysis into logical forms), but little with lexical (conceptual) equivalences. Secondly, it was found that in the process of abstraction to language-independent representations too much information was lost about text-oriented structure, e.g. whether a particular expression was the theme (subject) or rheme (comment) of a sentence. As a result, the TL output was often incoherent. In the transfer approach the intermediary representations are not intended to be language-independent; rather SL analysis is into a SL-oriented abstract representation and TL generation is from a TL-oriented representation, and between the interfaces is a SL-TL transfer component. The 'abstractness' of interfaces differs from one system to another, as does the nature and amount of different types of information (syntactic, semantic, pragmatic).

The second main distinction concerns the nature of the relationship between the mechanised translation processes and the operators and users of the systems. Systems can be 'fully automatic' in that no human intervention occurs between input of the text in one language and output of the text in another language, i.e. translation is a 'batch' process. Alternatively, systems can be 'interactive' involving human collaboration during translation processes. Further differences within these two basic approaches are also made, so that now there is a wide variety of system types.

Within the 'fully automatic' systems a distinction can be made between systems which are designed to accept input texts only of a particular subject domain (e.g. nuclear physics) or of a particular text type (e.g. patents) and systems which do not impose such restrictions. At present, probably only Systran (sect. 1 below) is capable of tackling, in principle, any text in most subjects – and this is primarily by virtue of the large dictionaries built up over many years. In practice, most MT systems are limited to particular 'sublanguages', the vocabulary (and structures) of a specific subject field. This may be regarded by the designers as an initial constraint, to be removed as the system develops into new subject fields. However, in some cases, the sublanguage limitation has been a deliberate design decision – cf. the Smart systems (sect. 3), the Johns Hopkins system (sect. 11), SEMSYN (sect. 16), the ISSCO project (sect. 22), TITRAN (sect. 26), etc.

The revision of MT output is now accepted universally as inevitable, given the limitations of computational processing of natural language. It is an accepted feature of almost any large translation service or agency that human translations are revised, and so the 'post-editing' of MT is equally acceptable. However, the revision of MT output is quite different from the revision of human translation; in the latter case, it is usually a matter of stylistic refinement and checking for consistency of terminology. In the case of MT, consistent translation of terminology is easily achieved; what is involved is a good deal of low-level correction of 'simple' grammatical mistakes which no human translator would commit: wrong choices of pronouns, prepositions, definite and indefinite articles, etc. However, much can be done to simplify the editing facilities for post-editors, as demonstrated in the PAHO environment (sect. 2 below). For certain purposes (e.g. for information acquisition), unedited or lightly revised versions are acceptable. At the other extreme, where high quality is demanded, the MT output may be regarded as a 'pre-translation' which human translators can use as a rough guide to their own version.

The low quality output of 'fully automatic' systems has encouraged the adaptation of texts to the limitations of MT systems. This can take two forms. In the 'pre-editing' of texts, expressions and constructions are changed to those which it is known the system can deal with – or alternatively, marks are included to indicate particular usages (e.g. indicating for *light* whether it is an adjective, a noun, or a verb). A more common practice at present is the restriction of input to a constrained language (restricted in vocabulary, in order to avoid homonyms and polysemes, and restricted in the range of syntactic structures). One example is the use of Multinational Customized English by the Xerox Corporation for documents which are to be translated by Systran into a number of languages. Another example is found in the systems developed by Smart (sect. 3 below) where documents are composed in an English which is less ambiguous and vague, is easier for foreigners to understand, and is more easily translated in a MT system. It is of course possible for systems to be both designed for a particular sublanguage and to be constrained in vocabulary and syntax.

It was the limitations of MT systems also which encouraged the development of 'interactive' systems. The involvement of human 'assistants' may take place at any stage of translation processes: during analysis, during transfer, during generation, or any combination of these. From developments in the past few years it is evident that we can identify the following types of interaction:

(a) interactive analysis: assistance in the interpretation of input text, principally in the disambiguation of polysemes and complex syntactic structures.

(b) interactive rewriting: computer-initiated requests to an author to reformulate input text in a form which the program can deal with (i.e. this is effectively interactive pre-editing) – cf. NTRAN project (sect. 20 below)

(c) interactive composition: the author composes text which the computer simultaneously attempts to analyse and translate (i.e. this overlaps with the notion of restricted language input) – cf. CMU projects (sect. 10 below)

(d) interactive transfer: assistance with the selection of TL equivalences; this may involve 'disambiguation' if there is for a single SL expression more than one TL option. (The SL form may not be monolingually ambiguous, but only in the context of a given TL.)

(e) interactive generation: assistance in producing fluent output, e.g. selection of appropriate constructions in context (thematisation, topicalisation, etc.). There are no known examples at present; the process would overlap with interactive post-editing.

None of these are mutually exclusive; in fact many systems combine several types. In addition, of course, interactive systems can be subject to the same set of design criteria that apply to 'batch' systems: they can be limited to particular sublanguages, they can be restricted in vocabulary and syntax, their input may be pre-edited (as in many Japanese systems), their output may be post-edited to various levels (for high quality products, for 'information-only' purposes). In overall strategy, interactive systems can be based on the 'direct translation' approach, or on transfer or interlingua approaches, and they can operate in a bilingual or a multilingual environment. Various combinations will be found in the survey below. Nevertheless, the great variety of interactive possibilities underlines the argument that the exploration of all possible machine-aided translation options has scarcely begun.

2. MT and understanding

The major theoretical issue which faces all MT researchers is the place of artificial intelligence in MT systems: briefly, how much 'understanding' of texts is necessary for translation. There are many systems under development which incorporate AI methods involving knowledge databases, semantic networks, inference mechanisms, etc. Some prominent examples are the ASCOF system at Saarbrücken (sect. 15), DLT at Utrecht (sect. 18), the Translator project (sect. 10), the NTT's LUTE system (sect. 36), and the research at ETL in connection with the Japanese ODA project (sect. 28). The notion of grafting AI techniques onto more traditional approaches has also been proposed (e.g. expert systems in the GETA project – Boitet/Gerber 1986.) By contrast, some researchers have deliberately eschewed AI approaches in the belief that the full potentials of essentially 'linguistics'-oriented models have yet to be demonstrated: the Eurotra project of the CEC is one example (sect. 12); another is the Rosetta project at Philips (sect. 17).

In discussion of this issue, it is important to remember the distinction between implicit knowledge and explicit knowledge. Implicit knowledge is that which is incorporated in the lexical and grammatical information of the system. It is the basic knowledge of the language which is a prerequisite for any 'understanding', and comprises therefore linguistic knowledge common to all of those competent in the language (i.e. morphological, syntactic and semantic 'competence'), and it encompasses linguistic knowledge specific to the particular sublanguage(s) of a text. Explicit knowledge is the extra-linguistic knowledge which is (or can be) brought to bear in the interpretation and disambiguation when implicit linguistic knowledge is insufficient. Explicit knowledge can in fact be of two kinds: the knowledge of the subject(s) of a text which a reader calls upon (i.e. both general knowledge of reality, facts and events, and a more specific 'expertise'), and the pragmatic knowledge acquired in the course of reading, interpreting and understanding the text itself (i.e. dynamically acquired or learnt knowledge of the facts, events, opinions, suppositions, etc. described in the text). Of course, the boundaries between all these kinds of knowledge are very fluid: what has been learnt from one text may be applied as knowledge in understanding another; sublanguage knowledge is inextricably bound up with subject 'expertise'; and what is 'common' linguistic knowledge changes over time to include what in the past may have been esoteric sublanguage knowledge.

The question is not whether understanding has a role in MT but how large a role it should have, and specifically how far MT systems should go in the direction of programs for natural language understanding (NLU). In general NLU programs (mainly in the context of AI) have been designed for specific purposes or tasks, e.g. in domain-specific retrieval systems, in systems for paraphrasing, and in systems for composing newspaper summaries; thus 'understanding' is effectively determined by specific expectations of text content or potential users' interests, often expressed in terms of 'scripts' or 'schemata'. NLU systems are concerned above all with the content and the message, and not the specific linguistic (discourse) framework in which the content is conveyed; once the 'message' has been extracted, the linguistic 'form' can be disregarded. But MT has to embrace all aspects of texts, only some of which are language-independent (universal) and only some of which involve extra-linguistic 'understanding'. It is argued (e.g. Tsujii 1986) that while interlingual concepts can be, indeed must be, defined in terms of extra-linguistic 'reality', facts and theories (i.e. the terminologies of the natural sciences, of engineering, of medicine, etc.), non-scientific vocabulary (which occurs in all texts as the basic 'linguistic' knowledge) cannot be defined other than intra-linguistically and language-specifically, e.g. as semantic networks within a particular language. In any case, the boundaries between 'scientific' sublanguages and 'non-scientific' common vocabulary are vague, indeterminate and changeable. Therefore, although some knowledge and text understanding is language-independent, much is specific to particular languages. Many processes of interpretation in MT are determined by the specific characteristics of the languages concerned; the choice of a TL lexeme may require information which is not expressed in the SL, e.g. when translating into Japanese from English, the relative status of speakers and hearers – the 'understanding' of the English text does not involve this information at all. For MT 'understanding' is not exclusively language-independent. MT must deal with a multiplicity of knowledge sources and levels of description: linguistic (implicit) data of both SL and TL (both sublanguage and common knowledge), information on lexical and structural differences between SL and TL, and explicit (a priori and dynamic) knowledge of the subject(s) of texts.

For such reasons, many MT researchers believe that MT systems should build upon well-founded and well-tested 'linguistics'-oriented approaches, with extra-linguistic knowledge bases as additional components alongside morphological, lexical, syntactic, semantic and text-grammatical information. The dominant framework for most MT systems under current development is essentially that of the transfer models represented by GETA (sect. 13), SUSY (sect. 15), Mu (sect. 26), METAL (sect. 5) and Eurotra (sect. 12). These projects are founded upon a solid body of well-tested and efficient methods of morphological and syntactic analysis. with modular flexible system architectures permitting progressive incorporation of newer techniques. Not surprisingly, many commercial systems recently marketed or under development have adopted this basic transfer model (particularly in Japan). However, as experience with sophisticated theoretical modelling of linguistic processes has increased, the popularity of the more ambitious interlingua approach has also grown, e.g. Rosetta (sect. 17), DLT (sect. 18), Translator (sect. 10), ATAMIRI (sect. 41), ETL (sect. 28), LUTE and LAMB (sect. 36).

3. Transfer

What distinguishes all MT systems from natural language understanding systems is the prominence of 'transfer' operations. At the most trivial level this means only that NLU systems are monolingual while MT systems are bilingual or multilingual. At the heart of MT are the conversion of SL lexical items into TL lexical items and the transformation of SL structures into TL structures. MT systems differ in the size and relationships of three basic processes: monolingual analysis of SL texts, bilingual conversion of SL expressions and structures into TL expressions and structures, and monolingual synthesis (or generation) of TL texts. Monolingual processing is language-specific and independent of any other language, bilingual processing is oriented to a pair of languages: the SL and the TL. At the two extremes are 'direct translation' systems and 'interlingua' systems. In 'direct' translation of the word-by-word variety there is no (or scarcely any) monolingual treatment, rather the program consists (almost) entirely of rules converting SL forms into TL forms. In 'interlingua' systems there are two monolingual components: SL analysis results in an intermediary (interlingual) representation which is the input for TL generation; there is no bilingual conversion from SL to TL, only transformation into and out of an intermediary language IL (interlingua). In practice these 'pure' forms of direct and interlingua MT are rare. Most MT systems incorporate some monolingual analysis and synthesis and some bilingual transfer. Where they differ is in the 'depth' of analysis, the 'abstractness' of transfer processes, and the amount and type of semantic and extra-linguistic information. Consequently, one way of classifying MT systems may be in the broad groups: morphological transfer, syntactic transfer, semantico-syntactic transfer, semantic-conceptual transfer.

Most of the early 'direct' MT systems were morphological transfer systems: monolingual analysis was limited generally to the establishment of word-class membership (grammatical categories), e.g. noun, verb, adjective, on the basis of inflections, conjugations and local cooccurrence rules; monolingual generation was likewise limited to the production of the correctly inflected TL forms; the bulk of the programs were devoted to SL-TL transfer processes – lexical translation and word order changes (often prompted by specific lexical items). A modern example of a 'morphological transfer' system is the CADA program for converting texts between closely related languages (sect. 9): the approach is valid only where there is a high degree of lexical correspondence, of morphological equivalences, and few (or no) differences of syntactic structures.

Syntactic transfer systems appeared early in MT research (the approach of Yngve at MIT is the best known example). Monolingual analysis concentrates on the establishment of 'surface' syntactic analyses (e.g. phrase structure or dependency trees), without seeking to eliminate structural ambiguities (e.g. the scope of negation, the relationship of a prepositional phrase within the sentence). In general, such syntactic analysis is normally preceded by morphological analysis, but sometimes there is a single morpho-syntactic stage: the decision is largely determined by the nature of the SL. Bilingual transfer involves both SL-TL lexical conversion and transformation of SL syntactic structures into equivalent TL syntactic structures. Monolingual TL generation may then establish the appropriate TL syntactic and morphological forms. Not infrequently, however, TL generation is embraced largely (even wholly) by processes within transfer. Recent examples of (basically) syntactic transfer systems are to be found in some of the Japanese commercial systems.

More common, however, is a semantico-syntactic transfer approach. In such systems, monolingual analysis seeks to eliminate syntactic ambiguities and to provide single representations for synonymous syntactic (sub)trees. An increasingly common method is the establishment of the case roles of nominal expressions (e.g. agent, patient, recipient, instrument, location, etc.) and their relations to verbal (action) expressions. Case roles and relations may be very similar for both SL and TL (indeed it is the assumed or presumed 'universality' of case relations which makes the approach so attractive). Transfer processes, therefore, may involve little change of SL structures into equivalent TL case structures; the burden of transfer is on SL-TL lexical conversion and any changes of structure resulting from differences of valencies. Monolingual generation involves the production of TL syntactic and morphological forms from the TL case-structure representations output by the transfer phase. This MT type has been found particularly appropriate for Japanese, with its relatively free word order; and many Japanese projects may be classed in this group.

A further level of abstraction is reached in what may be called 'semantic-conceptual transfer'. Monolingual analysis might include the determination of pronominal antecedents, the scope of coordination and negation, the logical relations of predicate and arguments, the textual functions of theme, rheme, and information presentation. The analysis procedures might be based on semantic features and semantic networks (hyponymic and thesaural relations), on knowledge databases and inference mechanisms; both linguistic (language-specific and universal) and extra-linguistic (language-independent) information may be invoked. The SL interface representations may combine 'linguistic' semantic (both language-specific and universal) and non-linguistic conceptual (language-independent) elements. They may well transcend sentence boundaries and embrace paragraphs. Transfer is then concerned with the conversion (perhaps minimal) of SL-specific lexico-conceptual elements into TL-oriented elements, and perhaps not at all with structural changes (since these may be interlingual). The theoretical distinctions between semantic and conceptual information are in practice blurred, although some MT systems concentrate exclusively on 'linguistic' processes (implicit knowledge) and make little use of extra-linguistic (explicit) knowledge. By contrast other AI-inspired models have been more 'conceptually' oriented (e.g. the conceptual dependency representations of Schank and his colleagues). At this higher level of abstraction or universality, the distinction between transfer systems and interlingua systems becomes less valid; all that remains of transfer is the 'adjustment' of a SL conceptual framework (determined by non-universal lexical and structural parameters) to a TL conceptual framework.

There are two basic approaches to interlingual representations. The first is to extend the progressive abstraction of SL and TL interface elements so that all elements (lexical as well as structural) are language-independent, interlingual and perhaps 'universal'. (The goal of nearly all interlingua MT projects is multilingual translation.

While, in principle, interlinguality may mean only shared neutrality for a particular SL-TL pair, it usually implies a presumed universality.). In the development of interlingual representations, the (assumed) universality of propositional and intensional logic has been particularly influential; logical formalisms have long constituted essential features of semantic representations (e.g. predicate and argument structures) in both linguistic theory and computational linguistics, and it has been further buttressed by the AI use of inferencing in language 'understanding'. This conception of a conceptual (semantic) and logical interlingua is to be found in various forms in many current projects, e.g. the Translator project, the LUTE project and the Rosetta project. The other approach to intermediary representations is to take an existing 'interlingua' (IL) – an international auxiliary language or a 'regular' natural language – and to devise procedures for converting SL representations into IL representations (texts) and from IL representations into TL texts. The first option has been taken by DLT, which has adopted Esperanto as its interlingua; the second is to be seen in the ATAMIRI project, where the interlingua is a South American language Aymara (sect. 41).

There is general agreement that at the semantic levels (whether in transfer or in interlingua systems) interface structures should retain lower-level information if satisfactory coherent TL texts are to be produced. Interfaces are thus often multi-level, combining syntactic categories, phrase structure relations, dependencies, case roles, thematic functions. Examples are to be found in the transfer systems GETA and Eurotra, and in the interlingua systems DLT and LUTE.

Recent developments in the variety and complexity of transfer and interface structures have highlighted the theoretical issues of transfer (e.g. Hauenschild 1986, Luckhardt 1987a, Somers 1987a, Tsujii 1987). Transfer was of course always recognised as important, but in the past the problems of NL analysis were seen as the more urgent, as the more intractable, and as the principal impediments to good quality MT output. Now transfer and generation are considered of nearly equal importance. Generation has received much attention in the AI field, because without good text production man-machine communication is deficient (e.g. in question-answering and information retrieval systems). It is also beginning to receive more attention in the MT context (McDonald 1987, Nagao/Tsujii 1986). However, it is transfer that distinguishes MT from monolingual NL processing in AI, and in most of computational linguistics – and it is transfer which must also represent a central feature of any 'theory' of translation. A valuable contribution is the monograph by Luckhardt (1987a), who discusses the relationship between analysis and transfer (in general the more analysis the less transfer, except that deeper analysis does not always simplify transfer or generation), the difference between explicit and implicit transfer, the types of unit transferred (lexical, structural, and categorial), and the importance of valency and case theories as the basis of transfer interfaces.

Recent contributions have indicated other areas of general agreement. One is that in bilingual systems, transfer and interfaces can be at a relatively shallow level (cf. the ENGSPAN system), while in multilingual systems interfaces must inevitably approach 'semantic-conceptual' levels of analysis (e.g. Eurotra) or the systems must adopt an interlingua approach (as in DLT). The context here is that of systems designed from the beginning as multilingual systems, not the adaptation of bilingual systems to new target languages (as in Systran, sect. 1 below). Another is that there may well be three aspects (perhaps stages) of transfer: the conversion of SL-oriented structures into SL 'neutral' interfaces (in which the structures peculiar to the SL are reduced), the conversion to TL 'neutral' interfaces, and the conversion to TL-oriented structures. The first corresponds to the Mu system's (sect. 26) 'pre-transfer loop' and the third its 'post-transfer loop'. Similar distinctions are made by Schubert (1987) in the 'metataxis' procedures for the DLT system. A third observation (Boitet 1987) is that in multilingual systems involving cognate languages it may well be feasible to establish common interfaces (e.g. a common interface for the Romance languages, or a common interface for Scandinavian languages), and thus reduce the complexity and number of transfer components. The increasing interest in case grammar as the basis for transfer systems (particularly in Japan) has demonstrated that traditional case and valency analyses are often unsuitable or insufficient and have to be changed or adapted for MT purposes – as they have, e.g., in Eurotra (cf. Schmidt 1986). In particular Somers (1986, 1987b) argues that valency analysis needs to be extended to nominal structures. Finally, the need for adequate treatment of discourse relations has become increasingly pressing. A number of researchers are investigating the place of text grammars in MT environments, e.g. at Grenoble (sect. 13), at Stuttgart and Saarbrücken (sect. 16 below), in the Translator project (sect. 10) and in the research at ETL (sect. 28).

In a sense all MT approaches have some merit because they are all attacking some aspect of the translation problem; all projects encounter the same issues in the end: semantic relativity, structural mismatch, no solid language universals, the complexity of dictionaries, the problem of 'ill-formed' texts, the treatment of metaphor, and of dynamic change. The difficulty lies in finding an overall strategy which can encompass most of the facilities required. At present the transfer approach still seems most suited. As Tsujii (1986) points out, it excludes neither interlingual elements nor 'understanding' nor inferencing, rather it encourages research on the precise role and contribution of these features to genuine translation.

4. Grammars and programming

As regards the computational aspects of MT there is a large measure of convergence on what are called 'unification grammar' formalisms (Kay 1984, Shieber 1986) and on non-transformational grammatical theories, particularly Lexical Functional Grammar (Kaplan/Bresnan 1983), Generalized Phrase Structure Grammar (Gazdar et al. 1985) and Montague grammar (Dowty et al. 1981). Implementation of LFG is to be seen in many MT projects, not only in experimental ones but even in the commercial development of Weidner systems (sect. 6); GPSG is favoured increasingly in experimental systems, e.g. NASEV (16) and NTRANS (20); and Montague grammar has been implemented in Rosetta (sect. 17) and in LUTE (36). At present the most appropriate programming environment for parsers and generators based on such formalisms is considered to be Prolog, which has begun to replace Lisp as the favoured language in many NLP situations (the relative merits of Lisp and Prolog for MT are discussed by Loomis 1987). Although Prolog was adopted as the basic programming language for the Japanese Fifth Generation project, it is to be found in relatively few MT projects in Japan – other languages, such as C, are favoured increasingly in systems designed for commercial development.

Increasing attention has been paid to creating linguistic software and appropriate workstations for linguists to develop grammars, parsers and generators. Examples are the software environments developed at Grenoble (sect. 13), at Saarbrücken (the SAFRAN workstation, sect. 15; cf. Licher et al. 1987), at Utrecht for DLT (sect. 18), at Kyoto (sect. 26: the GRADE language), and for the METAL system (sect. 5; cf. White 1987).

There is no pretension that the basic framework for the future has been decided. Among the many problems for future MT research (Tsujii 1986) are the content and structure of multi-layered representations, the integration of different levels of 'understanding', the development of robust (fail-safe) parsing of incomplete (or 'ungrammatical') texts and the treatment of weak semantic constraints (preference semantics and metaphorical usage), the development of robust and flexible frameworks for new developments, the efficient application and appropriate formalization of text linguistics, the problems of large and complex semantic networks, and the practical difficulties of ensuring consistent coding, particularly the lexical coding of large dictionaries.

5. Further developments

The emphasis of most MT research is towards systems which produce written translations and which start from complete finished texts. In recent years, research has expanded into new types of translation. There has been considerable interest in the prospects of telephone translation, a major project in Japan involving governmental sponsorship (the ATR investigation, sect. 28) and a project by British Telecom in the United Kingdom (sect. 20). There are also signs of interest by Japanese companies, e.g. Toshiba (sect. 32). There are few hopes of working systems in the near future; 15 years before a prototype is one of the more optimistic forecasts.

One new arena for MT offers more immediate prospects of working systems. It is recognised that AI knowledge-based systems produce 'paraphrases' of texts rather than translations, i.e. they concentrate on the essential 'message' and disregard surface expressions. There are already programs for checking scripts during composition (e.g. the 'expert editor' of Smart, sect. 3) and allowing interactive rewriting for reducing the complexities of MT operations. Soon there may well be systems which combine composition in the user's own language and simultaneous translation into another. The most immediate application would be conventional business correspondence, but extension to other spheres would surely follow, particularly if there were some speech input and output. The research at CMU, sect. 10, and at UMIST, sect. 20, is the first step in this direction.

A more distant prospect must be systems combining translation and summarization. The idea of producing summaries of foreign language documents for administrators, businessmen and scientists in their own language is almost certainly more attractive than rough translations of full texts. AI researchers and others have conducted small scale experiments on summarization in restricted domains, but it is already apparent that the complexities of the task are at least equal to those of MT itself.

Greater success is likely with the integration of MT and information retrieval systems. Sigurdson/Greatrex (1987) at the Research Policy Institute of the University of Lund have demonstrated that the technical means are already available for businessmen and scientists to access Japanese databases and obtain automatic translations of abstracts. A number of MT systems exist already which were designed for translating titles and abstracts (e.g. TITRAN and TITUS) and Systran has also been applied to patents (sect. 1). In the Japan-Info project of the EEC users will be able to ask for translations of Japanese abstracts (mainly of research reports and other 'grey literature'); they will be produced in Japan using Systran Japan and the Fujitsu ATLAS systems (sect. 29 and 30), transmitted to Europe and then to the requesters (Sigurdson/Greatrex 1987). The next step must be an integrated system – this is the aim of the MARIS project at present under development at Saarbrücken based on the SUSY translator (sect. 15; Zimmermann et al. 1987).

6. Operational systems

There are other examples of research groups looking for direct applications of their experimental work. They include the involvement of the Grenoble group in the French national project (Calliope), the development of the METAL system as a commercial German-English system by Siemens, and the second phase of the Mu project in Japan. Nevertheless, most operational and commercial systems have originated not from academic research groups but from independent companies.

The longest established, and still the leader for 'batch processed' MT, is Systran (sect. 1). Originally devised for Russian-English, then on behalf of the European Communities for English-French, Systran is now in worldwide use in an impressive range of language pairs. The recent coordination of separate developments of Systran version under the general ownership of Gachot and the recent online availability of Systran translations should mean the continued vigour of Systran for many years to come. Other 'batch' systems do not have the same international position. PAHO's systems for English and Spanish were created for in-house use only (sect. 2); Smart concentrates on large systems tailored to particular organizational needs, so far exclusively in North America (sect. 3); Logos has been successful in the German market but has so far made little impact elsewhere (sect. 4); and METAL, also for

German-English translation and probably the most advanced 'batch' system, is as yet only at the stage of trial implementations (sect. 5).

In the sphere of 'assisted' systems the current leader is undoubtedly WCC (previously Weidner), now owned by Bravis of Japan (sect. 6). It now offers an impressively wide range of languages for both VAX and IBM PC equipment, with particularly large sales of its microcomputer-based systems in Japan. Its main rival remains ALPS, which however has recently concentrated more on machine aids for translators rather than interactive systems, and has expanded its commercial base by purchases of translation agencies and bureaux. Other microcomputer 'interactive' MT systems have appeared in Europe and North America more recently, e.g. TII, Tovna and Socatra (sect. 8), but undoubtedly the greatest impact has come from Japan.

In the past five years there have appeared on the Japanese market systems for English-Japanese and Japanese-English translation from many of the large electronics and computer companies. Fujitsu and Hitachi were first with their ATLAS and HICATS systems respectively (sect. 30 and 31). They have been followed closely by Toshiba (32), Oki (33), NEC (34), Mitsubishi, Matsushita, Ricoh, Sanyo and Sharp (35). In design some of these are ambitious 'interlingua' systems, but most are relatively low-level transfer systems. Nearly all require in practical implementation a considerable pre-editing effort if satisfactory results are to be achieved: in large part, pre-editing is conditioned by the particular difficulties of Japanese (three scripts, lack of word boundaries, high degree of ellipsis, complex sentence structures). However, Japanese operators are accustomed to similar requirements when using Japanese word processors with no translation envisaged, so the extra costs of pre-editing are acceptable.

The range and diversity of MT products now available reflects the recognition of a large potential market. There is undoubtedly more translation work in technical, economic and scientific fields than can be dealt with by the present numbers of competent and qualified translators. Indications of the commercial expansion of the MT field are a survey of translators' work practices by DEC (Smith 1987), a large-scale evaluation of the potential market by Johnson (1985) and a technical evaluation by Balfour (1986). MT and machine-aided translation is now capable of offering at greater speed and at usually lower costs than human translation a diversity of translation products, which did not previously exist, and which can satisfy a wide range of requirements from rough unrevised MT output (for information purposes) to fully post-edited high quality versions.

However, the introduction of MT in any operational situation always demands considerable effort in creating special dictionaries for local needs, and their compilation requires appropriate translation expertise – which purchasers of MT systems are not always aware of. The practical problems of integrating MT in translation services are not trivial, but they can be overcome, as illustrated by the experience at CEC with Systran (sect. 1); numerous other examples are to be found in papers given at the Translating and the Computer conferences (Picken 1987, 1988), at the Japanese MT Summit (1987) and in the pages of *Language Monthly*; in nearly all instances, companies report higher throughput and greater consistency, but not always lower costs.

It is possible that in future the greatest expansion of MT will come in the provision of rough translations for those with sufficient subject knowledge to be able to overlook the grammatical and stylistic 'mistakes' of present MT systems. These are translations which would not have been done at all without MT, and in this respect MT will be satisfying urgent needs. Nevertheless, there are dangers; the limitations of MT may not be appreciated by those who are ignorant of translation or of languages. As long as systems are bought and operated by translators, translation bureaux and by companies with experience of translation, the recipients of unrevised MT output are likely to be made fully aware of the limitations of MT versions. The danger will come when, as we may expect, systems require less post-editing, are less restricted in subject coverage, and are purchased by non-translators and those with no foreign language knowledge. It is the duty of the translation and MT community to ensure that the general public is not mislead by unrealistic claims and promises.

Developments in the past five years have been more rapid than at any time since the 1960's; MT activity is growing not just in the developed countries of North America, Europe and Japan, but in less technologically advanced countries of Asia and South America. The internationalisation of MT research and of MT implementations is attributable to many factors: the trans-national commercial dimension of translation itself (Systran, Bravis/WCC, ALPS, Logos), explicitly multinational projects (Eurotra project, Japanese ODA project), international collaborative research (e.g. initiated by GETA, Siemens, Fujitsu, etc.), multinational companies (Xerox, IBM), the wider availability of increasingly powerful computer equipment, and the solid theoretical and practical achievements of natural language processing. The vigour of MT is reflected in its mixture of experimental speculative model building and of practically oriented development of operational systems. Machine translation is no longer a slightly suspect academic pursuit (as it was until the mid-1970's in many respects), it has established itself as an important branch of applied science (computational linguistics and artificial intelligence) and as a technology-based industry of international dimensions.

II. Survey of current and recent projects and systems

This survey of recent activity in MT research and production systems was completed in early 1988. It is intended to be as comprehensive and accurate as possible; it includes small scale experiments, large projects, government-funded projects and commercial systems, each with brief notes of recent developments as a guide to the extent of current activity. It represents a provisional supplement to the survey published in 1986 (Hutchins 1986), which covered MT research and production systems to the end of 1984. It includes therefore notices of systems already established in 1984 as well as new (or not previously noted) projects. Further information (or corrections) about any MT activity, whether mentioned or not in this survey, will be welcomed. The bibliography at the end of this paper, although substantial, is not designed to be comprehensive but to guide readers to the most recent (and usually most accessible) general accounts of particular systems. (The abbreviations *LM* and *LT* refer to the journals ***Language Monthly*** and ***Language Technology***, both of which carry regular items on MT.) The arrangement is broadly 'geographical', starting with systems originating or based in North America (nos. 1-11, including Systran, PAHO, Smart, LOGOS, METAL, WCC, ALPS, etc.), passing on to European activity (nos. 12-24, covering Eurotra, GETA, Saarbrücken, Rosetta, DLT, etc.), then to the numerous Japanese systems and projects (nos. 25-37), and ending with the rest of Asia and with South America (nos. 38-41).

1.

Systran is the oldest and the most widely used MT system. (Basic descriptions of the Systran design can be found in Hutchins 1986: 210-215). Ownership has now passed completely out of the hands of its original designer, Peter Toma (who has now set up a private university [Aorangi University] in Dunedin, South Island, New Zealand, in order to promote international conflict resolution) and almost wholly into the Gachot S.A. company. After a complex series of negotiations spread over a number of years, the **Gachot** company (Jean Gachot and Denis Gachot) has now united all US and European companies with Systran interests. The process had already begun with the acquisition by Jean Gachot of the Systran Institut GmbH and the World Translation Center (WTC) in La Jolla, California, and by Denis Gachot of Latsec, the US branch mainly concerned with military applications. Now the only company with Systran rights which remains outside is the IONA company (headed by Sadao Kawasaki) which owns the Systran Corporation of Japan (cf. 29 below) and the rights to the Japanese programs (Joscelyne 1988).

All the main organisations and users of Systran were brought together in February 1986 at the 'World Systran Conference' organised by the Commission of the European Communities and held in Luxembourg. The proceedings have been printed in special number of *Terminologie et Traduction* 1986, no. 1.

The longest standing user of a Systran system is the USAF Foreign Technology Division at Dayton, Ohio, where the Russian-English version has been in use for information scanning since 1970. By 1987 nearly 100,000 pages each year were being translated (Pigott 1988). The quality of raw output can be judged by the fact that only 20% of texts are edited (by the EDITSYS program) – this is the output which has been automatically flagged by the Systran program for not-found words, acronyms, potential rearrangement, potentially suspect adjective-noun and noun-noun compounds, uncertainty in disambiguation, and known problem words (Bostad 1986). The Russian-English system has recently been successfully adapted to the translation of Soviet patent abstracts (Bostad 1985). In addition, the USAF has now introduced German-English and French-English versions, and is developing Italian, Portuguese and Spanish as source languages (Pigott 88); there is apparently also a Japanese version under development (LT4 Dec 87).

Use of Systran at the Commission of the European Communities (CEC) began in 1976 with development of the English-French version, followed soon by French-English and English-Italian, and a pilot 'production service' for these language pairs in 1981. Since then versions have been also developed at Luxembourg for English to German, Dutch, Spanish and Portuguese as well as from

French into German and Dutch. Experience so far is that the best quality is achieved for translations into Romance languages and into English, the quality is lower for translation into German and Dutch, where there are particular problems of word order. In the near future, work is expected to begin on German into English and into French (Pigott 1988). Although the reception of MT output has steadily improved (helped by OCR input and links with a variety of word processors), usage is still relatively low – under 2% of CEC translations were post-edited Systran versions in 1987. Nevertheless, future growth is expected with more translators opting to use raw outputs as aids to quality manual translation (i.e. the use of MT versions as pre-translations), and with more recipients of information documents satisfied with rapidly post-edited texts (Pigott 1988).

Other long standing users are General Motors of Canada, where an English-French system produces literature for the Canadian market, and Xerox, where technical manuals written in a restricted English are translated at the rate of 50,000 pages a year into five TLs. Other users include the NATO headquarters in Brussels, the Dornier company in Germany, the German national railways (Bundesbahn), the Nuclear Research Center (Kernforschungszentrum) in Karlsruhe, and the International Atomic Energy Authority. A major user is the French company Aérospatiale, which after an initial trial with the CEC systems at Luxembourg, contracted directly with Gachot for use of English-French and French-English systems to translate aviation manuals. Aérospatiale hope that 50-60% of their needs will be met by unedited Systran output; Habermann (1986) has reported that researchers at the Kernforschungszentrum are very satisfied with the raw output from the French-English version.

In the last 5 years a number of bureau have started to offer clients translation services using Systran (Pigott 1988). Gachot in Paris is one of them; others include ECAT (European Centre for Automatic Translation, Luxembourg), the Mendez service bureau (in Brussels) and CSATA (Italy). Recently, Systran has been offered by ECAT to companies on Esprit projects as an on-line translation service (Siebenaler 1986).

The most striking development which Gachot has introduced has been to make Systran (and some of the Systran dictionaries) accessible to the 4.5 million users of the French Minitel network (cf. 14 below). Beginning with English-French, Gachot has now added Spanish-English, English-Spanish and English-Portuguese. The implications may well be revolutionary. Until now MT has been primarily for academics and for professional translators; Gachot has brought MT within reach of the general public. Its most effective use is likely to be for international business messages. The use by French students to help them with their homework is more dubious.

While the ownership of Systran rights was divided, systems developed in a relatively uncoordinated fashion. Development of Systran systems was undertaken with joint contracts between major users and the Systran companies such as (in the CEC case) the World Translation Center, World Translation Company of Canada, the Franklin Institut and the Systran Institut, and Informalux (Luxembourg). In most instances, the users developed the dictionaries, while the Systran companies worked on the software modules. Although WTC and Latsec, therefore, maintained a guiding role, there were inevitable divergences as long as dictionary construction was adapted to specific purposes, at USAF, Xerox, General Motors and within the CEC. Systran is essentially a lexicon-driven system (in common with most MT systems of the first generation) and inevitably the diverging 'philosophies' of dictionary construction resulted in diverging system types. The dangers were always recognised. Now, in bringing together Systran development in one organisation, Gachot can ensure that the coordination of divergent programs will continue more vigorously, with the aim being a total unification of all Systran systems. At the same time, Gachot benefits from the large dictionary databases which have been established by the CEC, Aérospatiale, etc.

The increasing modularity of the Systran designs will aid convergence. At the CEC the analysis programs for English and French have been adapted relatively easily to new target languages. The experience at Xerox with a single SL program (for English) and multiple TL programs is further evidence of the potential of Systran. According to Ryan (1987) there is now a 'common trunk' of procedures for the Romance languages, and the German and Dutch TL modules are also common to more than one pair. Just as the English SL modules are transportable to new targets, the French SL components are being adapted at present for multi-target systems. All this does not mean that Systran is a 'multilingual' system, since each version has to be specially designed for a particular language pair in one direction; but it does mean that the addition of a new version is becoming progressively easier. Gachot has been reported as developing a number of new versions: English-Italian, English-German, German-English, and to be working on Arabic, Portuguese and Spanish. (The problems of Arabic have been outlined by Trabulsi 1986.) In total, "Systran now offers 15 operational language pairs. These include English into 8 languages: French, German, Italian, Spanish, Portuguese, Russian, Japanese and Dutch; French into English, German and Dutch; and Russian, German, Japanese and Spanish into English. English-Arabic is under development, while pilot systems exist for 6 other language pairs: German into French, Spanish and Italian; and Chinese, Portuguese and Italian into English." (Ryan 1987)

There are now very large Systran dictionaries: USAF Russian-English has over 200,000 single words and over 200,000 expressions; CEC dictionaries for 4 languages have between 100,000 and 200,000 words; for the English-Japanese system it is planned to have 250,000 word dictionary of scientific and technical vocabulary and over 200,000 of medical terms. It is Gachot's aim to achieve by 1990 a quality level averaging over 96% for all the 12 language pairs currently available, although it is recognised that raising the quality of English-German and English-Russian, currently estimated at 67%, will be a major achievement in this time span.

After a period of threatening fragmentation into different 'dialects', Systran is entering a phase of consolidation guided by the Gachot interest in developing further what has for many years been the most widely used and undoubtedly most successful mainframe MT system.

2.
At the Pan American Health Organization (**PAHO**) there has been continued development of the Spanish-English (SPANAM) and English-Spanish (ENGSPAN) systems designed to translate a wide range of subjects and of document types in the broad field of medicine and health. The PAHO systems are well known as robust empirical systems based on well-tested MT techniques. The aim was practicality not experimentation. SPANAM became operational in 1980, ENGSPAN in 1985; the two systems are described in detail by Vasconcellos/Leon (1985/1988), and summarised by Hutchins (1986: 220-222)

Most research development has concentrated on ENGSPAN (Leon/Schwartz 1986). This is a batch-processing system with post-editing, but with no pre-editing and no restrictions on content or style. It is based on a transfer design, limited primarily to lexical and syntactic transfer, and with minimal semantic analysis. Morphological and syntactic analysis is by an ATN parser, written in PL/I. There are proposals to convert the PL/I code to the C language for running on a microcomputer.

SPANAM, fundamentally a 'direct translation' MT system, has undergone no basic changes since it first became operational, but there are proposals to incorporate features of the more advanced ENGSPAN in some future developments. It is now well-established at PAHO and for its on-screen post-editing special facilities have been developed, which are described by Vasconcellos (1986, 1987). The aim has been to devise functions ('macros') for frequently recurring actions: replacements, deletions and insertions (eg. of articles), inversions (eg. N *of* N $\rightarrow$ N N), etc. For the treatment of phrase structure changes it is argued that as far as possible the informational sequence (theme-rheme articulation and ideational presentation) of the original Spanish is to be preserved in the English version. For example, the 'raw' output:

For its execution there has been considered two stages...

could be changed to:

Its execution has been conceived in two stages...

As in this case this may mean that syntactic functions have to be altered, but it is often easier to do this than to shift around large segments of text. Undoubtedly such facilities would assist post-editing work in other practical MT operations.

3.

The unique feature of SPANAM and ENGSPAN is that they were designed for, researched by, and developed within and for the sole use of a single organisation. Whether this approach will ever be repeated is unlikely. In the future, the more probable course for organisations like PAHO will be to call in a company like that set up by John Smart in New York.

Smart Communications Inc. provides two basic products, the Smart Expert Editor and the Smart Translator (Mann 1987). The editor (MAX) is a batch-oriented text analyzer using a rule-based expert system and a specialized terminology knowledge base. The rule base contains 2500 generalized grammar and syntax rules for technical writing, the knowledge base includes information specific to the needs of a particular company (e.g. on dangerous chemicals). MAX acts like good copy editor, producing a report for the technical writer to act upon. As a by-product the result is easier to translate.

The Smart Translator thus operates on a restricted grammar and lexicon of a source language. It does not attempt to deal with ambiguities and vagueness, which are to be eliminated by the Editor. Smart's restricted language was based initially on Caterpillar English, devised for the Caterpillar company and subsequently modified and expanded by Xerox as their Multinational Customized English for use with the Systran system (sect. 1 above).

Smart Communications therefore provides tools for economical on-line help in writing clear, safe documentation and for translating it into several languages. It has been active since 1972, and there are now over 30 companies using SMART software, including Citicorp, Chase, Ford, and General Electric. Smart's largest customer to date is the Canadian Ministry of Employment and Immigration. A system was produced to translate job vacancies from English into French and vice versa. In operation since 1982, job descriptions are input at 5000 terminals across Canada, over 100,000 a year, and translated at a rate of up to 200 characters per second. The aim is not perfect translation; 90% accuracy is acceptable, since there are bilingual secretaries who can post-edit. The officials worked closely with Smart in tailoring the system to their particular requirements and they continue to maintain the knowledge base and update the dictionaries.

The Smart Translator has been implemented from English into French, Spanish, Portuguese, and Italian and vice versa. Some work has been done on German and on Japanese, and there are reports of future plans for English into Greek and Turkish (Rolling 1987b). There are no plans to implement cross-language pairs, e.g. French-Spanish, but Smart is investigating a French editor.

At present there are no customers outside North America, although there seem to be plans to open a base in England shortly. Like others, Smart has ideas also for a business letter writing 'kit' which would enable businessmen to write letters in any language by selecting parts needed. There might also be development of a more active interface, i.e. in effect an interactive MAT system, but Smart is doubtful that users really want this kind of system.

4.

The **LOGOS** English-German system was demonstrated in 1984 and joined the German-English version (first available in 1982) on the market, mainly in West Germany (largest user is the computer firm Nixdorf). Both systems run on a Wang OIS140 with a minimum of 80MB hard disk; and are now also available in versions for IBM (VM/CMS) mainframes. LOGOS has European offices in Frankfurt and

Zurich, with the former providing a bureau service since 1985. (Recent details of LOGOS are given by Wheeler 1985.)

Operation involves a preliminary run through the source text for missing vocabulary, the entry of new lexical items by the user (prompted by the computer for information on syntactic categories, grammatical case, inflection type, and semantic codes). The text is then translated in batch mode: morphological analysis, syntactic analysis, treatment of nominal subtrees, check for idioms, lexical transfer (guided by semantic codes), identification of subjects, objects, etc., and generation of target text – transfer and generation are combined (in a series of stages) in the fashion of some earlier 'direct translation' systems, i.e. LOGOS can be described now as a 'hybrid' syntax-oriented transfer system (Hutchins 1986: 255-257). Output is then post-edited using the Wang word processing facilities.

LOGOS provide customers with a basic bilingual dictionary of over 100,000, to which they can add their own specialised terminology; however, customers' additions cannot include verb entries, since these demand complex coding and have implications for the efficiency of the system as a whole. Software updates are supplied at no extra cost. There are reports of progress with more language pairs: English-French (in Canada), English-Spanish and German-French for the Walloon administration in Belgium (Rolling 1987).

5.
The **METAL** system was developed largely for bi-directional English and German translation at the University of Texas. Since 1978 it has been fully supported by the Siemens company in Munich. A commercial prototype is being tested at present, much earlier than Siemens had initially expected when they began sponsorship. A basic description of the system is to be found in Bennett/Slocum (1985/1988), and summarised in Hutchins (1986: 248-254): METAL has a modularized transfer design, with monolingual and bilingual/transfer dictionaries, a bottom-up chart parser, and fail-safe heuristics; it operates on a Symbolics 36-series Lisp machine and is designed for batch processing (estimated speed: 200 pages per day) with postediting on PC workstations, with sight either of both source text and target version together or of final target text only.

METAL will undoubtedly be the most sophisticated transfer system to be commercially available. The German-English version (the oldest) is being used to produce translations in several pilot operations (in Switzerland and elsewhere) and is due for imminent launch (Schneider 1987). METAL has been applied primarily in the fields of data processing and telecommunications. Future customers will benefit substantially in the construction of their specialised dictionaries by access to Siemens' multilingual term bank TEAM.

Other versions also under development involve Dutch, French and Spanish. Research is being sponsored by Siemens in Munich itself, at the University of Texas (Austin, Texas, USA), the University of Leuven (Belgium) and in Barcelona (Spain). An English-Spanish prototype is expected shortly (Schneider 1987), and some progress has been reported on a Dutch-French version (see also sect. 19 below). Most advanced appears to be the English-German system; the early stages of the research in Austin (Texas) on this version of METAL is reported by Liu and Liro (1987).

6.
While Systran is the most widely used mainframe MT system, the Chicago-based **WCC** (World Communications Center, formerly **Weidner** Communications Corporation) is the market leader in microcomputer systems. Since early 1988 the company has been wholly owned by the Japanese translation house, **Bravis** (which had a majority share in Weidner since 1984). Other WCC offices and bureaux have been established since since mid 1986 in Toronto and in Europe (where it trades under the name Weidner Translation Europe Ltd.)

The WCC systems (described in Hutchins 1986) now run in two versions: the MacroCAT systems on DEC MicroVAX II machines, and the MicroCAT systems on IBM PC/XT (and compatibles). Currently

(February 1988), MicroCAT is available for translation from English into French, German, Italian, Japanese, Portuguese and Spanish, and from French, Japanese and Spanish into English. Bravis has been particularly successful in sales of the Japanese to English systems, with a reported figure of 3000 packages sold in Japan (where it is marketed as MicroPack)

Other languages are being added in the near future. Arabic versions are at present under development, and, as reported by Darke (1986), under pilot testing in Saudi Arabia and to be marketed shortly. A MacroCAT system for English to Norwegian translation (ENTRA) was developed in a collaborative project between WCC and the University of Bergen, using as its starting point the existing English-German software (Brekke and Skarsten 1987). ENTRA is the first MT system for a Nordic language (except for the Danish component in Eurotra, and some very early experiments in the 1960's). It has been restricted initially to the language of the petroleum oil industry, with some current expansion of dictionaries to computing technology. The project's particular problems were getting word order right, treatment of English genitive relational phrases, and the problems of complex noun compounds. Preliminary evaluations indicate an acceptable quality for post-editing, but fuller quality testing has yet to be done.

More fundamental research is reported from the WCC research group at Provo, Utah. Significant progress has been made on more advanced software (System II) based on lexical-functional grammar (LM 54, March 1988). If so, this is confirmation of the desire of commercial companies to improve the quality of their product by exploiting the latest advances in computational linguistics. In this way, WCC systems may progress beyond what they are acknowledged to be, 'computer-aided translation systems', providing primarily facilities for dictionary lookup and text processing and only minimal translation.

7.
By contrast, **ALPS** (Automated Language Processing Systems Ltd.) appears to have drawn back from major aspirations in the MT market. In recent years ALPS has purchased a number of translation bureaux, notably TTI, and are starting to market medical expert systems (LM 50, Nov 1987). The ALPS aids for translators are now in three packages (for IBM PC AT's): 'Transactive' is the interactive translation program (now available for English into French, German, Italian and Spanish and from French into English); 'Autoterm' is an automatic terminology lookup package available for many languages (English, French, Spanish, Italian, German, Danish, Dutch, Portuguese, Norwegian); and the 'Translation Support System' is a multilingual word processor with facilities for terminology management, source text analysis, terminology frequency analyses, text transfer, and automatic word counting.

ALPS has expanded its text processing tools with three further packages: 'ABC Word', a "writer's assistance program", providing access from the user's terminal to a monolingual dictionary (Miriam Webster), to a thesaurus and to bilingual dictionaries (English into French, German and Spanish); 'PeriPhrase', a "rule-based linguistic software tool" suitable for the development of natural language interfaces, e.g. for computer assisted instruction and compiler development (for Unix and Xenix environments); and a 'Computer Analysis Program' for building tailored glossaries, and devising writing protocols.

It is clear that MAT is now becoming a less significant component of ALPS activities. The linguistic ingredient in the ALPS aids was always slight, and there is no evidence that research is being pursued on improving the quality of the ALPS translation modules.

8.
Within the last few years a number of rivals to ALPS and WCC have emerged in the area of interactive systems and machine aids. The following are those which have come to notice.

ALPS' glossary management package ('ABC Word') has a rival in LinguaTech's **Mercury** (distributed in Europe by InfoARBED under the name **Termex**). This represents the Level One of Melby's proposed translator's workstation (Melby 1985/1987). Mercury provides multilingual glossary construction (at present for English, French, German and Dutch) and telecommunication access to remote term banks. Level Two would provide facilities for analysing texts, producing text related glossaries, etc. (as already found in ALPS Translation Support System and in the INK Text Tools). Level Three would be the interface to a MT system, with facilities for post-editing.

Recently, the **TII** company (Telecommunications Industries Inc.) launched its 'translating word processor', the TWP/70, designed to run on IBM PC-compatible microcomputers with 768K RAM and a 30MB hard disk. The software will provide bi-directional translation for English-Spanish, English-Russian, English-French, shortly to be extended by software for English from and into Italian, German and Portuguese. The system is an interactive system (with split-screen dual language display), and designed expressly as an 'aid' for translators.

The **TOVNA** Ltd. (originallly Israel-based, now in London) have announced a system for Sun-level workstations (LT5 Jan 1988). The system (Tovna is a Hebrew homonym for 'software' and for 'insight') is claimed to be a 'learning system', augmenting and amending linguistic rules by AI inferencing, giving capacity for 'commercial quality' translation between any pair of languages: English-French is to be released in March 1988, to be followed by German, Spanish, Russian, and with plans for Arabic.

Linguistic Products (of Houston Texas) is a company set up by Ralph Dessau and George Mallard to market the interactive CAT packages they have developed for English and French, English and Spanish, English and Swedish and English and Danish. Their first product, an interactive stand-alone system for Spanish-English was launched in February 1985. It is apparently a straight word-for-word direct translation system, with differences of word-order dealt with by a syntax subroutine after lexical transfer and generation of TL word forms. Customers receive a 70,000 word dictionary, which includes all verb forms (i.e. there is no morphological analysis), but there are facilities for compiling personal word lists. The designers admit the limitations of the simple system, and the fact that it cannot handle complex text. Its selling point is cheapness (at $480 operating on IBM XT microcomputers); 80 copies of the Spanish-English system have been sold, and some in use by officers of the Customs and Excise in Texas. By 1988 the company expects to have 16 two-way language pairs on the market (LT4 December 1987).

In Canada, the **SOCATRA** company of Montreal (Societé Canadienne de Traduction Assistée), founded in 1981 by Claude Richaud, has developed a machine-aided system **XLT** for English-French translation and are offering to undertake translation for clients on a commercial basis. The system incorporates an ATN parser, context-free grammars, some semantic analysis and the use of 'fuzzy logic'. Text can be input by OCR, from diskettes and by telephone. Facilities for customized glossaries are provided. Clients can choose to receive output either unrevised, or revised by SOCATRA's own translators. Translation speeds of 60,000 words per hour are claimed. (SOCATRA brochure 1988).

9.

One consequence of increased awareness of MT and computational linguistic techniques is the development of limited systems for specific well-defined aims.

One example is the (apparently) one-off program, **TRANSOFT**, developed at Johns Hopkins University (Moore et al. 1986) to provide a draft translation of a German textbook. All the words were entered in a bilingual dictionary and assigned simple syntactic/semantic categories. The first stage of translation involved the rearrangement of German sentence structures into English-like structures – for this a set of 'parsing tables' were recursively applied. The second stage involved the replacement of German lexical items by English words. In brief TRANSOFT was a simple 'direct translation' system for word-by-word translation devised for one specific task. It is possible that further exercises of this nature will become common in the future.

A much more significant example, and one which may have implications for other MT projects, is the Computer Assisted Dialect Adaptation (**CADA**) approach to translation between closely related dialects, which has been under development since 1979 by David Weber (Summer Institute of Linguistics) and others in South America. The method, it is stressed, is designed for members of language families which are closely related lexically, syntactically and semantically. It is not seen as a MT system but as a computer aid for translation within well defined situations. The method focuses on systematic differences, aiming to account for 80% of translation work between the dialects. Residual problems are left to human editors who also make any stylistic changes. Programs are written in the C programming language and operate on DEC microcomputers. There are the following stages: input (erasing information not required: capitalisation, punctuation, non-alphabetic characters), morphological analysis (decomposition into roots, suffixes, dealing with morphemic variation; indication of grammatical functions of suffixes), lexical transfer (using bilingual root dictionary), synthesis (using TL morphemes and information about suffix functions). In overall strategy the method is of the 'direct translation' type operating essentially at the morphological level only; it is valid primarily for translation between dialects of agglutinative languages. A description of CADA for dialects of the Tucanoan family is given by Reed (1985), Kasper/Weber (1986) and Barnes (1987).

The designers and users emphasise the amount of linguistic preparatory investigation demanded if CADA is to work well. It has in fact been used widely in South America, for languages in Peru (Quechua, Campa), Colombia (Tucanoan), Guatemala (Cakchiquel), and is now being developed in the Philippines, Ecuador (Quichua), Brazil (Tupi). Whether the method can be adapted for language families where more syntactic analysis is necessary is still an open question. Nevertheless, it has been suggested that the approach might also be valid for some Romance language pairs (e.g. Spanish and Portuguese) and perhaps between Scandinavian languages.

10.

In recent years there have been a growing number of experimental MT projects in the United States and Canada. Many of them have been inspired to exploit the power of new programming languages (such as Prolog), to experiment with recent advances in formal linguistics (e.g. lexical-functional and unification grammars) and to apply techniques and methods of Artificial Intelligence in Knowledge Based MT systems.

One of the earliest experiments of this kind has been the project at **Colgate** University on the interlingua system **TRANSLATOR** (Nirenburg et al. 1986, 1987, and summarised in Hutchins 1986: 282-283). Extra-linguistic knowledge is incorporated in SL and TL dictionaries, and is utilized by the 'Inspector' module during the transfer stage to assist disambiguation. A major distinctive feature of TRANSLATOR is the inclusion of discourse information in the interlingua representation (the 'IL text' representation). Recent developments in the treatment of discourse phenomena are reported by Nirenburg and Carbonell (1987). They describe the means adopted for recording information about co-reference and topic-comment structures. The purpose of the 'IL text' component is to combine (a) 'meaning representations' of the text derived from semantic relations of the text itself and extra-textual inferences and enrichments derived from a 'knowledge base', and (b) structures relating tokens of the IL lexicon which reflect the discourse presentation (including cohesion markers, modal context) of the SL original. While the eventual aim is a fully automatic system, the designers intend to incorporate interactive facilities for analysis and disambiguation in order to augment the knowledge bases dynamically.

At **Carnegie-Mellon** University (CMU) research continues on the knowledge-based MT system designed by Tomita and Carbonell (1986; also Carbonell/Tomita 1987). The project intends to capitalise on the advantages of the entity-oriented approach of Hayes (1984) for the representation of language-independent conceptual knowledge in a specific domain (in the case of CMU the domain is doctor-patient communications). The formalism of Functional Unification Grammar (Kay 1984) will be employed to represent language-specific (but domain-independent) information about the grammars of the languages involved (initially English and Japanese, but later Spanish, French, German and Italian).

From these two knowledge bases will be compiled automatically at the time of translation a single large Lisp program for a "very efficient real-time parser".

The other MT research at CMU is that of Tomita (1984, 1986), who has been concentrating on the best methods of conducting interactive dialogues for MT. Part of the answer is the establishment of suitable general-purpose templates, e.g. to disambiguate a PP relation (whether linked to preceding NP or VP) the templates might be: "*The action* (VP) *takes place* (PP)" and "(NP) *is* (PP)":

I saw a man in the park.
1. The action (*saw a man*) takes place (*in the park*)
2. (*the man*) is (*in the park*)

The other part of the solution is to delay asking for disambiguation assistance until all possible parses, i.e. those which have not so far been deleted, are available together. However the procedure is not without considerable problems as Whitelock et al (1986) point out.

The CMU Center for Machine Translation is also reported to be organisers of a joint international project involving IBM, Hewlett-Packard, and a number of Japanese computer companies (Sigurdson/Greatrex 1987); Carbonell (at MT Summit, September 1987) spoke of the Center's ambition to become a major research centre for MT on a broad front, utilizing AI and knowledge engineering techniques, text understanding, and speech input. It would be building on the existing achievements of Carbonell and his colleagues in AI, computational linguistics and experimental MT. The goals are high quality systems that work, which for MT implies the interlingua approach, and the utilization of specific domain knowledge bases.

Research continues also at **New Mexico** State University by X. Huang (previously at University of Essex) on an experimental English-Chinese system **XTRA** using the Definite Clause Grammar formalism (Huang/Guthrie 1986). The project has developed a parsing system which comprises component 'parsers' to test for sentence structure, to try out all possible adjective and noun relations within noun phrases, to check for subject-verb and verb-object compatibilities. The components operate in parallel and can be called interactively by each other. There are clear implications for efficient MT analysis programs.

11.

Experimental MT systems such as these are often short lived. There do not, for example, appear to have been further developments of the AI (or knowledge-based) systems at Yale and at Georgia Institute of Technology – descriptions are to be found in Nirenburg (1987) and summaries in Hutchins (1986: 279-280,282). On the other hand, new AI-inspired systems have been reported; some are no more than toys (e.g. Lee (1987) on English-Korean), others are more substantial, even if still on very small scales.

At the University of **California (Irvine)**, Yoshii (1986) has been experimenting with a Japanese-English system **JETR** – a small-scale knowledge-based MT experiment, based on a corpus of Japanese cooking recipes and instructions for digital watches. The structural analysis of Japanese is based primarily on the identification of particles, which are treated as indicators of case roles. It combines a top-down processing looking for the fulfilment of predictions and a bottom-up processing to narrow down multiple parses and to resolve slot mismatchings. A major feature is the ability to deal with incomplete and elliptical input, e.g. missing subjects and verbs, missing particles and unknown words, by reference to domain knowledge and an 'inferencer'. JETR distinguishes between information inferred from (incomplete or elliptical) text and information explicitly given in the text. Other knowledge-based MT systems, which do not make this distinction, generate from semantic representations and produce paraphrases rather than translations. Generation of English is in fact performed as soon as there is sufficient information from the Japanese analysis to produce a coherent phrase. Thus, for example, a Japanese phrase translated so far as '*Turn the crown quickly clockwise...*' is changed, when encountering the Japanese subordinator *'to'*, to *'When you turn the crown quickly...'* In this way, the phrase order of the original is largely maintained, and, it is claimed, the system preserves "the syntactic and semantic content of both grammatical and ungrammatical sentences." Although clearly a knowledge-based approach in that inferencing and role-filling are dominant features, JETR is similar in certain respects to earlier 'direct translation' systems, being designed specifically for two particular languages, intertwining analysis and generation and preserving SL phrase order as far as possible in TL output.

From the University of **British Columbia**, Sharp (1986) has described a small-scale experiment applying the Government and Binding theory of syntactic analysis. The basic argument is that GB-theory provides a principled foundation for designing grammars which comprise a set of universal features and a set of language-specific features. In a translation system for English and Spanish there are three grammatical components: a universal grammar component (a phrase structure grammar based on X-bar syntax and including rules of Move Affix and Move Alpha) and two language-specific components for English and for Spanish. The latter consist of a lexicon (lexical entries and tables of inflections) and grammar rules characteristic of the language in question; in the case of English it would include rules of Subject-Aux inversion, *have-be* raising, *it*-insertion, etc; for Spanish it would include rules for Verb preposing, Null subject, etc.

The University of **Texas** has long been a centre for MT activity in the United States (its major project METAL has been sponsored since 1978 by the Siemens company and is shortly to be available commercially, cf. 5 above) The tradition of experimental MT research has been continued with an investigation by Alam (1986) of the potential of Lexical-Functional Grammar as a formalism for MT, with particular reference to problematic aspects of Japanese syntax, and with a study by Jin/Simmons (1986) of the feasibility of writing a single set of bi-directional procedural grammar rules which could accomplish both parsing into logical form and generation from logical form, and of paraphrase rules to convert from logical form of one language into logical form of another and vice versa. The languages selected were English and Chinese; the goal was thus one single grammar which both parses and generates Chinese and one single grammar which both parses and generates English. Analysis was in the form of deep case 'semantic representations'; paraphrase (transfer) rules mapped SR structures of one language to SR structures of the other language. The corpus was very small but it was concluded that "it is definitely possible to write grammars to translate between two subsets of natural languages using symmetric rule forms". (The research has clear affinities and relevance to the Rosetta project, see 17 below.)

A similar concentration on basic MT design is evident in the recent work of two ex-members of the TAUM project (a final summary and survey of the substantial achievements of the TAUM-AVIATION system has been given by Isabelle and Bourbeau 1985/1988). Isabelle and Macklovitch (1986) have begun an experimental English-French and French-English system, written in Prolog, which applies a strictly modular transfer approach. SL analysis is strictly TL-independent, and transfer is limited to strict lexical equivalence with no details of constructional features: thus in a transfer dictionary neither English *know* nor French *savoir* and *connaitre* would indicate any structure constraints. (In basic philosophy the approach pursues the rigorous minimisation of transfer seen in the Eurotra specifications, cf. 12 below.)

Finally, mention should be made of the revival of MT research at **Georgetown** University, under Michael Zarechnak (LT4 Dec 87), and the alleged continued interest in MT development by the 'father of Systran', Peter Toma, who is reported to be working on a new system **Textus**, for English-French and French-English translation.

12.
The **EUROTRA** project is the largest MT project in the world (in number of personnel, and possibly in expenditure also) and it remains one of the most ambitious and most experimental, in that it is attempting to define the foundations of multilingual high-quality translation.

Eurotra began in 1978, with two basic aims: to construct a prototype MT system for the official languages of the European Community, and to develop expertise in MT and related areas within the Community. The languages are Danish, Dutch, English, French, German, Greek and Italian. The implications of the addition of Spanish and Portuguese are still not clear (Arnold/Des Tombe 1987). The domain has been limited to information technology and official community documents, and the initial prototype is to have relatively small dictionaries of 20,000 items for each language. The project has been extremely ambitious in terms of the number of languages involved, the high quality of system design, and the political logistics.

Eurotra has an estimated 100 full or part-time researchers in 16 different locations: Belgium (Louvain/Leuven, Liège), Denmark (Copenhagen), France (Centre d'Etudes Linguistiques pour la Traduction Automatique, Nancy), Germany (Saarbrücken, Stuttgart, Berlin, Bielefeld), Netherlands (Institute for Applied Linguistics, Utrecht), Greece (Athens), Ireland (Dublin Institute of Technology), Italy (Institute of Computational Linguistics at the University of Pisa), Luxembourg, United Kingdom (University of Essex, University of Manchester Institute of Science and Technology). In addition there is a Central Unit of about 12 specialist linguists, computer scientists and translators, and a secretariat provided at ISSCO (Geneva). The project is administratively complex thanks to the deliberate policy of decentralisation.

A general account of the current status of the project is provided by Arnold (1986), Arnold et al. (1986), Arnold/Des Tombe (1987) and by a special issue of *Multilingua* (Somers 1986b), which includes accounts of each of the language teams. Earlier stages are represented by Johnson et al. (1984, 1985) and are summarised in Hutchins (1986). Other speculative theoretical contributions of a more specific nature are given by Schmidt (1986) on valency, by Hauenschild (1986) on AI approaches, and by Rohrer (1986a, 1986b) on unification grammar.

The Eurotra project has always stressed the need for explicit and appropriate formalism (e.g. Johnson et al. 1984), firstly for the practical reason that decentralisation of research requires each team to be fully clear of the framework in which it has to work, and secondly for the theoretical reason that multilinguality demands a level of abstraction not previously attempted by any MT project. In the course of the last few years the previous dependence on a GETA-type formalism has been dropped, and there has now emerged a more firmly based theory which embodies the strict application of the compositionality principle, a unification grammar, lexical-functional grammar ideas, etc. The new <c,a>t framework is intended to overcome problems of the older unconstrained 'standard', which allowed too much latitude to alternative formulations (Arnold et al. 1986). The framework is designed to conform to the basic theoretical principles of differentiation (i.e. that meaning distinctions are preserved), simplicity, specificity (inc. perspicuity to researchers) and 'isoduidy' (i.e. that structures must have the same interpretation).

The transfer approach is seen as not only the most practically feasible design for MT, but also as the most appropriate from theoretical considerations. The basic premiss is that the translation process should be regarded as a series of relations between representations (of sentences and texts) which are necessarily linguistic in nature. Translation involves more than the preservation of meaning (unlike 'paraphrase'); in MT representations must be linguistic, and less abstract than content representations. It is argued that the representation languages at the interfaces of analysis and transfer and at the interfaces of transfer and generation have to be formalisms which, having resolved language-specific 'ambiguities', are capable of distinguishing all those interpretations leading to different translations; furthermore, the representation languages must be readily understood and easily learnable by linguists working on the system (i.e. they must be theoretically 'coherent' formalisms). The latter requirement is achieved by defining representation languages as generative devices ('grammars'), which evaluate for 'well-formedness'. A particularly pressing requirement in a multilingual system is for the transfer component to be as 'simple' as possible; consequently, further levels of representation are necessary within SL analysis and TL generation (giving a 'stratificational' model) – at present five levels are being suggested for each language: case frame structure (the interface semantic dependency structure), relational syntax (equivalent to LFG f-structures, and including surface grammatical relations such as subject, object, etc.), configurational syntactic structure (surface structures as represented e.g. in GPSG), morphological structure (decompositions of word structures), and normalised text. Relations between representations are defined by 'translators', a set of rules which are constrained by the principles of 'one-shot'-ness and compositionality. The first principle requires simply that no intermediary representations are created. The second states that the interpretations of structures are functions of the interpretations of their components in a formally defined way. By the notion of compositionality is meant that the translation of a complex expression should be a function of the translation of the basic expressions it contains together with their mode of combination – in this respect Eurotra shows the influence of Landsbergen's Rosetta project (below), whose influence on the Eurotra formalism is readily acknowledged. In Eurotra, however, there is uncertainty whether 'translators' should operate between representations or (as in Rosetta) between derivation trees. The Eurotra approach is also less stringent with respect to the 'isomorphism' of grammars, i.e. it does not extend to the requirement that grammars should be 'attuned' to each other and be truly isomorphic.

The main grammar formalism is the nondeterministic tree-tree transducer (as found also in TAUM and GETA); representations are in the form of dependency trees, at all levels: morphological, surface syntactic, deep syntactic, and interface. The latter are, as in GETA, multi-level representations including morpho-syntactic features as well as semantic features. In general, the formalism is regarded as equivalent in power to that of lexical-functional grammar (Arnold 1986).

There can be no doubt that the theoretical activity of Eurotra researchers has contributed substantially to the theoretical foundations of MT. However, it is conceded readily and frankly that "the results of this research are not very clear yet" and that the obvious limitation is "the lack of a principled account of the lexicon" (Arnold/Des Tombe 1987). Eurotra remains an explicitly 'linguistic' system; it does not attempt to incorporate any knowledge bases or cognitive modelling of the AI kind. It has, therefore, been obviously open to strong criticism for its concentration on abstract formalism, for neglecting the construction of actual grammars, parsers, generators and dictionaries, its insufficient empirical testing, and what is seen as a 'narrow' exclusion of discourse phenomena and advances in knowledge based approaches to natural language processing. Its design was beginning to look 'obsolete', a batch system with no interactive component, an exclusively 'linguistic' model with no AI. In addition, the project was behind schedule; a small prototype was very slow (over 20 minutes for one sentence!); and it had received about $40million from the CEC and contributing countries (LT1 June 1987). The European Parliament set up an independent evaluation.

The report appeared in late 1987 (the Pannenborg report, CEC 1987). It was certainly not uncritical: problems of management had not resolved; there was a lack of central resources; the exclusive emphasis on linguistic foundations had led to a neglect of computational possibilities (e.g. of interactive approaches); there had been insufficient attention to dictionary compilation. The project was criticised for excessive research and for straying from its mandate to create an operational system; the report confirmed fears that the project will fail to produce a prototype by 1990 or a commercial system by 1993. Nevertheless, the project had made fundamental progress in the specification of interfaces and had succeeded in promoting computational linguistics research in member countries. It concluded that it would be a retrograde step for CEC to abandon the project at this stage; what was needed was more realistic deadlines, and it recommended that the research phase should come to an end in 1988 and that the project should then establish closer links with industry and start development of a practical system.

13.

The French MT research group at **Grenoble** is now the longest established. In the 1950's and 1960's its CETA system explored the interlingua approach to MT system design; since 1971 the GETA project has done some of the most fundamental research on the transfer design. The latest version Ariane-85 is a further development of the now well known **Ariane**-78 system described, e.g. by Boitet (1984/1987), Vauquois/Boitet (1985/1988) and summarised in Hutchins (1986: 239-247). The fullest descriptions of Ariane-85 are given in Boitet 1986, 1987a, 1987b. The basic design retains the modular structure, separate SL, TL and bilingual dictionaries and grammars, in the following stages: morphological analysis (strings to trees), structural analysis (producing abstract multilevel tree representations which combine syntactic, logical and semantic relationships), lexical transfer (lexical substitution with some structural changes), structural transfer (tree transduction), syntactic generation, morphological generation (trees to strings).

The long-term aim of the GETA project is a multilingual system producing 'good enough' results, i.e. accepting the need for post-editing. The system is essentially, like Eurotra, a linguistics-oriented system; it does not claim to use any 'deep understanding' or 'intelligence', and hence no AI-type explicit 'expertise' is incorporated in GETA-ARIANE – although the possibility of grafting on an 'expert' error correction mechanism was investigated by Boitet and Gerber (1986). However, unlike other linguistics-based systems, Ariane extends translation analysis to sequences of several sentences or paragraphs, in order to deal with problems of anaphora and tense/aspect agreement. For practical production the system permits optional pre-editing, primarily the marking of lexical ambiguities; post-editing can be done using the REVISION program developed for ARIANE-78. It is a mainframe batch system with no human interaction during processing. However, Zajac (1986) has investigated an interactive analysis module for GETA, somewhat on the lines of Tomita's research at Carnegie-Mellon (Tomita 1986).

One important development has been the refinement of the theoretical basis, particularly the clarification of the distinction and the relationship between dynamic and static grammars in the system. Static grammars (or SCSG 'structural correspondence static grammars') record the correspondences between NL strings and their equivalent interface structures in a formalism which is neutral with respect to analysis and synthesis. The processes of analysis and generation are handled by 'dynamic grammars' written in appropriate 'special languages' (SLLPs or Special Languages for Linguistic Programming): ATEF for morphological analysis, ROBRA for structural analysis, structural transfer and syntactic generation, EXPANS for lexical transfer, and SYGMOR for morphological generation. (The distinction between 'static' and 'dynamic' grammars is now found in many advanced transfer systems; the GETA project has been a leading force in this theoretical development.)

Equally important have been the improvements to the research environment, in tools for the development of systems, such as ATLAS for lexicographic work and VISULEX for viewing complex dictionary entries. Such tools are components of a 'linguistic workstation' for MT research (an idea also being developed by the Saarbrücken and the Kyoto groups, 15 and 26 below). Within this environment the work of the Calliope project has taken place: the compilation of the static grammars for English and French during 1983-84, their corresponding dynamic grammars, and the substantial lexicographic work.

The Grenoble group has always encouraged and supported other MT projects using GETA software, and thereby helped to train MT researchers. ARIANE is regarded above all as "an integrated programming environment" for the development and building of "a variety of linguistic models, in order to test the general multilingual design and the various facilities for lingware preparation..." The ARIANE software has been tested on an impressive range of languages, often in small-scale experiments (Vauquois/Boitet 1985/1988; Hutchins 1986: 247-8; Boitet 1987a), but sometimes in larger projects, e.g. the English-Malay project mentioned elsewhere in this survey.

The largest GETA-ARIANE system has been for Russian-French translation, which built upon previous experience with CETA. Since 1983 this system has been extensively and regularly tested in an experimental 'translation unit'; large corpora of text have been translated, including some 200,000 running words during one 18-month period (Boitet 1987b). Another large-scale system was the German-French system developed by Guilbaud and Stahl, using the same generator programs as in the Russian-French system. Its principal features were the attention given to morphological derivation and inflection, and the restriction of structural analysis almost wholly to morphological and syntactic data, with little or no use of semantic information. The system has been described by Guilbaud (1984/1987), but there has been little development of the system since 1984 (Boitet 1987b).

The most important practical application of a large-scale system has, however, been through GETA's involvement in the French national computer-assisted translation project (NCATP). Launched in November 1983 (after a preparatory stage in 1982-83, the ESOPE project), the **Calliope** project has been financed 50% from public funds (administered by the Agence d'Informatique) and 50% from private sources. One source has been B'VITAL, founded in 1984 by the Grenoble group, which is responsible for the machine-readable dictionaries and for the 'static grammars' (Joscelyne 1987). Another has been Sonovision, which was to provide the aeronautics terminology for the major French-English system Calliope-Aero. After a demonstration of a prototype of Calliope-Aero at Expolangues in February 1986, it was decided to develop also an English-French system for the translation of computer science and data processing materials, Calliope-Info. In addition to these MT systems, both batch systems, the project was also to produce a translator's workstation (Calliope-Revision, organised around a Bull Questar 400 microcomputer) for preparing and post-editing texts and for access to remote term banks and including OCR and desk-top publishing facilities. This was essential if the systems were to be fully integrated into an industrial documentation environment. However, given the expected delays there have been plans by SG2 (one of the backers) to develop a terminology aid with split-screen word processing, Calliope-Manuel.

Whatever the commercial feasibility of the Calliope project, which came to a formal end in February 1987 (Boitet 1987a), the experience will no doubt be put to good use by the GETA project, in particular the experience of dealing with complex dictionaries and the type of scientific and technical sublanguage presented by aeronautics. Boitet (1986), for example, mentions the successful treatment of complex noun phrases (eg. *la jonction bloc frein et raccord de tuyauterie*) and complex adjectival phrases (eg. *comprise entre les deux index noir*). Other problems did not occur in the sublanguage and were thus put aside, e.g. interrogatives, relative clauses introduced by *dont*, imperatives, certain comparatives, nominal groups which do not only consist of nouns, and so forth.

The NCATP has had other consequences. It stimulated the conversion of the ARIANE-85 to run on IBM PC AT (with a minimum 20MB hard disk), adequate for MT development but not for a production system. It also encouraged the writing of new software in a French dialect of Lisp (Boitet 1986; Boitet 1987a, 1987b), with the aim of creating a fully multilingual system with a single 'special language' for processing strings and trees (TETHYS). Clearly, GETA has continued to advance the boundaries of MT research.

14.

While GETA is the main MT research centre in France, there are other MT projects in Nancy and Poitiers. At **Nancy**, Chauché (1986; Rolf/Chauché 1986) continues his research, begun at Grenoble, on algorithms for tree manipulation which are suitable for MT systems. Tests of the algorithms have been applied to Spanish-French and Dutch-French experiments (in collaboration with Rolf of Nijmegen University). From Poitiers, Pocsco (1986) reports a small-scale knowledge-based MT experiment for translating Rumanian texts on three dimensional geometry into French. The ATN parser produces a conceptual frame-slot representation from which the generator devises a 'plan' for producing TL output.

The restricted language system **TITUS**, designed for multilingual treatment of abstracts in the textile industry, has expanded in its latest version TITUS IV (Ducrot 1985) in order to deal with a wider range of subjects and to allow somewhat freer expression of contents.

As elsewhere, there is commercial interest in translators' workstations: **Cap Sogeti** Innovations is proposing a "language engineering workshop", providing 'intelligent' language tools, a dedicated multilingual word processor, a natural language knowledge base, a technical summary writer, and a 'text analyzer' which will produce abstract meaning representations. Details are necessarily vague at present (Joscelyne 1987).

Attitudes to MT in France are most likely to be changed by the provision of MT services on **Minitel**. The availability of Systran has already been mentioned (sect. 1 above). Other services include a number of dictionaries and term banks: the Harrap French and English slang dictionary, the Dictionary of Industries, Normaterm (the term bank of the French standards organisation AFNOR), the DAICADIF lexicon for telecommunications, and (next year) FRANTEXT the historical dictionary Trésor de la Langue Française.

15.

The largest and most long-established MT group in Germany is based at **Saarbrücken**. It began in the mid-1960's with research on Russian-German translation, sponsored from 1972 to 1986 by the Deutsche Forschungsgemeinschaft. The SUSY project expanded into a multilingual system, based on the transfer approach, with the source languages German, Russian, English, French, and Esperanto, and the target languages German, English and French. Detailed descriptions of the latest version SUSY II as at the end of 1984 are given by Maas (1984/1987) and by Blatt et al. (1985), and summarised by Hutchins (1986: 233-239).

The most recent developments of MT research at Saarbrücken are to be found in Zimmermann et al. (1987). The most significant are the changes introduced into the basic design by the introduction of English as a SL (in SUSY-E project), the development of explicit formalisms and software tools for testing natural language processing and MT models and for general computational linguistic experimentation (SAFRAN: Software and Formalism for the Representation of Natural Language – see Licher et al. 1987), the planned application of SUSY as the foundation of a production-oriented system (STS), the new direction of Saarbrücken MT research in the ASCOF project for French and German translation, and the involvement of SUSY personnel in the Eurotra project.

The greater emphasis on product-oriented research has arisen in part from the ending of direct DFG funding in 1986. The project **MARIS** (Multilinguale Anwendung von Referenz- Informationssystemen) was established in mid-1985 at the University of the Saar to develop a multilingual information retrieval system, in particular to meet the needs of German-speaking users of English-language documentation (Zimmermann et al. 1987; Luckhardt 1987b). For this purpose, the MARIS team is developing a computer-assisted translation system STS (Saarbrücker Translationsservice) based on the Saarbrucken MT research. Initially only English-German will be developed, and it will restricted to the translation of abstracts and titles of journal articles. There are three phases to the project: first a manual system in which translators can have access to computer-based term banks, secondly the addition of automatic lookup of terminology, and thirdly the application of SUSY as a post-edited MT system. The chief emphasis will be on lexicographic data and sublanguage information in the particular fields of application: housing and construction, environment, standards, social sciences. At a later stage it is hoped to add French-German and German-French versions. The MARIS project is a natural continuation of basic MT research on SUSY, some earlier experience with a prototype translator's workstation (SUSANNAH) and the long-established research at Saarbrücken under Harald Zimmermann on information retrieval systems.

The **ASCOF** project (Projektbereich C at Saarbrücken) grew out of research at Saarbrücken on computational methods for the analysis of the 'Archive du Français Contemporain' (established in mid-1960's). The project team initially worked in close collaboration with GETA. However, from the mid 1970's, after the elaboration of French analysis programs for SUSY, the team established closer links with the Saarbrücken MT projects. For a while the research was using both GETA and SUSY algorithms, but since 1977 it has concentrated on SUSY-type methods, and in 1981 it emerged as an independent MT project at Saarbrücken (Scheel 1987). Its distinctive features are: the use of the COMSKEE programming language, the integration of syntactic and semantic analysis, the adoption of ATN parsers, and the use of semantic networks as a 'knowledge base' for disambiguation.

ASCOF (Biewer et al. 1985/1988; Stegentritt 1987) is a system for French-German translation with a multilevel modular transfer design. Programs are written in COMSKEE (Computing and String Keeping Language), the programming environment developed at Saarbrücken. The object of ASCOF

(= Analyse und Synthese des Französischen mit Comskee) is fundamental MT research not a practical system.

Analysis is in three basic phases. The first phase of morphological analysis is followed by a second phase in three parts: disambiguation of word class homographs, identification of non-complex syntactic groups, and segmentation of sentences into independent (unrelated) parts, e.g. noun, verb and prepositional phrases. In the third phase, structural analysis is realised by a series of cascaded ATN parsers which combine syntax (e.g. functional relations) and semantics (e.g. case frames or valencies), with no priority given to either one or the other. Analysis modules operate not sequentially but interactively: thus analyses of verb phrases, complex noun phrases, complements, coordination etc. interact with each other. The integration of syntax and semantics in ASCOF analysis contrasts with procedures in SUSY and other linguistics-based transfer systems. Lexical disambiguation is achieved by reference to semantic networks which include information on synonymy, homonymy, hyponymy (e.g. whole-part, genus-species), and semantic-functional frames for verbs. As in GETA and EUROTRA, the results of analysis are not interlingual representations but SL canonical trees in which SL-specific lexical and syntactic ambiguities have been resolved.

Transfer operates in a familiar way with bilingual lexical substitution and structural tree transduction, and it is followed by TL syntactic synthesis and morphological synthesis for the production of TL text output. Most of the ASCOF research effort has concentrated on problems of analysis and on testing the semantic network approach to disambiguation. Consequently the transfer and synthesis components have not yet been fully developed; there is no French synthesis program and only a small German one, so only partial implementation of translation from French into German has been possible so far (Stegentritt 1987). The system is to be tested on EEC agricultural texts, and this corpus has provided the data for the illustrative semantic networks. The quality of the output is considered to be crucially dependent on the development and elaboration of the semantic networks, the linguistic 'knowledge base' of the system. ASCOF is an example of a transfer system of the third generation of MT, incorporating AI-style 'knowledge base' semantic analysis, and aiming in the long-term for high quality (batch) translation.

16.

ASCOF has not been the only context in which research on knowledge based approaches to linguistic analysis has been conducted at Saarbrücken. There has been activity in text-oriented MT by Weber and Rothkegel. Weber (1986, 1987) has investigated a small-scale text-oriented system for MT. **COAT** (= Coherence Analysis of Texts) is a program, written in COMSKEE, which establishes text coherence, using information about valencies, arguments and roles, and produces complex representations of SL texts which might be translated into equivalent TL text representations. Analysis is not to the depth of AI-type understanding, only sufficient for translation. A speculative extension is OVERCOAT (not implemented) for establishing global text structures (paragraph sequencing) and AI-type discourse frames, and involving 'knowledge' of stereotypical situations and events. Rothkegel's (1986a, 1986b, 1987) research between 1981 and 1986 was devoted to TEXAN, a system for recognising text-linguistic features (illocution, thematisation, coherence, etc.), for identifying text types (specifically EEC treaties) and consequently enabling text-specific semantic and structural analysis, disambiguation and transfer.

The Saarbrücken group had collaborated with Kyoto to develop a system for translating German journal titles into Japanese. SUSY was used for the analysis of German titles and TITRAN for the generation of Japanese titles (Ammon/Wessoly 1984-85). There has subsequently been a similar project at Stuttgart to produce German translations of Japanese journal titles in the information technology field (Laubsch et al. 1984, Rösner 1986a, 1986b). The **SEMSYN** (Semantische Synthese) system takes as input the semantic interface representations of Japanese texts produced by Fujitsu's ATLAS/II system (cf. 30 below). ATLAS was designed for Japanese-English translation and so the semantic interface representations were not completely sufficient for German synthesis, since they gave few indications of number, definiteness, or tense. SEMSYN is a semantics-based MT system (or rather partial system); it incorporates a frame description formalism (cases, roles, modalities, scopes, purpose, part-whole relations, etc.) from which German titles are generated by reference to a restricted knowledge base of linguistic and extra-linguistic information. Like many AI-inspired systems, SEMSYN is written in Lisp.

The Saarbrücken group was an early participant in the Eurotra project and it has contributed a number of theoretical studies. Two recent examples are the work of Steiner (1986) on generation and of Schmidt (1986) on valency structures. However, the West German Ministry for Research and Technology (Bundesministerium für Forschung und Technologie) has also established three groups in Berlin, Bielefeld and Stuttgart to undertake theoretical research on behalf of the Eurotra project. The BMFT project as a whole is known as **NASEV** (Neue Analyse- und Syntheseverfahren zur maschinellen Übersetzung).

At Stuttgart, Rohrer (1986a, 1986b) has been investigating the relevance of formal linguistics to the theoretical basis of MT. He advocates unification grammars (e.g. LFG, GPSG, FUG) as offering the most appropriate general frameworks for future advances in MT research. At the Technical University of Berlin, Hauenschild (1986) has been investigating AI approaches to problems of MT transfer. This research, under the acronym KIT (Künstliche Intelligenz und Textverstehen), commenced in April 1985, and can be regarded as a continuation of her previous work on the CON3TRA project at the University of Konstanz and on the earlier SALAT project at Heidelberg. Hauenschild's model proposes (i) SL analysis in terms of a modified Generalized Phrase Structure Grammar, (ii) conversion into an intentional logic representation directly from the GPSG analysis (applying compositional semantic rules in the manner of Montague grammar), and then (iii) conversion into two levels of semantic representation: a level of 'referential nets' linking text referents, and a level of global 'text argument' structures recording intersentential relations. Transfer would operate at multiple levels: lexical (at semantic representations), sentence-semantic (at intentional logic representations, i.e. in order to preserve informational structure of SL texts), and syntactic (i.e. from 'superficial syntactic' GPSG analyses). The semantic representation language is a propositional logical formalism (with variables and operators), and includes knowledge of facts, rules and objects. The 'argument structure' representation is regarded as genuinely interlingual in so far as logical, case and argument features may be 'universal'. However, the precise division of levels is still fluid. As a MT model, Hauenschild's work represents the convergence of many recent strands of MT theory.

17.

Two of the most innovative MT projects at present time are based in the Netherlands. Both have chosen to develop interlingua models. At Philips in Eindhoven, the Rosetta project is exploring a system based on Montague grammar; at the BSO software company in Utrecht, the DLT project is building a system with Esperanto as the interlingua.

The basic principles of **Rosetta** derive from its foundations on Montague grammar (Landsbergen 1984/1987, Appelo/Landsbergen 1986, Leermakers/Rous 1986, Landsbergen 1987). The main characteristic of Montague grammar is the derivation of meaning representations (interpretations) from the syntactic structure of expressions. A fundamental principle is compositionality, namely the premiss that the meaning of an expression is a function of the meaning of its parts. Since the parts are defined by syntax, there is a close relation between syntax and semantics. The link is the correspondence of syntactic derivation trees and semantic derivation trees. Syntactic derivation trees represent the processes by which syntactic rules are applied to produce a syntactic analysis (parsing) of a sentence. For each rule of a syntactic derivation tree there is taken to be a corresponding semantic operation; hence, the semantic value of a full syntactic derivation is given by its corresponding parallel semantic derivation tree. From such semantic derivation trees may be derived logical expressions (in an intentional logic formalism), and this is frequently the preferred option by Montague grammarians.

One model for a MT system based on Montague grammar would, therefore, be to use these logical expressions as interlingua representations. But this would entail the loss of information about the surface 'form' of messages or texts, and this is information which can be vital for generating satisfactory translations. Furthermore there would be the problem of devising a single logical formalism for a wide variety of languages. Consequently, the Rosetta project has taken a different approach: it aims to use the semantic derivation trees as interlingual representations. This is done by making the syntactic derivation trees of the languages in the system isomorphic, and isomorphism is achieved by attuning the grammars of the languages in question (their 'M-grammars') so that for every syntactic rule in one language there is a corresponding syntactic rule in the other with the same meaning operation, i.e. so that the processes of constructing or deriving sentences in one language are parallel to the processes of constructing and deriving (translationally) equivalent sentences in the other language. Thus the corresponding semantic derivation trees are identical and in effect interlingual representations for the languages whose grammars have been 'attuned' appropriately. Rosetta is thus intended as a multilingual interlingua system; initial research (in the six-year project starting in 1985) will concentrate on developing successively more sophisticated M-grammars of three languages, English, Dutch and Spanish; with other languages to be added at later stages.

Rosetta adds another principle to those of compositionality and isomorphism. This is the reversibility principle: a single grammar of a language (M-grammar) should be the basis of procedures for both analysis (M-parser) and synthesis (M-generator), so that for each analytical rule there is a reverse generative rule, i.e. grammar rules should be reversible in a bi-directional MT system. Explicitness and rigour of grammars, formalisms and theoretical foundations are natural and expected concomitants of a MT model based so firmly on achievements in formal linguistic theory. Rosetta is, then, deliberately and explicitly a linguistics-oriented model. Specific linguistic problems and their treatment have been reported: temporal verbs (Appelo 1986), idioms (Schenk 1986), and synonymy (de Jong/Appelo 1987). The need for extra-linguistic knowledge is recognised in a practical translation system, but the incorporation of AI-type extra-linguistic data in the model is to follow at a later stage of the project.

18.
The MT project in Utrecht at the software company, Buro voor Systeemontwikkeling (BSO) began in 1982 with a feasibility study supported by the EEC. BSO set up a six-year project in 1985, with the assistance of a substantial grant from the Netherlands Ministry of Economic Affairs, to build a prototype system for translating from English into French, with a commercial version expected in 1993.

DLT (Distributed Language Translation) is designed as an interactive multilingual system operating over computer networks, where each terminal acts as a translating machine from and into one language only; texts are transmitted between terminals of the network in an intermediary language, a version of Esperanto. DLT is not, therefore, a 'translating machine' or a tool for translators but primarily a tool for interlingual communication, enabling monolingual users (authors) the means to generate their texts in other languages. Users will know only the language of source texts; hence they will interact during analysis and transfer in their own language – in some cases, interaction may lead to rephrasing original texts in order to remove ambiguities or translation problems. A description of the present DLT system is given by Schubert (1986), and more extensive treatments of the semantics and syntax in Papegaaij (1986) and Schubert (1987).

As an interlingua system, DLT has two basic parts: analysis of SL texts into IL (Esperanto) representations, and generation of TL texts from IL representations. Analysis is by far the most complex, since the results must be unambiguous for both the SL and for any of the potential TLs. In the DLT system the decision has been made to restrict linguistic analysis of SL sentences to morphological and syntactic features and to concentrate all semantic disambiguation at IL stages. There are therefore no SL and TL semantic components, all semantico-lexical knowledge is represented in an IL (Esperanto) database. The arguments in favour of Esperanto as an IL are given as being its NL-like expressiveness and flexibility, its regularity and consistency, and its independence from other NLs (its autonomy) – i.e. unlike the IL in Rosetta, the DLT IL is not 'attuned' (adapted or refined) to the SL and TL involved.

Analysis passes through the following stages: SL syntax parsing, SL-IL transfer, IL semantic 'word expert' system (SWESIL), SL dialogue, IL linearization. In the DLT English-French prototype texts are composed in Simplified English (a 'restricted grammar'), with the aim of free unrestricted input by 1990. Syntactic analysis is performed by an ATN parser producing dependency tree representations; multiple analyses are common because no resolution of non-syntactic homography or ambiguity is undertaken. SL(English)-IL transfer involves three aspects: (a) replacement of English words by tentative IL words, (b) arrangement of IL lexical items in syntactically correct IL trees, and (c) selecting the semantically and pragmatically best tree. The first step is done by straightforward substitution via a bilingual English-IL dictionary. The second step is done by 'metataxis' rules which take as input subtrees relating groups of (English) lexical items and produce as output their corresponding IL subtrees; a detailed account of metataxis and its linguistic foundations is given by Schubert (1987).

At this stage, there will be a number of IL subtrees representing different interpretations of the SL (English) input sentence. It is the task of the IL 'word expert' system to determine which is the correct or most probable interpretation. SWESIL (Semantic Word Expert System for the Intermediate Language) tests pairs of IL words linked by a dependency relationship (expressed by an IL relator, e.g. preposition) for meaning compatibility, computes a score which indicates the probability of the given two words occurring in the given dependency relation, ranks the probability scores for all the possible relationships and determines which meanings and which relationships are to be selected. In this way SWESIL resolves syntactic ambiguities of SL input which cannot be solved by monolingual syntactic information, and at the same time it defines unambiguous IL interfaces from which TL forms are generated. The knowledge required by SWESIL is both syntagmatic, i.e. lists of acceptable IL word pairs and their relators, and paradigmatic, i.e. taxonomies of IL words, tree-structures of part-whole, genus-species, hypernym-hyponym relations, etc. It also contains both linguistic and world knowledge, and is thus modelled on AI-type knowledge-based systems, although unlike many systems DLT does not use semantic features or 'primitives'. (More details of SWESIL are given by Papegaaij 1986.)

Any residual ambiguities are presented for resolution to the user in a computer-initiated interactive dialogue in the user's own language, i.e. not in Esperanto. (It is intended that the results of these interactions will be incorporated in the SWESIL knowledge base, which will thus become a 'learning' system.) Finally, the 'unambiguous' IL text is linearized as quasi-Esperanto sentences for transmission in the network. At earlier stages of the DLT project it was anticipated that Esperanto would have to be extensively modified; in practice little modification has been found to be necessary and so the linearized IL representations are consequently readily understood by anyone familiar with 'normal' Esperanto (thus facilitating inspection of DLT system performance by researchers).

The conversion of the IL text into TL text is to be performed without any human intervention. Synthesis is the inverse of analysis: problems of TL word choice are resolved by reference to SWESIL information, a bilingual IL-TL (French) dictionary and a set of IL-TL metataxis rules converts IL structures into TL (French) dependency trees, which are in turn linearized as French sentences.

A launch of the DLT prototype in December 1987 (LT5;LM52), though based on a small 2000 word vocabulary, demonstrated the basic feasibility of the approach; the present operational slowness is expected to be overcome by future advances in parallel processing. Most research effort will concentrate on building the Esperanto based knowledge bank. The DLT group have recognised the importance of tackling lexical problems of MT from the beginning, instead of leaving them (as many MT projects have done) until after procedures for morphological and syntactic analysis and synthesis have been fixed. For this reason, an initial test of the lexical adequacy of the system was undertaken independently by Melby (1986; Sadler/Papegaaij 1987).

19.

Although there is no large MT project in Belgium there is an impressive amount of activity in this area and in the related fields of computational linguistics and artificial intelligence. Researchers at the universities of Liège and Leuven (Louvain) in Belgium participate in both the Eurotra project (the Belgo-Français and the Belgo-Dutch groups respectively) and in the development of the Siemens

METAL system for Dutch-French translation (which also has input from the University of Mons). In addition, there is an independent project at the Free University of Brussels to develop a microcomputer system for English-French translation of computer manuals (Luctkens/Fremont 1986). The ultimate aim is a multilingual transfer design, but as yet the experiment has concentrated primarily on developing an ATN parser for syntactic analysis.

20.
In the recent past MT research in Great Britain was negligible; now there are some signs of greater interest and support. The centres for the Eurotra project are the University of Essex and the University of Manchester Institute of Science and Technology (UMIST). Both centres have made substantial and important contributions in the areas of software development, linguistic theory, and the formalization of the basic environment. The MT experience at UMIST has been augmented by a grant from the governmental Science and Engineering Research Council (under the so-called Alvey initiative), and with substantial support from the computer company ICL. A joint project has been set up with the University of Sheffield: the UMIST team are undertaking research on an English-Japanese system, the Sheffield group on a Japanese-English model. Knowles (1987) gives a general outline of the two projects, due to come to an end in October 1987.

The English-Japanese prototype (**NTRAN**) at UMIST is an interactive transfer system, written in Prolog with Lexical Functional Grammar providing the basic framework for parsing, transfer and generation. A bottom-up parser produces LFG-type F-structures; from these are derived the S-structure interface representations which are converted into equivalent Japanese interfaces; these S-structures are the source of the F-structures for Japanese surface strings.

In this project the approach to interactive MT differs from the familiar one (although shared by the DLT project). It is argued that a MT system should concentrate on producing good TL output on the basis of SL texts interpreted interactively with users of the system (Johnson/Whitelock 1987; Whitelock et al. 1986). The user is thus freed from the need to know anything about the TL. Any deficiencies of the MT system in knowledge of the SL or in the subject matter of the texts will be made good by the user in computer-initiated dialogues (on lines indicated by Tomita 1986). The intention is that users of the system would be authors who compose documents in their own language (English) and are prompted for explanation (and resolution) of ambiguities in their own language. Disambiguation would take place not during analysis but during transfer, when it will be known not only what SL ambiguities are present but also what particular translation problems are prompted by the language-specific characteristics of the TL. Although the aim is essentially to solve translation difficulties, it is envisaged that the mechanism could also act as 'intelligent style-checker', i.e. an interactive rewriting component. NTRAN is deliberately underdetermined in SL syntax and lexicon semantics; the emphasis is on the knowledge base of linguistic and extra-linguistic information necessary for transfer and generation. In this way, the 'expertise' of the MT system resides in its 'knowledge' of the TL and the problems of interpretation from the perspective of that language. It is not an 'expert' in the SL and the subject; that knowledge is provided interactively by the operator (or author).

The Sheffield (**AIDTRANS**) model for Japanese-English translation is derived from research on teaching people with little linguistic talent how to 'decode' Japanese texts by using a sophisticated grammar-dictionary in an 'automaton-like' fashion. (The integrated grammar-dictionary was devised by Jiri Jelinek who had worked on MT in Czechoslovakia before emigrating to Britain.) The system is strictly uni-directional (Japanese-English) and, in terms of MT design, based on the 'direct translation' model of linear predictive analysis. The intention of the project is to computerise the almost 'mechanical' procedures of the human learners ('decoders'), and to produce a type of machine-aided system of translation.

As elsewhere, there are in Britain small-scale experiments. One is the **SLUNT** system, an interlingua model based on numerical coding of vocabulary items, which is described with a demonstration microcomputer program in Goshawke et al. (1988). Another is **TRANPRO**, a translator's aid (essentially a multilingual word processing package) providing access to remote dictionaries and in-house glossary updating (LM34 July 1986). A third is the research reported from **ICL** (International Computers Ltd.) on Telex message translation for the language pairs English and French and English and German (LT5 Jan 1988).

More widely reported is the research by **British Telecom** on a speech translation system for business telephone messages (Stentiford/Steers 1987). The system, first announced in August 1987, has been under development since 1984; a marketable system is hoped for in the mid 1990's. The speaker utters his message clearly and deliberately into a microphone attached to a Merlin 2000 microcomputer. The message is confirmed by a synthetic repetition, then translated and spoken by a speech synthesis program in a TL. The languages involved at present are English, French, German, Italian, Spanish and Swedish. The corpus is limited to a set of 400 common business phrases involving some 1000 different words. The computer program is designed to recognise (by pattern matching) 100 keywords from which it can select the intended phrase and generate (synthesise) a spoken phrase in another language. Speech recognition is prone to considerable error, but errors can be reduced by restricting the domain and by limiting identification to a small number of keywords. The researchers claim that for this limited corpus, any phrase can be identified by three or four keywords (not necessarily 'content words' only). At present, the speech recognizer has to be trained for each individual speaker; the aim is for the system to be speaker-independent, to handle a larger vocabulary and to produce more natural output.

21.
Spain is a newcomer to MT research. Mention has already been made of activity in connection with Siemens' METAL project (sect. 5 above). There are recent reports (LT2 August 1987) that the **IBM** Research Centers in Spain and Israel will be directing a study of the feasibility of MT systems for English-Spanish and English-Hebrew (probably batch systems with post-editing), for use within IBM itself. The company had earlier invested heavily in a trial of ALPS machine aids for English-French translation. The principle aim will be "to develop internal IBM knowledge and expertise in machine translation", involving other IBM Centers in Europe and inviting university participants (Helsinki is already committed). It appears that the system will be written in Lisp and will not be IBM-hardware specific, and that it will probably use the English parser developed at the Yorktown Center in the United States for the EPISTLE system.

22.
The Dalle Molle Institute for Semantic and Cognitive Studies (**ISSCO**) in Geneva, Switzerland, has been active in the Eurotra project from the beginning, functioning for a while as the secretariat of the project and convening seminars on MT and related aspects of computational linguistics (e.g. the proceedings of the 1984 Lugano tutorial edited by Smith 1987). The Institute has also undertaken experimental work itself, for example, the project described by Buchmann et al. (1984). This is a prototype MT system (SEPPLI) for translating job advertisements from German into French and Italian. The corpus is limited to posts in administration taken from a Swiss government weekly publication. The objective of the project is to define the depth of linguistic analysis necessary in this particular domain and sublanguage – which exhibits a high proportion of noun phrases, few finite verbs and no relative phrases and dependent clauses. The hypothesis is that analysis can be relatively 'shallow', with dependency trees representing only partial analyses. For example, there is no attempt to establish the correct relationships of prepositional phrases, coordination, etc. since the surface linearity of the SL texts is retained in the TL output. The limited lexical domain of the sublanguage obviates the need for a semantic component. The model – a familiar transfer design, with independent modules for SL analysis and TL generation – is seen primarily as a didactic and research tool; no large-scale operational system is planned.

23.
Scandinavian activity has been mentioned already: the involvement of researchers at Copenhagen University in the Eurotra project, the **ENTRA** (English-Norwegian) system developed in collaboration with Weidner (WCC) at Bergen University, the report of collaboration by researchers at Helsinki

University in the IBM project (cf. 21 above), and the use of MT for translating Japanese databases at the Research Policy Institute of Lund University (Sigurdson/Greatrex). Mention should also be made of the experimental work by Sigurd, also at Lund, on the multilingual Prolog-based **SWETRA** system.

24.
In recent years there has apparently been little new research activity directly on MT as such in Eastern Europe. In the Soviet Union it would appear that development of the AMPAR, NERPA and FRAP systems (cf. Hutchins 1986: 308-313) has not progressed significantly. The same seems to be true of MT research at Charles University **Prague**, which has always been a strong centre for computational linguistics (e.g. Hajičová and Sgall) and experimentation on advanced MT would seem likely in the future. In the meantime there are just reports of work on the dictionary formats for machine-aided English-Czech translation (Strossa 1987). Other relatively small projects are reported from Hungary and Bulgaria. At **Szeged** University (Hungary) Fabricz (1986) has been studying problems of modal particles (e.g. *only, nur*) in connection with an experimental English-Hungarian project. In **Sofia** (Bulgaria) a project for an English-Bulgarian system has been reported (Pericliev 1984, Pericliev/Iliaronov 1986) – the researchers argue that sentences which are ambiguous in the SL (English) do not need to be disambiguated if there exist parallel structures in the TL (Bulgarian) which maintain the same ambiguities. For example '*He promised to please mother*' and the corresponding Bulgarian '*Toj obešta da zaradva majka*'; in both cases the subordinated constructions (*to please mother, da zaradva majka*) can refer either to the object of the 'promise' or to the manner of the 'promise'. There are clear advantages in not having to disambiguate pronoun references if there is an equally 'ambiguous' pronoun in the TL. Further evidence of renewed interest in MT in Bulgaria was the holding of a conference in Sofia in May 1987 (LM48 Sept 1987).

25.
Without any doubt the country which has seen the most rapid expansion of MT research of all kinds is Japan. MT activity in Japan has been stimulated by a number of factors: the great demand for translations from English, in particular of scientific and technical information, the demand for companies to produce English-language marketing and technical documentation for their products, the rapid growth of the Japanese export trade and of international competition, the great difficulties experienced by Japanese in learning European languages, the promotion of the Fifth Generation Project to give Japan a leading position in the future 'information society'. There are estimated to be now some 800-900 people presently engaged on research (Sigurdson/Greatrex 1987), with probably 60% of these in commercial companies, mainly involved in computer manufacture or in computer software.

The Japanese language has presented challenges to MT system design that were absent when most research concentrated on European languages. There are problems of the script: the combination of Japanese alphabets (hiragana and katakana) and Chinese characters, with no capitals and no spaces between words; and problems of language structure: a verb-final and modifier-modified language, no distinction of singular and plural nouns, no definite and indefinite articles, frequent omission of subjects (particularly pronouns), a largely free word order, numerous embedded compound clauses in sentences. much use of particles, and a 'logical' tense system. As a consequence, analysis of Japanese is oriented to the identification of semantic (case) relations rather than syntactic (phrase) structures, and operational systems often rely heavily on pre-editing (breaking up long sentences, inserting the omitted subjects, marking the modifying clauses, indicating the functions of particles). Most Japanese-English systems are intended for Japanese users who can do the pre-editing; Western users with no knowledge of Japanese will therefore get poor results, although the output may be good enough for information purposes (Sigurdson/Greatrex 1987).

Most systems and research projects are for translation between English and Japanese, although there is also interest in Japanese-Korean. General descriptions of current MT activity in Japan are to be found in Nishida/Doshita (1986), Whitelock (1987), Sigurdson/Greatrex (1987), and papers given at the MT Summit (1987).

26.
A pioneering centre for MT research has been **Kyoto** University under Makoto Nagao, whose influence is evident in many current projects. The Japanese government MT project (the Mu project) at Kyoto was completed in March 1986 (Tsujii 1987). Its aim was to develop a prototype system for Japanese-English and English-Japanese translation for a restricted subject domain and restricted document types. Mu is a bilingual transfer system, with dependency grammar analysis, a pre-transfer 'loop' to convert SL structures into more neutral forms, transfer proper (lexical and structural substitution), a post-transfer 'loop' for further adjustments to TL structures, and generation. Whereas analysis and generation of Japanese is wholly case grammar based, analysis and generation of English is partly based on a phrase structure grammar. An important contribution of the Kyoto research has been the development of a programming environment for grammar writing, the GRADE system (in conception similar to the 'special languages' of GETA.) A description of the Mu system is given by Nagao et al. (1985/1988, 1986), Nagao/Tsujii (1986), Nagao (1987). Evaluation of the output showed that unedited MT output was good enough for rough understanding of the gists of documents.

The Mu-II project is a four-year project (1986-1990) to transform the research prototype into a practical system for daily use by the Japan Information Center for Science and Technology (JICST) for translating abstracts. The project's aims are to reduce processing speeds and memory requirements, to enhance the dictionaries, to reduce the need for pre-editing, and to integrate text editing facilities. The development is being undertaken by researchers at Tokyo University, at the Electrotechnical Laboratory and at JICST, with the support of the Japanese government's Science and Technology Agency. It has been reported that more than 50 researchers at JICST are working full-time on MT: mostly on dictionaries, but 10 on grammar and 10 on software (Sigurdson/Greatrex 1987). Sakamoto et al. (1986) describe the development of semantic markers, principally case frame features, to improve the quality of Japanese-English translation.

The other system developed at Kyoto, the restricted language system **TITRAN** for translating titles of scientific and technical papers, which was originally developed for English-Japanese, has now been extended to Japanese-English and Japanese-French. The English-Japanese version was evaluated and has been implemented in the Tsukuba Research Information Processing System of the Agency of Industrial Science and Technology. A collaborative project with Saarbrücken was also undertaken to adapt TITRAN to translating Japanese titles into German.

Since the ending of the research phase of Mu, the Kyoto MT team has been concentrating on basic theoretical work. Small scale projects have included research on a system written in Lisp for Chinese and Japanese, by Yang/Doshita (1986).

27.
There are numerous Japanese university research groups, e.g. at Tokyo Institute of Technology, Oita University, Kyushu University, Toyohashi University of Technology, University of Osaka Prefecture, Kobe University (where Sanamrad/Matsumoto (1986) have developed PERSIS, an analysis program for Persian). From the University of Tokyo Chung/Kunii (1986) have reported on the NARA system to translate from Korean into Japanese and vice versa; they claim that the syntactic structures of the two languages are sufficiently similar (both being agglutinative and verb-final languages) for the formal transfer mechanism to be relatively simple. The project has concentrated so far on syntactic matters, adopting the formalism of Generalized Phrase Structure Grammar.

28.
The Japanese government is funding MT research through the Overseas Development Agency (ODA) and through its Key Technology Center (KTC), set up from capital resulting from the privatisation of NTT.

The Electronic Dictionary Research Institute (**EDR**), with 70% support from KTC and 30% from 8 electronics companies (Fujitsu, Hitachi, Mitsubishi. Matsushita, NEC, Oki, Sharp, Toshiba), is to collaborate with ICOT, the research facility established for the Fifth Generation Project (Sigurdson/Greatrex 1987). It will undertake basic research into dictionary systems and in the production of computer software programs for dictionary compilation. The project will develop two types of dictionaries (Kakizaki 1987). Word dictionaries, with entries under headwords giving definitions (concepts expressed) and grammatical features, will be developed both in English and in Japanese for 'basic' vocabulary (200,000 words of 'daily life') and for specialised terminology (100,000 words from the field of information processing). Concept dictionaries will be constructed using a 'knowledge representation language' which indicate possible (binary) relations between concepts: dependencies (e.g. cause-effect), synonymy, hypernymy, hyponymy, and thesaural relations by means of a concept classification. Major problems are recognised to be the maintenance of consistency, uniformity and accuracy. The dictionaries are to be evaluated by testing on MT systems, Information Retrieval systems and voice recognition systems. The main goal is the construction of dictionaries for interlingual MT systems (e.g. the ODA project, see below), and extension to other languages is envisaged.

Longer term research is being supported by KTC at **Osaka**, the seven-year project for Basic Research of Automatic Translation Telephone, funded 70% by KTC and 30% by the NTT and KDD telephone companies (Sigurdson/Greatrex 1987). The project has close links with the **ATR** (Advanced Telecommunications Research) project for automated telephony. At least 15 years basic research is anticipated; ATR originally offered collaboration with European and US companies (LM26 Nov 85). The approach at ATR has been particularly influenced by the MT research at NTT (see 36 below) by Nomura and his colleagues (e.g. Kogure/Nomura 1987).

The **ODA** project is an ambitious scheme to develop a multilingual system for translating between Japanese and languages of the Pacific economic region, Malay, Bahasa Indonesian, Thai and Chinese. It will be a collaborative project involving teams to be set up the countries concerned. The six-year R&D project is receiving central funds from MITI (Ministry of International Trade and Industry) via CICC (Center of the International Cooperation for Computerization). The political aim is to promote technological and cultural exchange between Japan and other Asian countries, and to encourage the research capabilities of the countries concerned in the area of computer technology. Initial plans have been reported by Tsuji (1987); it will be an interlingua (text-analysis) system for two-way translation of industrial and technical information between Japanese and Thai, Japanese and Malay, Japanese and Indonesian, Japanese and Chinese (and with an eventual potential as a fully multilingual system supporting translation from and to Thai, Malay, Indonesian and Chinese). The aim is 80-90% accuracy with pre-editing, and a speed of 5000 words per hour. The project will concentrate on the development of general and special dictionaries, on the interlingua, on text analysis and generation procedures, and on a translation support system. In many respects the project is as ambitious in both political and linguistic terms as the Eurotra project (sect. 12 above).

The research at the Japanese government **Electrotechnical Laboratory** (Tokyo) is now linked to the ODA project. It represents preliminary investigations of the ambitious text-based approach envisaged for the interlingua system. Ishizaki (1987) describes work on a small-scale experimental Japanese-English system using contextual information: CONTRAST (Context Translation System). Texts are interpreted ('understood') using information from a concept dictionary as well as grammatical and lexical information; in effect the concept dictionary will be the IL lexicon. The system will not adopt the Schank approach of semantic primitives and inference rules, but will attempt successive matching, reanalysis and conversion of SL input against concept structures. The results of 'contextual analysis' will be language-independent paragraph-based interface representations. The system has the following stages: syntactic analysis (augmented context free parser), semantic analysis, contextual analysis, paragraph-level generation, sentence-level generation, and word-level generation.

29.
At present, the operational MT systems in most common use in Japan are the batch-processing Systran system and the microcomputer-based Bravis system. However, they are rivalled now by other systems which have recently entered the market (29-34 below).

Systran Corporation of Japan (a company independent of the Systran companies owned by Gachot – cf. 1 above) has developed English-Japanese and Japanese-English versions, running at speeds up to 2 million words per CPU hour on the FACOM M-380 (Akazawa 1986). Two major users of the English-Japanese system are a large Tokyo translation bureaux, which has been supplying post-edited Systran output since 1984 (over 10,000 pages per year), and the Tokyo branch of the Arthur Andersen accountancy company for the translation of its documentation into Japanese. The Japanese-English system has also been used outside Japan by the US Department of Defense and National Aeronautics and Space Administration and by the EEC for its Japan-Info project (Sigurdson/Greatrex 1987).

Bravis International (now owners of WCC, cf. 6 above) have developed two versions of a Japanese-English system based on the Weidner design. The Minipack JE was introduced in 1984, running on DEC microcomputers under Unix, at a translation speed of 5-6000 words per hour. The Micro-Pack JE system was introduced in 1985, running under MS-DOS (640K memory, 20MB disk) at a translation speed of 1500 words per hour and integrating with word processor packages. Bravis is at present developing a MicroPack system for Japanese-Korean (Sigurdson/Greatrex 1987).

30.
The **Fujitsu** MT activity, which began in 1978, has taken place in the context of a wide range of long-term advanced research in the field of artificial intelligence (described by Sato/Sugimoto 1986). Fujitsu has developed and now markets two systems: ATLAS/I for English-Japanese and ATLAS/II for Japanese-English. Current MT work also includes collaboration with the Korean Advanced Institute of Science and Technology on a Japanese-Korean system.

ATLAS/I, based on the 'direct translation' design (syntax-based, phrase structure grammar, coded in assembler) has been operational since 1982 (on test at the Central Research Institute for Electrical Power Industries), and in 1984 appeared as the first commercial English-Japanese system (Sigurdson/Greatrex 1987).

ATLAS/II is a more advanced 'transfer' system for Japanese-English translation, written in the programming language C. It incorporates an AI-type 'world model' representing semantic relations between concepts for checking analysis and interface structures. SL and TL interfaces are conceptual dependency representations (case relations and semantic features), of sufficient abstractness to minimise transfer to conceptual and lexical differences as much as possible (i.e. many interface components are intended to be interlingual). The basic stages are as follows (Uchida 1986, 1987): morphological segmentation; simultaneous syntactic and semantic analysis (with a context-free grammar referring to the 'world model' for verification and disambiguation, checking of resulting SL semantic structure etc.); transfer of SL conceptual structure into TL conceptual structure; generation of TL linear form (dealing with syntactic and morphological restructuring simultaneously). The eventual aim is expansion into a multilingual system; there have been experiments in translating into French, German, Swahili, and Inuit: the most significant is the joint project with Stuttgart (SEMSYN) on Japanese-German (cf. 16 above). ATLAS/II has been commercially available, within Japan only, since 1985, and has been ordered by EEC for the Japan-Info project to translate abstracts (Sigurdson/Greatrex 1987).

31.
The **Hitachi** company has also been involved for some years in two MT systems for Japanese-English and English-Japanese. There are now apparently over 100 people involved in MT, with perhaps 10-15 of these engaged on basic research (Sigurdson/Greatrex 1987).

The **HICATS/JE** (Hitachi Computer Aided Translation System/ Japanese to English) has been on the market since May 1987, in Japan only. Written in PL/I it is implemented on Hitachi M series computers (5MB memory, 100MB hard disk support) and is designed to handle scientific and technical documents, manuals and catalogues, with a processing speed up to 60,000 words an hour. The system was demonstrated at Geneva in 1987, via a satellite link (LT5 Jan 1988). Previously known as ATHENE/N (Nitta et al. 1984), the system is based on a transfer model with semantics-directed dependency structures as interface representations. The stages are: morphological analysis (segmentation into words); syntactic analysis (dependency grammar approach, using semantic features); semantic analysis (establishing case relations, performing disambiguation based on semantic features, producing conceptual dependency structure); transformation of dependency graph (conversion of SL-oriented representation to appropriate TL-oriented graph, and lexical substitution); syntactic generation (phrase grammar approach); morphological generation (Kaji 1987). The system provides for pre-editing, e.g. marking (bracketting) structurally ambiguous sections, and for post-editing (e.g. selection of alternative English words) in a split-screen interactive mode. It is supplied with a 250,000 base dictionary, and with facilities for users to compile their own dictionaries via a menu-driven editor.

The **HICATS/EJ** system for English-Japanese (also in PL/I and previously known as ATHENE/E) is not yet commercially available. In this case the transfer approach is more syntax-oriented, with the intention of adding a semantic component to generation later. However, it is believed that because of the relatively free word order of Japanese stylistically awkward output may be acceptable - as long as the correct particles have been assigned. English analysis employs a phrase structure grammar, Japanese generation a case grammar approach.

Hitachi have recently (LM52 Jan 1988) announced the completion of a Japanese-Korean system developed in collaboration with the Korean Institute of Economics and Technology, with further plans for setting up a translation centre in Seoul and for developing a Korean-Japanese system.

32.
Toshiba's English-Japanese system **AS-TRANSAC** became available commercially during 1986, running at present only on Toshiba AS3000 minicomputers operating under Unix (8MB memory, 140MB disk support), with a claimed speed of 5-7000 words an hour (Sigurdson/Greatrex 1987). The Japanese-English version is still under development.

The English-Japanese system (known during its research phase as TAURUS, Toshiba Automatic Translation System Reinforced by Semantics) is a standard batch-processing bilingual transfer system, written in the C programming language. Its stages are as follows (Amano et al.1987): morphological analysis (assigning syntactic features); syntactic analysis (ATN parser producing a single purely syntactic representation, with all ambiguities remaining implicit); semantic analysis and transfer (using case frames and semantic features in an analysis oriented towards the requirements of Japanese, and also incorporating lexical transfer); syntactic generation (from Japanese conceptual representation, involving determination of word order and attachment of Japanese particles); and morphological generation.

Toshiba have demonstrated the potential of the two MT programs for international communication over telephone links (LT5 Jan 1988). The system is known as ATTP (= Automatic Translation Typing Phone). An English message is typed at a Toshiba AS-3000 engineering workstation, translated into Japanese by "station-resident software", and then transmitted via satellite; the reply is typed in Japanese at a similar workstation, translated into English, and "transmitted back almost simultaneously". The workstation displays messages sent and replies received on a split screen. ATTP is still a research prototype, with no date yet for a commercial product.

33.
The **PENSEE** systems from the Oki computer company are designed for Japanese-English and English-Japanese translation. The Japanese-English version has been commercially available since autumn 1986, running on Unix-based personal computers with 8MB memory and 80MB hard disk

support, at a speed of 4000 words per hour. The English-Japanese version is still under development (Sigurdson/Greatrex 1987, MT Summit 1987).

PENSEE is described (Sakamoto/Shino 1987) as having these stages: morphological analysis, syntactic analysis, and English morphological synthesis. Analysis involves the identification of case relations and disambiguation using semantic features. The results are dependency (case) tree representations, which are then converted into English phrase structure representations by means of bilingual transfer dictionaries and tree transduction rules. It is basically the familiar syntactic transfer approach with limited semantics. The system is programmed in the C language, it includes facilities for bilingual editing and for in-house glossary compilation, and it provides for both sentence by sentence (i.e. 'interactive') and full text translation (i.e. batch). The designers acknowledged that translations are "literal" and "unnatural", and therefore need post-editing; also that some pre-editing may be necessary for poor Japanese input.

34.

The **PIVOT** system from **NEC** has been commercially available since 1986, running on an ACOS System 4 microcomputer (4MB memory, 120MB support disk), with a claimed maximum translation speed of 100,000 words per hour (Sigurdson/Greatrex 1987). Unlike other commercial Japanese systems, PIVOT (Pivot Oriented Translator) is based on the interlingua approach. Designed for bi-directional English and Japanese translation, the eventual aim is a multilingual system (Muraki 1987). Interlingua representations are in the form of networks of 'conceptual primitives' and 'case' labelled arcs, incorporating structural information, pragmatic information on topic and focus, theme and rheme, scopes of quantification and negation. In addition a knowledge base of extralinguistic information interacts at interface and interlingua levels for disambiguation. Written in the C programming language, processing passes through the stages of "morphological analysis, grammatical and semantic analysis, semantic extraction, conceptual wording, grammatical generation, morphological generation." (MT Summit 1987). The problems of defining lexical items in terms of conceptual primitives are expected to be tackled within the EDR project on a conceptual dictionary (see 28 above). At present, PIVOT operates on dictionaries of 40,000 entries for Japanese and 53,000 entries for English, and covers some 20 different subject domains. In practical operation PIVOT can be used in batch mode or interactively. Facilities are provided for dictionary maintenance and for the essential processes of pre-editing and post-editing.

35.

The **MELTRAN** (Melcom Translation) from **Mitsubishi** is an interactive Japanese-English system which is to be available during 1988 (known during research as THALIA). It is a transfer system, with pre- and post-editing, either batch or interactive modes, with 'logic programming' in a version of Prolog (ESP), and running only on Melcom machines (10MB memory and 50MB disk support).

Ricoh's RMT (Ricoh Machine Translation system), a transfer system for English-Japanese, is expected to be available commercially in 1988. Its features include English parsing with an augmented context free grammar, dependency trees with semantic features as interface representations, implementation in the C programming language, split-screen editing, OCR input, and a claimed translation speed of 4500 words per hour. Ricoh also has a Japanese-English system under development (MT Summit 1987, Sigurdson/Greatrex 1987).

The **Sharp** system OA-110WB for English-Japanese translation is also expected to reach the market in 1988. This is an interactive transfer system with pre- and post-editing essential, Written in C and operating under Unix, and running on Sharp machines OA-110WS, OA-210, OA-310 and IX-7, with a translation sped of 5000 words per hour. Analysis involves an augmented context free grammar, case frames, and some limited semantics. There is a basic dictionary of 60,000 words and technical dictionaries (up to 40,000 words) in the subject fields of economics, information processing, electronics, and mechanical engineering (MT Summit 1987, Sigurdson/Greatrex 1987).

The **Sanyo** system SWP-7800 system is advertised as a 'Translation Word Processor' for Japanese-English translation, performing at a speed of 3500 words per hour. It became available in April 1987. It is basically a syntactic transfer model with pre- and post-editing, written in C and with augmented context free parsing and case grammar dependency structures. The basic dictionary contains 55,000 entries.

36.
The **LUTE** project at **NTT** (Nippon Telegraph and Telephone), which began in 1981, continues to represent one of the most advanced experimental systems. LUTE (Language Understander Translator Editor) is designed as an AI-oriented (knowledge-based) transfer system for bi-directional translation between Japanese and English. Recent accounts (Nomura et al. 1986; Kogura/Nomura 1987) describe the present configuration.

The basic formalism is a dynamic frame-network memory structure, comprising linguistic and non-linguistic knowledge, which is invoked by input text and which is used to interpret texts. As result of text processing and interpretation, the system assimilates the meaning of texts into its memory structure. Discourse structure, analogous to long-term memory is defined by Local Scene Frame, a collection of cases and predicates of previously analysed sentences. Episodic (short-term) memory is modelled by the Extended Case Structure, a linguistic formalism for representing text meanings and for simultaneous representation of syntactic and semantic relations. It is not language-independent, thus there are separate ECS's for English and Japanese. The components of ECS are concepts (prototypes and instances), semantic categories, and semantic relations (whole-part, possession, case relations, modification, apposition, conjunction, time and cause relations, etc.) Therefore, the MT system analyses a Japanese sentence into a J-ECS, and its transfer process generates an equivalent E-ECS for English. Analysis ('extended case analysis') integrates semantic and syntactic information, intertwining bottom-up and top-down parsing. It includes establishment of syntactic patterns, semantic structures, case relations, modalities (passive, causative, etc.), resolution of ambiguities, and use of AI-type demons to perform specific tests, etc. Transfer processes are regarded as essentially frame manipulations. LUTE has monolingual dictionaries for analysis and generation (containing semantic categories, case frames, event relation frames, heuristics for resolving ambiguities, etc.), and a bilingual (concept) dictionary for transfer.

LUTE, implemented in ZetaLisp on a Symbolics Lisp machine, is undoubtedly one of the most sophisticated experimental projects at the present time; the researchers are not aiming to produce a prototype system but to provide a research environment for basic MT theoretical activity, in particular to investigate the relative roles of linguistic and non-linguistic knowledge at every stage of translation.

Another knowledge-based experimental transfer system is the **LAMB** system for Japanese-English translation under development by **Canon**. This is also written in Lisp, for a Symbolics 3620 machine. The PAROLE experimental system at Matsushita is another example: a Japanese-English transfer system with case-frame dependency structure, tree transducer, written in Prolog and Lisp (MT Summit 1987). And IBS KK are reported to be at any early stage in developing a bi-directional English and Japanese system (Sakurai 1987).

37.
Other companies have developed or are developing MT systems for internal use. These include the VALANTINE system at KDD; the prototype English-Japanese system at Nippon Data General Corporation (MT Summit 1987); and the English-Japanese system using a Lexical-Functional Grammar approach, developed by the CSK Research Institute (Kudo/Nomura 1986).

Best known, however, is **IBM Japan**'s prototype English-Japanese system for translating IBM computer manuals (Tsutsumi 1986). The aim is a high-quality system within this particular restricted domain. The system is based on the transfer model, with the following stages: English analysis (using the augmented phrase structure grammar developed by Heidorn for the EPISTLE text-critiquing program); English transformation, in which some of the characteristically difficult structures of English are transformed into more Japanese-like structures (e.g. *'There are several records in the file'* → *'Several records exist in the file'*); English-Japanese conversion (transfer proper) divided into semantic disambiguation (based on semantic markers appropriate for the domain of computer manuals), lexical conversion using 3 bilingual transfer dictionaries (for verbs, nouns and prepositions), substitution of expressions deemed to be idiomatic in this domain ('simple noun phrases'), and conversion of whole sentence structures (again employing semantic information); finally, Japanese generation.

38.
As we have seen, a number of Japanese projects involve Korean MT. Current research in **Korea** itself is reported by Kisik/Park (1987). As in Japan early efforts were devoted to the problems of character recognition, developing a Korean word processor, basic linguistic analysis of the language, and experimental application of different formalisms (case grammar, LFG, TG, etc.). Since the early 1980's MT research has been supported by the Korean Ministry of Science and Technology at the Systems Engineering Research Institute (SERI) of the Korean Advanced Institute of Science and Technology (KAIST), and at four universities (Seoul, Inha, Hanyang, Graduate School of KAIST). The research at Seoul National University has concentrated on a Korean-English transfer system (based on TG) and on a collaborative project with IBM on an English-Korean system. At Inha University there has been research on a prototype for bi-directional Korean and Japanese translation, involving semantic pattern matching and inference functions. The project at Hanyang University has been a LFG-based Japanese-Korean system in collaboration with Waseda University in Japan. The Graduate School of KAIST has undertaken fundamental research on computational parsers for Korean, experimenting with case grammar, Montague grammar, LFG and GPSG formalisms; recently a collaborative project with NEC has started on a multilingual system including Korean-Japanese and Korean-English. The SERI/KAIST project was the national Korean MT project for Korean and Japanese bi-directional translation based on a syntactic transfer model; the result has been KANT/I for Korean-Japanese running on a 16-bit Unix machine, and the cooperative development of a Japanese-Korean system with Fujitsu (see 30 above). SERI has also collaborated with GETA (see 13 above) on English-Korean and French-Korean systems using the ARIANE software. There is clear evidence of vigorous support for MT in Korean at a national level. The greatest demand is for translation between Korean and English, but for initial experiments Korean and Japanese offered more immediate expectations of success because of the affinity of the two languages. With the exception of the SERI/KAIST-Fujitsu project, few systems approach any kind of commercial feasibility.

38.
China's interest in MT can be dated back to the 1950's. A number of centres were active until the mid 1960's when internal political events brought them to an end for more than a decade. Recent activity began in 1979 with a cooperative project involving the Computational Institute of the Academy of Sciences, the Linguistic Institute of the Academy of Social Sciences and the Institute of Scientific and Technical Information. This was a project to translate titles of English metallurgical literature into Chinese. The most successful project so far has been KY-1, a transfer system developed at the Military Academy of Sciences. It is a post-edited batch transfer MT system (written in a derivative of COBOL) with some minimal pre-editing; analysis involves a "logical semantic theory" based on case grammar; an average accuracy of 75% is claimed. The system includes components for the compilation of English to Chinese dictionaries and for statistical analyses of English texts. It system is intended initially for translation in the fields of military science, electronics, chemistry and economics; it is to be marketed shortly as Transtar-1 and was demonstrated in December 1987 at a translation conference in Hong Kong (Kit-yee 1988; Du/Li 1987).

Other projects are an English-Chinese system under development at Tsinghua University of Beijing, a Chinese-English interactive system at the East China Normal University in Shanghai and an English-Chinese system at the National Tsing Hua University at Hsinchu (Taiwan). At Xi'an University researchers are developing a microcomputer-based English-Chinese system written in Prolog and operating in either batch or interactive modes. It is limited initially to the translation of catalogue titles.

The system uses Wilks-type semantic templates to assign case frames and for disambiguating prepositions (Xi'an Univ. 1987).

Other non-university centres were mentioned by Dong Zheng Dong at the 1987 MT Summit conference. They include: the Institute of Linguistic Research, the Institute of Scientific and Technical Information, the Institute of Computer Software, the Academy of Posts and Telecommunications, the Academy of Military Sciences. Evidence of the growing interest in China are the establishment of a national committee for MT set up by the Institute of Scientific and Technical Information, numerous regional and national conferences, and the international conferences organised by the Chinese Information Processing Society in 1983 and 1987. A number of Chinese scientists have been sent abroad to study MT, to Europe (particularly Grenoble) and to the United States (e.g. Texas).

40.
MT activity in other Asian countries has been growing rapidly. A joint project was started in 1979, involving the Grenoble group GETA and the University Sains **Malaysia**, to develop an English-Malay system based on the ARIANE-78 software (Vauquois/Boitet 1985/1988, Warotamasikkhadit 1986; Tong 1986). The initial aim was the translation of secondary-level teaching materials in technical fields and the basic system was completed in 1982. A test on a chemistry textbook in 1985 showed that 76% of sentences were 'understandable' without post-editing. Particular problems were English grammatical homonymy, prepositions, coordination, and Malay pronoun generation. In 1984 a permanent project was established to develop an industrial prototype within the next 3 years for texts in the field of computer science. The project will also be devoted to the development of a translator workstation for English-Malay translation, on the Melby model (cf. 8 above), with automatic dictionary lookup, split-screen text processing, and eventual incorporation of the MT module (Tong 1987).

A similar cooperative project in **Thailand** involving the GETA group was set up in June 1981 using ARIANE software for an English-Thai system. This is being developed by researchers at the universities of Chulalongkorn, of Rakhamhaeng (Bangkok), and of Prince of Sonkia (Had-Yai); the project is being undertaken in cooperation with the English-Malay research at the University Sains Malaysia (Vauquois/Boitet 1985/1988, Warotamasikkhadit 1986).

The very early stages of MT activity in **Indonesia** have been reported by Sudarwo (1987). The national Agency for the Assessment and Application of Technology is at present developing a prototype machine-aided system for English-Indonesian, and is preparing the ground for involvement in the Japanese ODA multilingual project (cf. 28 above).

In **India** research on MT began in 1983 at the Tamil University in South India. The TUMTS system is a small-scale 'direct translation' system specifically designed for Russian as SL and Tamil as TL and running on a small microcomputer with just 64K memory and restricted to a small corpus of astronomy text. The researchers readily admit the shortcomings and limitations of their work, but no doubt this modest start will encourage them and others in India.

41.
This 'geographical' survey ends with South America. The CADA project involving South American languages has been mentioned earlier (sect. 9). However, what has attracted much attention is the Bolivian MT project **ATAMIRI**. This is the system designed and developed by Iván Guzmán de Rojas (1985, 1986) of La Paz, Bolivia. It is a multilingual interlingua system using Aymara (an Indian language of South America) for intermediary representations (ATAMIRI is Aymaran for 'translator' and is an acronym for Automata Traductor Algoritmico Multilingue Interactivo Recursivo Inteligente). Guzmán claims that the regularity of Aymara morphology and syntax make it ideal as an interlingua. After initial experiments with Spanish to Aymara translation Guzmán began to investigate the use of Aymara as a 'pivot' language for multilingual translation of English, Spanish and German. Analysis and synthesis operate by matching structural patterns and transforming matrix representations; there is no use of tree structures. Updating of the dictionary is through the medium of Spanish. At present the

system is purely syntactic, with no treatment of lexical and structural ambiguity. However, ATAMIRI is intended as an interactive system referring to professional translators for assistance. The system has been demonstrated at a number of places, including the World Monetary Fund and World Bank in Washington, and there are reports of its use by a translation centre in Panama for English-Spanish translation.

References

Akazawa, E. (1986): Systran Japanese systems.
In: *Terminologie et Traduction* no. 1, 1986, 78-79.

Alam, Y. S. (1986): A lexical-functional approach to Japanese for the purposes of machine translation.
In: *Computers and Translation* 1(4), 1986, 199-214.

Amano, S. / Hirakawa, H. / Tsutsumi, Y. (1987): TAURUS: the Toshiba machine translation system.
In: MT Summit (1987), 15-23.

Ammon, R. von / Wessoly, R. (1984-85): Das Evaluationskonzept des automatischen Übersetzungsprojekts SUSY-DJT (Deutsch-Japanische Titelübersetzung).
In: *Multilingua* 3(4), 1984, 189-195; 4(1), 1985, 27-33.

Appelo, L. (1986): A compositional approach to the translation of temporal expressions in the Rosetta system.
In: Coling '86, 313-318.

Appelo, L. / Landsbergen, J. (1986): The machine translation project Rosetta.
Eindhoven: Philips Research Laboratories, 1986.

Arnold, D. J. (1986): Eurotra: a European perspective on MT.
In: *Proceedings of the IEEE* 74(7), 1986, 979-992.

Arnold, D. J. et al. (1986): The <C,A>,T framework in Eurotra: a theoretically committed notation for MT.
In: Coling '86, 297-303.

Arnold, D. J. / Des Tombe, L. (1987): Basic theory and methodology in Eurotra.
In: Nirenburg (1987), 114-135.

Balfour, R. W. (1986): *Machine translation: a technology assessment.*
London: BMT Consultants, 1986.

Barnes, J. (1987): User perspective on computer-assisted translation for minority languages.
In: *Computers and Translation* 2(3), 1987,131-134

Bátori, I. / Weber, H. J. eds. (1986): *Neue Ansätze in maschineller Sprachübersetzung: Wissensrepräsentation und Textbezug.*
Tübingen: Niemeyer, 1986.

Bennett, P. A. et al. (1986): *Multilingual aspects of information technology.*
Aldershot: Gower, 1986.

Bennett, W. S. / Slocum, J. (1985/1988): The LRC machine translation system.
In: *Computational Linguistics* 11(2/3), 1985, 111-121. Repr. in: Slocum (1988), 111-140.

Biewer, A. et al. (1985/1988): ASCOF: a modular multilevel system for French-German translation.
In: *Computational Linguistics* 11(2/3), 1985, 137-155. Repr. in: Slocum (1988)

Blatt, A. / Freigang, K. H. / Schmitz, K. D. / Thome, G. (1985): *Computer und Übersetzen: eine Einführung.*
Hildesheim: Olms, 1985.

Boitet, C. (1984/1987): Research and development on MT and related techniques at Grenoble University.
In: King (1987), 133-153.

Boitet, C. / Gerber, R. (1986): Expert systems and other new techniques in M(a)T.
In: Bátori/Weber (1986), 103-119.

Boitet, C. (1986): The French national MT-project: technical organization and translation results of CALLIOPE-AERO.
In: *Computers and Translation* 1(4), 1986, 239-267.

Boitet, C. (1987a): Current state and future outlook of the research at GETA.
In: MT Summit (1987), 26-35.

Boitet, C. (1987b): Current projects at GETA on or about machine translation.
Presented at II World Basque Congress, San Sebastian, September 1987.

Bostad, D. A. (1985): Soviet patent bulletin processing: a particular application of machine translation.
In: *CALICO Journal* 2(4), June 1985, 27-30.

Bostad, D. (1986): Machine translation in the USAF.
In: *Terminologie et Traduction* no. 1, 1986, 68-72.

Brekke, M. / Skarsten, R. (1987): Machine translation: a threat or a promise?
Paper presented at Translating and the Computer 9, November 1987.

Buchmann, B. / Warwick, S. / Shann, P. (1984): Design of a machine translation system for a sublanguage.
In: Coling '84, 334-337.

Carbonell, J. G. / Tomita, M. (1987): Knowledge-based machine translation, the CMU approach.
In: Nirenburg (1987), 68-89.

Chauché, J. (1986): Déduction automatique et systèmes transformationnels.
In: Coling '86, 408-411.

Chellamuthu, K. C. / Rangan, K. / Murugesan, K. C. (1984): *Tamil University Machine Translation System (TUMTS), Russian-Tamil.*
Research report, phase-I. Thanjavur: Tamil Univ., 1986.

Chung, H. S. / Kunii, T. L. (1986): NARA: a two-way simultaneous interpretation system between Korean and Japanese.
In: Coling '86, 325-328.

Coling '84. *10th International Conference on Computational Linguistics, 22nd Annual meeting of the Association for Computational Linguistics: proceedings of Coling84.* Stanford: University, 1984.

Coling '86. *11th International Conference on Computational Linguistics: proceedings of Coling '86.* Bonn: University, 1986.

Darke, D. (1986): Machine translation for Arabic. In: *Language Monthly* 28, 1986, 10-11.

De Jong, F. / Appelo, L. (1987): Synonymy and translation. Eindhoven: Philips Research laboratories, 1987.

Dowty, D. R. / Wall, R. E. / Peters, S. (1981): *Introduction to Montague semantics.* Dordrecht: Reidel, 1981.

Du, C. Z. / Li, R. (1987): An overview of MT research in China. Xi'an University, 1987.

Ducrot, J. M. (1985): TITUS IV: System zur automatischen und gleichzeitigen Übersetzung in vier Sprachen. In: *Sprache und Datenverarbeitung* 9(1), 1985, 28-36.

Fabricz, K. (1986): Particle homonymy and machine translation. In: Coling '86, 59-61.

Gazdar, G. et al. (1985): *Generalized phrase structure grammar.* Oxford: Blackwell, 1985.

Goshawke, W. et al. (1987): *Computer translation of natural language.* Wilmslow: Sigma Press, 1987.

Guilbaud, J. P. (1984/1987): Principles and results of a German to French MT system at Grenoble University (GETA). In: King (1987), 278-318.

Guzmán de Rojas, I. (1985): Hacía una ingeniería del lenguaje. In: *Boletín de Informática RCII* 3, 1985, 1-10 & 18-25.

Guzmán de Rojas, I. (1986): Seminario sobre traducción multilingue por computadora utilizando el sistema ATAMIRI, Roma, noviembre de 1986. Roma: Intergovernmental Bureau for Informatics, 1986.

Habermann, F. W. A. (1986): Provision and use of raw machine translation. In: *Terminologie et Traduction* no. 1, 12986, 29-42.

Hauenschild, C. (1986): KIT/NASEV oder die Problematik des Transfers bei der maschinellen Übersetzung. In: Bátori/Weber (1986), 167-195.

Hayes, P. J. (1984): Entity-oriented parsing. In: Coling '84, 212-217.

Huang, X. / L. Guthrie (1986): Parsing in parallel. In: Coling '86, 140-145.

Hutchins, W. J. (1986): *Machine translation: past, present, future.* Chichester: Ellis Horwood, 1986. (New York: Halstead, 1986)

Hutchins, W. J. (1987): Prospects in machine translation.
In: MT Summit (1987), 48-52.

Isabelle, P. / Bourbeau, L. (1985/1988): TAUM-AVIATION: its technical features and some experimental results.
In: *Computational Linguistics* 11(1), 1985, 18-27. Repr. in: Slocum (1988), 237-263.

Isabelle, P. / Macklovitch, E. (1986): Transfer and MT modularity.
In: Coling '86, 115-117.

Ishizaki, S. (1987): Machine translation using contextual information.
In: MT Summit (1987), 53-54.

Jin, W. / Simmons, R. F. (1986): Symmetric rules for translation of English and Chinese.
In: *Computers and Translation* 1(3), 1986, 153-167

Johnson, R. L. / Krauwer, S. / Rosner, M. / Varile, G. B. (1984): The design of the kernel architecture for the Eurotra software.
In: Coling '84, 226-235.

Johnson, R. L. / King, M. / des Tombe, L. (1985): Eurotra: a multi-lingual system under development.
In: *Computational Linguistics* 11(2/3), 1985, 155-169.

Johnson, R. L. / Whitelock, P. (1987): Machine translation as an expert task.
In: Nirenburg (1987), 136-144.

Johnson, T. (1985): *Natural language computing: the commercial applications.*
London: Ovum Ltd., 1985.

Joscelyne, A. (1987): Calliope and other pipe dreams.
In: *Language Technology* 4 (Nov/Dec 1987), 20-21.

Joscelyne, A. (1988): Jean Gachot resurrecting Systran.
In: *Language Technology* 6 (March/April 1988), 26-29.

Kaji, H. (1987): HICATS/JE: a Japanese-to-English machine translation system based on semantics.
In: MT Summit (1987), 55-60.

Kakizaki, N. (1987): Research and development of an electronic dictionary: current status and future plan.
In: MT Summit (1987), 61-64.

Kaplan, R. M. / Bresnan, J. (1983): Lexical-functional grammar: a formal system for grammatical representations.
In: Bresnan, J. (ed.): *The mental representation of grammatical relations.*
Cambridge: MIT Press, 1983.

Kasper, R. / Weber, D. (1986): *User's reference manual for the C Quechua Adaptation Program.*
Dallas, TX: Summer Institute of Linguistics, 1986.

Kay, M. (1984): Functional unification grammar: a formalism for machine translation.
In: Coling '84, 75-78.

King, M. ed. (1983): *Parsing natural language.*
London: Academic Press, 1983.

King, M. ed. (1987): *Machine translation today: the state of the art.* Proceedings of the Third Lugano Tutorial... 2-7 April 1984. Edinburgh: Edinburgh Univ. Press, 1987.

Kisik, L. / Park, C. (1987): The machine translation researches and governmental view in Korea. In: MT Summit (1987), 66-72.

Kit-yee, P. C. (1988): The future of Chinese translation. In: *Language Monthly* 53 (February 1988), 6-10.

Knowles, F. E. (1987): The Alvey Japanese and English machine translation project. In: MT Summit (1987), 73-78.

Kogure, K. / Nomura, H. (1987): Computer environment for meaning structure representation and manipulation in machine translation system. Paper presented at International Conference on Information and Knowledge, November 1987, Yokohama.

Kudo, I. / Nomura, H. (1986): Lexical-functional transfer: a transfer framework in a machine translation system based on LFG. In: Coling '86, 112-114.

Landsbergen, J. (1984/1987): Isomorphic grammars and their use in the Rosetta translation system. In: King (1987), 351-372.

Landsbergen, J. (1987): Montague grammar and machine translation. In: Whitelock, P. et al. (eds.) *Linguistic theory and computer applications.* (London: Academic Press, 1987), 113-147

Laubsch, J. et al. (1986): Language generation from conceptual structure: synthesis of German in a Japanese/German MT project. In: Coling '84, 491-494.

Lee, C. (1987): Machine translation: English-Korean. In: *The Thirteenth LACUS Forum 1986*, ed. I. Fleming (Lake Bluff, Ill.: Linguistic Association of Canada and the United States, 1987), 410-416.

Leermakers, R. / Rous, J. (1986): The translation method of Rosetta. In: *Computers and Translation* 1(3), 1986, 169-183.

Lehrberger, J. / Bourbeau, L. (1988): *Machine translation: linguistic characteristics of MT systems and general methodology of evaluation.* Amsterdam: Benjamins, 1988.

Leon, M. / Schwartz, L. A. (1986): *Integrated development of English-Spanish machine translation: from pilot to full operational capability.* Washington, D. C.: Pan American Health Organization, 1986.

Lewis, D. (1985): The development and progress of machine translation systems. In: *ALLC Journal* 5, 1985, 40-52.

Licher, V. / Luckhardt, H. D. / Thiel, M. (1987): Konzeption, computerlinguistische Grundlagen und Implementierung eines sprachverarbeitenden Systems. In: Wilss/Schmitz (1987), 113-153.

Liu, J. / Liro, J. (1987): The METAL English-to-German system: first progress report.
In: *Computers and Translation* 2(4), 1987, 205-218.

Loomis, T. (1987): Software design issues for natural language processing.
In: *Computers and Translation* 2(4), 1987, 219-230.

Luckhardt, H. D. (1987a): *Der Transfer in der maschinellen Sprachübersetzung*.
(Sprache und Information 18). Tübingen: Niemeyer, 1987.

Luckhardt, H. D. (1987b): *Von der Forschung zur Anwendung: das computergestützte Saarbrücker Translationssystem STS*.
Saarbrücken: Univ. d. Saarlandes, 1987.

Luctkens, E. / Fermont, P. (1986): A prototype machine translation based on extracts from data processing manuals.
In: Coling '86, 643-645.

Maas, H. D. (1984/1987): The MT system SUSY.
In: King (1987), 209-246.

McDonald, D. D. (1987): Natural language generation: complexities and techniques.
In: Nirenburg (1987), 192-224.

Mann, J. S. (1987): Get Smart! industrial strength language processing from Smart Communications.
In: *Language Technology* [3] (September/October 1987), 12-15.

Melby, A. K. (1986): Lexical transfer: a missing element in linguistics theories.
In: Coling '86, 104-106.

Moore, G. W. et al. (1986): Automated translation of German to English medical text.
In: *American Journal of Medicine* 81, 1986, 103-111.

MT Summit (1987): *Machine Translation Summit, manuscripts & program*
September 17-19, 1987, Hakone, Japan.

Muraki, K. / Ichiyama, S. / Fukumochi, Y. (1985): Augmented dependency grammar: a simple interface between the grammar rule and the knowledge.
In: *Second Conference of the European Chapter of the Association for Computational Linguistics...* March 1985, University of Geneva, 198-204.

Muraki, K. (1987): PIVOT: two-phase machine translation system.
In: MT Summit (1987), 81-83.

Nagao, M. (1985/1987): Role of structural transformation in a machine translation system.
In: Nirenburg (1987), 262-277.

Nagao, M. / Tsujii, J. I. / Nakamura, J. I. (1985/1988): The Japanese government project for machine translation.
In: *Computational Linguistics* 11(2/3), 1985, 91-110. Repr. in: Slocum (1988), 141-186.

Nagao, M. / Tsujii, J. I. / Nakamura, J. I. (1986): Machine translation from Japanese into English.
In: *Proceedings of the IEEE* 74(7), 1986, 993-1012.

Nagao, M. / Tsujii, J. I. (1986): The transfer phase of the Mu machine translation system. In: Coling '86, 97-103.

Nirenburg, S. ed. (1987): *Machine translation: theoretical and methodological issues.* Cambridge: Cambridge Univ. Press, 1987.

Nirenburg, S. / Raskin, V. / Tucker, A. B. (1986): On knowledge-based machine translation. In: Coling '86, 627-632.

Nirenburg, S. / Raskin, V. / Tucker, A. B. (1987): The structure of interlingua in TRANSLATOR. In: Nirenburg (1987), 90-113.

Nirenburg, S. / Carbonell, J. (1987): Integrating discourse pragmatics and propositional knowledge for multilingual natural language processing. In: *Computers and Translation* 2(2), 1987, 105-116.

Nishida, T. / Doshita, S. (1986): Machine translation: Japanese perspectives. In: Picken (1986), 152-174.

Nitta, Y. et al. (1984): A proper treatment of syntax and semantics in machine translation. In: Coling '84, 159-166.

Papegaaij, B. C. (1986): *Word expert semantics: an interlingual knowledge-based approach.* (Distributed Language Translation 1). Dordrecht: Foris, 1986.

Pericliev, V. (1984): Handling syntactical ambiguity in machine translation. In: Coling '84, 521-524.

Pericliev, V. / Ilarionov, I. (1986): Testing the projectivity hypothesis. In: Coling '86, 56-58.

Picken, C. ed. (1985): *Translation and communication: Translating and the computer 6. Proceedings of a conference... November 1984.* London: Aslib, 1985.

Picken, C. ed. (1986): *Translating and the computer 7. Proceedings of a conference... November 1985.* London: Aslib, 1986.

Picken, C. ed. (1987): *Translating and the computer 8: a profession on the move. Proceedings of a conference...* November 1986. London: Aslib, 1987.

Pigott, I. M. (1986): Essential requirements for a large-scale operational machine-translation system. In: *Computers and Translation* 1(2), 1986, 67-72

Pigott, I. M. (1988): *Systran machine translation at the EC Commission: present status and history.* [Luxembourg: CEC, January 1988.]

Popesco, L. (1986): Limited context semantic translation from a single knowledge-base for a natural language and structuring metarules. In: *Computers and the Humanities* 20, 1986, 289-295.

Reed, R. B. (1985): CADA: an overview of the Tucanoan experiment. In: *Notes on Computing (SIL)* 11, 1985, 6-20.

Roesner, D. (1986a): SEMSYN – Wissensquellen und Strategien bei der Generierung von Deutsch aus einer semantischen Repräsentation.
In: Bátori/Weber (1986), 121-137.

Roesner, D. (1986b): When Mariko talks to Siegfried.
In: Coling '86, 652-654.

Rohrer, C. (1986a): Maschinelle Übersetzung mit Unifikationsgrammatiken.
In: Bátori/Weber (1986), 75-99.

Rohrer, C. (1986b): Linguistic bases for machine translation.
In: Coling '86, 353-355.

Rolf, P. C. / Chauché, J. (1986): Machine translation and the SYGMART system.
In: *Computers and the Humanities* 20, 1986, 283-288.

Rothkegel, A. (1986a): Textverstehen und Transfer in der maschinellen Übersetzung.
In: Bátori/Weber (1986), 197-227.

Rothkegel, A. (1986b): Pragmatics in machine translation.
In: Coling '86, 335-337.

Rothkegel, A. (1987): Semantisch-pragmatische Aspekte in der maschinellen Übersetzung.
In: Wilss/Schmitz (1987), 163-180.

Ryan, J. P. (1987): SYSTRAN: a machine translation system to meet user needs.
In: MT Summit (1987), 99-103.

Sadler, V. / Papegaaij, B. C. (1987): The Melby test on knowledge-based lexical transfer.
Utrecht: BSO, 1987.

Sakamoto, M. / Shino, T. (1987): Japanese-English machine translation system 'PENSEE'.
In: *Oki Technical Review* 126, April 1987, 9-14.

Sakamoto, Y. et al. (1986): Concept and structure of semantic markers for machine translation in Mu-project.
In: Coling '86, 13-19.

Sakurai, K. (1987): On machine translation.
In: *Information, Information Processing, Information Retrieval/Joho Kagaku* 23(4), 178-181. (In Japanese; Japan Technology 0119542)

Sanamrad, M. A. / Matsumoto, H. (1986): PERSIS: a natural language analyzer for Persian.
In: *Journal of Information Processing* 8(4), 1986, 271-279.

Sato, S. / Sugimoto, M. (1986): Artificial intelligence.
In: *Fujitsu Science and Technology Journal* 22(3), 1986, 139-181.

Scheel, H. L. (1987): Bericht über die Arbeit des Projektbereichs C.
In: Wilss/Schmitz (1987), 211-223.

Schenk, A. (1986): Idioms in the Rosetta machine translation system.
In: Coling 86, 319-324.

Schmidt, P. (1986): Valency theory in a stratificational MT-system.
In: Coling '86, 307-312.

Schneider, T. (1987): The METAL system, status 1987.
In: MT Summit (1987), 105-112.

Schubert, K. (1986): Linguistic and extra-linguistic knowledge.
In: *Computers and Translation* 1(3), 1986, 125-152.

Schubert, K. (1987): *Metataxis: contrastive dependency syntax for machine translation.*
(Distributed Language Translation 2). Dordrecht: Foris, 1987.

Siebenaler, L. (1986): Systran for ESPRIT and ECAT bureau service.
In: *Terminologie et Traduction* no. 1, 1986, 54-60.

Sharp, R. (1986): A parametric NL translator.
In: Coling '86,124-126.

Shieber, S. M. (1986): *An introduction to unification-based approaches to grammar.*
Stanford, Ca: Center for the Study of Language and Information, 1986.

Sigurdson, J. / Greatrex, R. (1987): *Machine translation of on-line searches in Japanese databases.*
Lund: Research Policy Institute, Lund Univ., 1987.

Slocum, J. (1985/1988): A survey of machine translation: its history, current status, and future prospects.
In: *Computational Linguistics* 11(1), 1985, 1-17. Repr.in: Slocum (1988), 1-47.

Slocum, J. (1987): Concept-lexeme-syntax triangles: a gateway to interlingual translation.
In: *Computers and Translation* 2(4), 1987, 243-261.

Slocum, J. ed. (1988): *Machine translation systems.*
Cambridge: Cambridge Univ. Press, 1988.

Smith, D. (1987): Translation practice in Europe.
In: Picken (1987), 74-82.

Somers, H. L. (1986a): The need for MT-oriented versions of case and valency in MT.
In: Coling '86, 118-123.

Somers, H. L. ed. (1986): *Eurotra special issue.*
= *Multilingua* 5(3), 1986, 129-177.

Somers, H. L. (1987a): Some thoughts on interface structure(s).
In: Wilss/Schmitz (1987), 81-99.

Somers, H. L. (1987b): *Valency and case in computational linguistics.*
Edinburgh: Edinburgh Univ. Press, 1987.

Stegentritt, E. (1987): Überblick und Bericht zum ASCOF-System des Projekts C.
In: Wilss/Schmitz (1987), 225-231.

Steiner, E. (1986): Generating semantic structures in Eurotra-D.
In: Coling '86, 304-306.

Stentiford, F. / Steer, M. G. (1987): A speech driven language translation system.
Presented at European Speech Technology Conference, Edinburgh, September 1987.

Strossa, P. (1987): SPSS – an algorithm and data structures design for a machine aided English-to-Czech translation system.
In: *Prague Bulletin of Mathematical Linguistics* 47, 1987, 25-36.

Sudarwo, I. (1987): The needs of MT for Indonesia.
In: MT Summit (1987), p. 113.

Tomita, M. (1984): Disambiguating grammatically ambiguous sentences by asking.
In: Coling '84, 476-480.

Tomita, M. (1986): Sentence disambiguation by asking.
In: *Computers and Translation* 1(1), 1986, 39-51

Tomita, M. / Carbonell, J. G. (1986): Another stride towards knowledge-based machine translation.
In: Coling '86, 633-638.

Tong, L-C. (1986): English-Malay translation system: a laboratory prototype.
In: Coling '86, 639-642.

Tong, L-C. (1987): The engineering of a translator workstation.
In: *Computers and Translation* 2(4), 1987, 263-273.

Trabulsi, S. (1986): Difficultés de la traduction en langue arabe.
In: *Terminologie et Traduction* no. 1, 1986, 90-95.

Tsuji, Y. (1987): Research and development project of machine translation system with Japan's neighboring countries.
In: MT Summit (1987), 116-120.

Tsujii, J. I. (1986): Future directions of machine translation.
In: Coling '86, 655-668.

Tsujii, J. I. (1987): The current stage of the Mu-project.
In: MT Summit (1987), 122-127.

Tsutsumi, T. (1986): A prototype English-Japanese machine translation system for translating IBM computer manuals.
In: Coling '86, 646-648.

Tucker, A. B. (1987): Current strategies in machine translation research and development.
In: Nirenburg (1987), 22-41.

Uchida, H. (1986): Fujitsu machine translation system ATLAS.
In: *Future Generations Computer Systems* 2, 1986, 95-100.

Uchida, H. (1987): ATLAS: Fujitsu machine translation system.
In: MT Summit (1987), 129-134.

Vasconcellos, M. / Leon, M. (1985/1988): SPANAM and ENGSPAN: machine translation at the Pan American Health Organization.
In: *Computational Linguistics* 11(2/3), 1985, 122-136. Repr. in Slocum (1988), 187-235.

Vasconcellos, M. (1986): Functional considerations in the postediting of machine translated output. I. Dealing with V(S)O versus SVO.
In: *Computers and Translation* 1(1), 1986, 21-38

Vasconcellos, M. (1987): Post-editing on-screen: machine translation from Spanish into English.
In: Picken (1987), 133-146.

Vauquois, B. / Boitet, C. (1985/1988): Automated translation at Grenoble University.
In: *Computational Linguistics* 11(1), 1985, 28-36. Repr. in Slocum (1988), 85-110.

Warotamasikkhadit, U. (1986): Computer aided translation project, University Sains Malaysia, Penang, Malaysia.
In: *Computers and Translation* 1(2), 1986, 113.

Weber, H. J. (1986): Faktoren einer textbezogenen maschinellen Übersetzung: Satzstrukturen, Kohärenz- und Koreferenz-Relationen, Textorganisation.
In: Bátori/Weber (1986), 229-261.

Weber, H. J. (1987): Wissensrepräsentation und Textstruktur-Analyse.
In: Wilss/Schmitz (1987), 181-209.

Wheeler, P. (1985): LOGOS.
In: *Sprache und Datenverarbeitung* 9(1), 1985, 11-21.

White, J. S. (1987): The research environment in the METAL project.
In: Nirenburg (1987), 225-246.

Whitelock, P. J. et al. (1986): Strategies for interactive machine translation: the experience and implications of the UMIST Japanese project.
In: Coling '86, 329-334.

Whitelock, P. J. (1987): Japanese machine translation in Japan and the rest of the world.
In: Picken (1987), 147-159.

Wilss, W. / Schmitz, K. D. eds. (1987): *Maschinelle Übersetzung, Methoden und Werkzeuge: Akten des 3. Internationalen Kolloquiums des Sonderforschungsbereichs 100...* Saarbrücken... September 1986. Tübingen: Niemeyer, 1987.

World Systran Conference (1986).
= *Terminologie et Traduction* 1986, no. 1 special issue.

Xi'an University (1987): *Resarch of machine translation on microcomputer.*
By MT Group Xi'an Jiaotong University.

Yang, Y. / Doshita, S. (1986): The construction of a semantic grammar for Chinese language processing and its implementation.
In: *Transactions of the Information Processing Society of Japan* 27(2), 1986, 155-164. (In Japanese: Japan Technology 0049845)

Yoshii, R. (1986): A robust machine translation system.
In: *Proceedings of SPIE 635, Applications of Artificial Intelligence* III, 1986, 455-463

Zajac, R. (1986): SCSL: a linguistic specification language for MT.
In: Coling '86, 393-398.

Zimmermann, H. H., Kroupa, E. / Luckhardt, H. D. eds. (1987): *Das Saarbrücker Translationssystem STS: eine Konzeption zur computergestützten Übersetzung.* Saarbrücken: Univ. d. Saarlandes, 1987.

W. John Hutchins

Lastatempaj evoluoj en perkomputila tradukado
Revuo de la pasintaj kvin jaroj

Resumo

La unua publike funkcianta komputila traduksistemo (METEO), la unuaj vendataj tradukhelpiloj (ALPS, Weidner, Logos) kaj la ekesto de AI-esploroj grave spronis la fortan kreskon de traduksistemkonstruado kiu okazis dum la pasintaj kvin jaroj. La akcento ŝoviĝis de Eŭropo-Usono pli al Japanujo kaj de universitatoj pli al la industrio.

Evoluis tri bazaj modeloj de komputilaj traduksistemoj: rektaj, interlingvaj kaj transiraj. Iliaj respektivaj malavantaĝoj estas la nekongruo de lingvostrukturoj, la malfacileco konstrui interlingvon kaj la informperdo pro tro profunda disanalizo. Krome eblas klasi sistemojn laŭ la roldivido inter homo kaj maŝino kaj laŭ la speco de limigoj: temspecifaj, antaŭredaktaj, postkorektaj, interagaj. La interago povas okazi en tre diversaj procespaŝoj.

Grava teoria demando estas la rolo de artefarita inteligento (AI), alivorte, kiom da "kompreno" necesas por traduki? Oni uzas sciobankojn, semantikajn retojn, konjektilojn, ekspertsistemojn (ASCOF, DLT, LUTE, ETL, ODA, GETA). Aliaj intence evitas AI preferante lingvistikajn rimedojn (Eurotra, Rosetta). Gravas distingi implicitan kaj eksplicitan scion kaj difini kiugrade (do ne ĉu) rolu kompreno. Traduksistemoj intersekcas kun (unulingvaj) tekstkomprenaj, respondaj kaj informserĉaj sistemoj. Alia grava demando estas la nivelo kaj maniero de transiro de unu lingvo al alia (morfologia, sintaksa, semantika, koncepta ...). Oni uzas du formojn de interlingvoj: artefaritajn (logikajn, universalajn ...) kaj homajn (Esperanton, ajmaran). En la transirproceso oni distingas preparajn, efektive transirajn kaj malpreparajn paŝojn.

Komunaj problemoj de ĉiuj klopodoj estas semantika relativeco, struktura nekongruo, manko de fidindaj universalaĵoj, komplekseco de vortaroj, eraraj tekstoj, metaforo, dinamika ŝanĝiĝo. Sur la tereno de gramatiko oni multe tendencas al "unuigaj" kaj "netransformaj" modeloj. Ĉefaj programlingvoj estas Prolog kaj Lisp, la unua anstataŭanta la duan. Oni pli dediĉas sin al kreado de laborprogramaro por lingvistoj.

Plejparte oni okupiĝas pri tradukado de kompletaj skribitaj tekstoj, sed ankaŭ aperis aliaj celterenoj, kiel ekz. telefonaĵoj. Iuj uzas tradukdevenan fakscion por aliaj aplikoj, ekz. "inteligentaj" tekstredaktiloj, resumiloj, informserĉiloj k.s.

Malmultaj sistemoj estas efektive uzataj. La aplikterenoj estas tre diversaj (unusola organizaĵo, ĉiaj klientoj ...). La plej grandaj ŝancoj por la estonteco apartenas al krudaj tradukoj kun neglekteblaj formaj eraroj. Ili devos resti en la manoj de fakuloj.

Perkomputila tradukado fariĝis rapide disvolviĝanta, impeta kaj respektata branĉo de aplika scienco.

Ne estas resumita la dua parto de la artikolo, kiu ne estas parto de la konferenca prelego. Ĝi donas superrigardon pri unuopaj komputilaj traduksistemoj.

Language and the Computer Society

Tibor Vámos

Magyar Tudományos Akadémia
Számítástechnikai és Automatizálási Kutató Intézete
Hungarian Academy of Sciences
Computer and Automation Institute
Victor Hugo u. 18-22
H-1132 Budapest
Hungary

Language as the unique instrument for human communication of any cooperative activity is always in the focus of interest, since the circumstances in the media and in the application of this basic ingredient of human society keep changing. The mystic, divine role of naming through language can be followed from the earliest mythologies, the Bible (the name of this holy book is also a communication concept), and the Greek philosophers up to recent times. In the course of this long history, which can hardly be separated from the general history of human thought, there was a close, intrinsic relationship between language and other areas: only for short periods and for scientists of very limited interest was language a topic per se, not related to history, psychology, logic, neurology, pedagogy and many other disciplines of human development and brain activity. This relationship did not bear fruit of itself, but rather by becoming a conscious direction of research for pioneers in these fields, as can be seen by referring only to quotations from Aristotle, Leibniz, or John Stuart Mill. Similarly to the relationships between neurology and ophthalmology, where the eye is not considered as a device developed by nature, but as a relevant part of the brain exposed outside the skull and therefore an open window for exploration, language is such a window-like interface of the thought processes, i.e. the only relevant and distinguishing human attribute.

Four revolutionary epochs can be specified in this historical process: first the evolution of the spoken language parallel with the evolution of the primitive human societies; second, the invention of writing systems, making possible the origins of human culture, science, intergenerational continuity, and the social consciousness of mankind; third, printing, making possible the Epoch of Reason, of modern science, of the modern state and social concepts; and fourth, our electronics based computer and communication revolution. Similarly to the earlier three, this final period has initiated fundamental changes in all areas of human activity with a renewed interest in the new-old roles of language. The first revolution created communication between people who spent all their lives together; the second bridged remote groups separated by time and distance, the third broadened this communication by orders of magnitude connecting very different semantic fields, and peoples of heterogenous cultural backgrounds, i.e. language emerged step-by-step from the environment of metalinguistic communication and had to represent the message in an increasingly distilled way, so that the role and responsibility of linguistic representation increased dramatically. This has never been true to such an extent as in our epoch, which is justly termed the information revolution. As communication networks and autonomous or semi-autonomous computer systems evolve, becoming intermediate or final participants in human activities by replacing the human element at an increasingly high level of intelligence, the linguistic representation of concepts, actions, and procedures becomes the most responsible and powerful human operation and can develop into a terrible boomerang, if misused or not used in a professional way. Awareness of this radical change entails several consequences:

1. The above mentioned relationships with other disciplines move into the forefront. The broader and nearly exclusive application of language for organization of cooperation among people and artificial environments excludes any perspective on language per se, since it is always related to the usage of those transformations which occur in its transmission to machines, people, and actuators. The relativity of text becomes an absolute and any earlier beliefs about absolute concepts and linguistic representations become dangerous nonsense.

2. Mankind should be educated, trained and retrained not only for using the new devices like any others, but for a new culture which eliminates many obsolete, outdated issues.

Being a specialist from the computer side rather than a linguist and realizing the decisive importance of linguistics, I would like to mention some problems of and some approaches to these unlimited broad issues.

Computer-based linguistic intelligence

The problem is an old, dual complex which was solved case by case by experts in special fields, librarians, and other people who had the opportunity, erudition and time to do this for themselves. If we want to access some information on anything, we have to know where it is available, in what kind of structural order it can be found (e.g. a directory, library, reference book, schedule), the definitions, special words, symbols used, how we can get the needed contextual information, information on the validity of the information received (authenticity, reliability, time limitations etc.); sometimes the information is not available in the mother tongue or is given in a distinct professional vernacular (e.g. medical, legal, railroad). The second problem is to put new information into the right context. This entails similar difficulties and uncertainties. Everybody has experience in the problems with the traditional procedures and surely knows the annoyances with dull computer-based information systems. Several projects have tried to develop a more intelligent system which could be a flexible, extensible and self-controlled, intelligent and intelligible knowledge base.

The technical form is defined by the hypertext and the electronic encyclopaedia concept. The hypertext, with its pages movable in every dimension, can be used for creating special-purpose windows, or for focussing on specific words, browsing, windowing, zooming. It should possess a multidimensional reference system. The reference system is not so much a usual index in alphabetical order as a dictionary, a thesaurus and an encyclopaedia all in one.

Systems like the Webster, the Roget or the Longman-type work with different conceptual frames, topical indexing, explanatory and cross-referencing facilities, evaluating synonyms and contextual relations as well.

If we evaluate text processor programs, we see that an increase in services in general causes a decrease in user-friendliness. Only very sophisticated solutions can maintain a balance between complexity and human interface simplicity. Here we meet a problem which is more complex and has several orders of magnitude: instead of orthography, grammar and some typographic services we require a complete partnership, whose verbal description provides a hint to its complexity. The completion of the above-mentioned dictionaries is and was the task not only of industrious collectors but of practitioners of high-level linguistics. An automatic or semiautomatic system of such complexity cannot be imagined without substantial new efforts in this discipline. The project which we outlined briefly is only an initial step towards a further goal. The usual text processing systems and the electronic encyclopedia under development possess some graphic facilities. Graphical representation is used now in most dictionaries and an important result was the Duden-like pictorial dictionary. On the other hand, morphological descriptions are used in all kinds of explanatory works, especially in crystallography, biology, criminology, topics related to textures, surfaces, and shapes. No real linguistic interface exists between the verbal and pictorial representations, no transformations in either direction, if we neglect some relevant but very limited results of pattern recognition programs.

The problem is by far not exhausted: it starts just at the point that a very comprehensive knowledge base which can be accessed and manipulated in a simple and fast way becomes available for several related, unrelated, or seemingly unrelated topics.

Any human dialog is in some sense vague and incomplete. This is due to the lack of the meticulous art of colloquial talk, due to a supposed tacit knowledge of the partner and to the lack of knowledge of the inquirer. We label all these as Low Quality Information. Fuzziness of attributes is only one characteristic of this regular phenomenon; we can say that exact information is the exceptional or at least the trivial case (e.g. answering to prefixed questionnaires, operations on primitive menues). The understanding of a natural language can be identified with this task but in some sense this can be divided into further layers. In most cases, the expression *natural language* covers a well-formed sentence sequence which contains all information needed for the dialog, yet permits all the syntactic diversity admitted by the language concerned and similarly all ambiguities of semantic representation. Here we meet incompleteness, contradictory, and vague formulations as we would from any inquirer who is either not fully aware of the contextual, structural relations of the topic, or is not capable of using the right words, or is not even sure what he/she wants to say. This is the regular case in most occasions when somebody is looking for a commodity in a shop without having decided at which price, what colour, type, fashion etc. would suit him/her or a patient consulting a doctor, a client a lawyer, a traveller for a convenient itinerary and lodging and a research worker who would like to find some analogy, a feasible solution, an appropriate instrument, material, technology.

We have now reached what are perhaps the most complex problems of human and man-machine communication and whose degree of solvability will have a decisive impact on the whole future. A total solution is excluded; even the brightest and closest interhuman communication is unable to achieve, to possess the same background knowledge and get a perfect model of the partner's behaviour. One of the reasons why we cannot express ourselves perfectly is that we are often taken by surprise. We can describe our idea, a certain vaguely defined concept, but the feeling can immediately change after receipt of further information or the viewing of something else. Conscious human creativity is also directed to a very limited extent by a predetermined rule. In any dialog between man and a system, we have to suppose certain limits of understanding, but achieving a higher freedom in this respect is an achievement of higher intelligence.

It is not necessary to emphasize the linguistic challenges here to an audience much more experienced than our modest computer community. I shall, however, briefly outline two major subproblems.

The first is the handling of uncertainty. Uncertainty of attributes and concepts is mostly dealt with by the fuzzy approach. Although many other ways exist (e.g. certainty factors, measures of belief etc.), we should not elaborate here discussions which have lasted for decades among the different philosophies of probability interpretations (frequency, subjective) and others, especially the fuzzy-possibility approaches. I can only mention that I have the impression that this depends on the model-type used, different models permit different interpretations, and the results do not diverge much from each other. From the viewpoint of linguistic understanding, these methods provide solutions only in the very simple cases, that the dimension of the attribute or concept is linear, i.e. if we can define a one-to-one symmetric mapping between the verbal and the numeric representation. E.g. if we say *long* and this is marked by a value 0.8, then in this context 0.8 should answer: long. As we mentioned in the case of morphology, this symmetric and transitive correspondence is far from a solution!

The other view of uncertainty is related to logic, the validity of certain inference mechanisms, results related to the model of discourse (modalities, intentions etc.). This is also a long-term research program (as long as the evolution of human thought). Its linguistic aspect is obvious. We could say that the whole problem is really a linguistic one, although it is treated in symbolic logic and by computer science, too, but cognitive psychology also claims to play a role. Both views of uncertainty relate to the models of discourse and this leads us to the second related topic which I would like to mention: the models behind the dialog.

In the case of not complete, low quality information the crutches that we use are models. We can create two kinds of model: a model of the person, the inquirer (customer, patient, client, research worker etc.) and a model of the knowledge. Both have a delimiting, guiding role. Let us illustrate this by a simple example, the patient-doctor dialog. The patient can be a middle-aged neurotic person, low income, obese, fingers yellow from nicotine, face typical of an addict to alcohol. This model of the patient provides a fast further process of diagnostics based in models of syndromes. The match of the two models is a key for heuristics as it is done by the human expert, and this analog can serve as a guide for computer realization.

Models of the individuals are in some respect linguistic problems as well. Bernard Shaw's play *Pygmalion* is a nice hint to that really everyday usage.

Even if we could reach this point after all the steps outlined above, we would still not have reached the final goal, a realistic dialog.

In some cases the dialog is easy to control, if the environment and the goal are clear. In the medical examination example based on the hypothesis of the doctor, a relatively straightforward dialog can be generated from the knowledge base, questions, inquiring data which can assert or refute the diagnosis. Most difficult is the case in which we are not progressing towards a predetermined goal or assertion, but a negotiation should be conducted until a compromise is reached. This is e.g. mostly the case if a purchase (compromise on existing models, features, prices etc.) of a legal procedure (compromise among ethical, social principles, aggravating and attenuating circumstances) or any other open problem should be solved. Although operations research and decision theory has developed a big store of multi-objective and multi-person optimization procedures, well-designed dialog protocols, adapted to specific cases and individuals, are only in an embryonic status. We should somehow approximate the delicate conversation psychology which can lead to a reasonable compromise in bargaining and is furthermore a very rare and occasional characteristic of human negotiators.

A well-designed, impressively high standard protocol system governed by rules of fair play, is not an unrealistic objective of research beauty, but it is an extremely important contribution to a new world where bargaining of cooperative systems is the everyday modus procedendi of life. Several processes have started to require such a speed that control and execution by machines cannot be left to ad hoc human considerations. The cooperation of energy systems and traffic control in a case of congestion are typical examples for such a need at present, but the requirement of extension is growing fast, since computer controlled networks play a major role in everyday activities. How computer networks can even deteriorate and destabilize the performance of inadequately designed applications, was several times demonstrated in the stock exchange events of 1987. The other extreme, i.e. fast changes not created by a computer, was exemplified by the big black-outs. I am convinced that the design of these negotiation protocols is no less a linguistic task than a logical, mathematical, process analysis exercise.

If I had to review what is being done and has been achieved in all the various branches of linguistics and those fields related to them, I would be confused. All of them are in a more or less advanced research or development phase, but practically none or very few of them have reached their goals and become usable in practice. This statement is also confusing, because the attainment of the final goal and thereby a real satisfaction lies in the heavens: an imitation of a perfect, ideal human performance, a level which has never been reached by humans and most probably is forever unattainable both for humans and machines. We could observe this when discussing the problems of human understanding or that of the negotiations for a mutually satisfactory compromise or just the translation problem.

We are troubled by the difficulty of a clear judgement of claims, advertisements, publications, and demonstrations. As with any more complex system, a longer experience is needed to provide justification, if the product is not trivially shoddy. In this country, we try to keep up to the level of international development both on the linguistic side and of the computer. Some preparations are going on in the field of electronic encyclopedias, in finding contextual contents in written text, my group is working on the dialog problem in expert systems where we meet many related issues. The results are modest but in several cases sufficient to cooperate with worldwide efforts.

Education for a new society

We have outlined above some features of a new convergence brought into focus by language. This furnishes some lessons for education.

One is a hint to think more about the consequences of the new synthesis in education. The originally homogeneous but limited human knowledge has fallen into parts, each one specified further and this process of specification created very professional, sometimes surprisingly efficient but detached knowledge, people who had a sharp shortsightedness and therefore depending on the knowledge, professional structure of time and circumstances as this was acquired. The new world is somehow different. It demonstrates fast changes in human requirements, skills, knowledge, environment, a much higher level of adaptation is needed than before in less turbulently changing historical periods. Adaptation in this respect means a relatively broad but well-digested basic knowledge. Basic knowledge should also be open to new paradigms and flexible application; it should be more a culture of thinking in the dynamics of natural and human processes (e.g. physics, economics, history) than a catechism-like solid foundation. An excellent but sometimes misused example is the teaching of new math; another one is the teaching of physics with an eye on technology or history (in the spirit of the French Annales-group). The emphasis on verbal and written expressive abilities helps develop not only these skills but also ways of thinking, communication, i.e. the most important future human activities. Learning a minimum of one foreign language is important (especially for countries of smaller language groups), not only because it opens windows to international communication, but is (and can be, if taught and applied well) a wonderful paradigm for other paradigms. This statement means that another language illustrates another way of thinking, expression and a different culture which in its dissimilarity reflects other valid values.

A society which would like to cope with the future should prepare the whole nation for the human use of the those devices, communication media and knowledge apparatus which were partly outlined in this paper too. It is easy to realize that this requirement is situated on a much higher level than any other one before, but it is extremely difficult to put this realization into a nationwide education scheme. Structural unemployment, the loss of hope for an increasing percentage of society, which falls behind the requirements, is only the first signal of further consequences. We envisage for the first half of the next century a totally computerized knowledge-engineered society, equipped with such an abundance of robots as the present society is equipped with cars and for the next few years personal computers. Those who do not master their use are unable to perform any job and therefore excluded from any participation in society. We do not believe in the health of a society where the majority is not active, but only getting benefits from those who are able and willing to work.

Equal opportunity becomes much more significant than at any time before, although the conditions, the instruments for it, and even the definition are unclear; it is only clear that all these lie overwhelmingly in education and especially in those features of language which have been mentioned before.

This does not imply a simplified view of computer literacy. For some time, ideas about computer literacy have been misunderstood. They have meant for educators and general public a primitive knowledge of programming (we had a nationwide TV school for BASIC with some voluntary exams) and a dexterity in using the keyboards. Computer games were considered to be a step toward computer literacy, although it led more to a new kind of narcotics than to a higher understanding of the processes behind them. There is no doubt that some versatility in handling the computers is needed to an extent which might be similar to the need for non-professional drivers. The ability for further application, for being an emancipated member of a computer and communication-based society is quite different. It requires to a much greater extent the mastery of the already mentioned active, hypertext-like, associative knowledge bases, professional consultation systems, and the art of cooperation through computer networks.

Through education, we must avoid the danger of becoming addicted to computers as this is the case and task with other modern media, such as TV, video, etc. They should not abolish the thirst for reading, as the telephone, dictating machines, etc. have sometimes done, nor the intrinsic need for writing. Education should not lead to enslavement by machines, but to mastery of them.

Here I risk being interrupted by any experienced observer with the following statement: "You draw a picture of an elitist education, but what about the majority and especially about those who are practically illiterate, and not just with respect to computers!"

Here we meet the basic dilemma of the educational system not only in Hungary, but anywhere. A democratic society with equal opportunity requires a standard basic education for everybody, i.e. equalized to all who are not mentally disabled. On the other hand, we have had very bad experiences with any kind of such human standardization, this can mean the planned decay of a nation, a tragedy for any progress. One example of a need for flexible compromises – as yet unfulfilled. We in Hungary face an extremely significant example of the problem, the education of a Gypsy minority which is about 4% of the population and has a fast increasing portion because of the much higher birth rate. Most of the Gypsy population has a very low economic basis, they are not accustomed to regular work, not even to a settled way of life, their social habits, values, and concepts are different from those of a well-established population; even their language is not rich enough for expressing higher concepts, modern thoughts. If we do not solve the problem of integrating the Gypsy groups into the society, it will be a disaster not only for them but also for the Hungarian majority. The issue of coeducation or separate education comes up every year; several studies have been prepared about the role of school-computers in education of Gypsy children, but the results are rather limited.

The Gypsy education problem is an extreme case of the general problem. Views, arguments, and emotions are divergent. My personal view is in favour of creating elitist education as well, a devoted elite is or should become a vehicle for the elevation of the general population just by a positive elitist consciousness, by a vocational drive. These people can also be a counterbalance in another negative trend of computer-based activities, against mental uniformization.

Another aspect of education for the future is the preparation of the citizen. One of our projects is directed toward this objective. This project was reported several times elsewhere and the progress is till now limited; here I shall speak only about the main issues. The general public opinion considers the computers to be new menaces to civil rights, new instruments in the hands of powers striving for total control. We would like to demonstrate a totally different usage, an expert system in the hands of the citizen which makes the process of administration transparent and exhibits the alternatives involved in the decisions, rules, regulations, and laws which can be applied. This system should be more than a lawyer-consultant; it can be operated at home and at any time; it can check the progress of the case continuously and can reach an acceptable resolution by means of a dialog. The system should serve to let the citizens check the policies and practices of the authority. It should let them check whether the decision process follows the principles declared by them and voted on at the elections. The citizen can also check whether the principles work in the desired way or not. Recent election practice, based more on slogans, emotions, publicity, and popularity, is unduly subjective and specially designed for a manipulable lower or medium level publicity. A more objective mirror of principles would serve mainly to distinguish a rather traditional, conservative law and order view, focussed on efficiency and stimulation, from a rather progressive, compliant, empathy-oriented attitude, focussed on equity and humanistic ideas. This can provide a better overview of the society's main actual emphasis. Several examples indicate the need for such an approach; these include pros and cons in regulations against pornography, cruelty in motion pictures, capital punishment, regulations of prisons, or the previously discussed attitudes in education. The citizen should be emancipated in his/her own case and in public affairs as well. All the problems of education mentioned for a society regulated by computer and communication are closely related to our new relation to language.

Returning to the thesis in the introduction, we note that the linguistic interface should be elevated to a new level of expressive power and responsibility because the feedback will be direct and vitally significant. An immense task lies before us.

Note

The author expresses his appreciation to Dan Maxwell not only for the careful revision of his English but for improvements in clarification of the text.

Tibor Vámos

Lingvo kaj la komputila socio

Resumo

Kiel unika homa komunikilo lingvo ĉiam estis objekto de atento kaj intereso. Ĝi rolas en mitologio kaj religio, kaj preskaŭ en ĉiuj epokoj scienca pensado konsideris ĝin ne nur en si mem, sed lige al historio, psikologio, logiko, neŭrologio, pedagogio kaj aliaj prihomaj kaj pricerbaj disciplinoj. Kiam en la nuna epoko oni klopodas antstataŭi homajn agojn de alta intelekta nivelo per komunikadsistemoj kaj komputiloj, la rolo de la homa lingvo fariĝas des pli grava.

Informserĉado estas malnova problemo, laŭokaze solvita de bibliotekistoj k.a. Nuntempaj komputilaj sistemoj por la sama celo ofte estas malagrable "stultaj". Ili ankoraŭ malhavas taŭgajn trovmekanismojn. Krome ĝenerale validas, ke ju pli kompleksa tia sistemo estas, des malpli senpere uzebla ĝi fariĝas por laikoj.

La esprimo natura lingvo *estas kutime uzata por vicoj da korektaj frazoj, dum natura homa dialogo ofte tute ne estas tia. Pensu pri homo en vendejo kiu ankoraŭ ne tute bone scias kion li volas, nek scias la ĝustajn vortojn. Tial komputilsistemoj devas povi trakti necertaĵojn. Necerteco havas lingvajn, psikajn, logikajn kaj aliajn aspektojn, kies esplorado estas same longdaŭra kiel la studo de la homa penso mem. La ĉi-rilataj esplorklopodoj estas multnombraj. Ili atingis malsamajn gradojn de progresinteco, sed la celo, imiti la homan dialogon, restas malproksimega.*

Socio kiu volas bone regi sian estontecon devas prepari kaj eduki la tutan popolon por uzi la sistemojn de la estonta, rapide ŝanĝiĝanta homa vivo. La nuna struktura senlaboreco, la minaco ke partoj de la socio estos esceptitaj de la evoluo, jam anoncas ontajn grandajn konsekvencojn. La unua duono de la venonta jarcento estos tiel plena de scioteknologia ilaro, ke nepriĝas eduko kiu kapabligas ĉiujn, kaj ne nur ian aktivan malplimulton, uzi la ilojn. Egalŝanceco fariĝas multe pli grava ol ĝis nun.

Ĉi tiu postulo ne celas al primitiva speco de komputila alfabetismo. Por esti samrajta ano de komunikada kaj komputila socio necesas altnivela scipovo uzi sciobankojn, profesiajn konsultsistemojn kaj komputilajn retojn. Tamen la edukado ne fariĝu kvazaŭ drogdependa de komputiloj, kiel okazis pri televido, video ktp. Legi kaj skribi nepre restu esencaj. Edukado instruu ne sklaviĝi al maŝinoj, sed regi ilin.

Ĉu ĉi tiu pledo estas elitisma? Hungarujo frontas gravan edukan problemon ekz. rilate al sia cigana minoritato. Miaopinie oni solvu tiajn problemojn, sed ja samtempe paralele eduku eliton, en pozitiva senco. La elitanoj dank' al sia eduko ankaŭ povus kontraŭagi negativan sekvon de komputado: animan unuformecon.

Konkreta ekzemplo por sistemo kiu ne limigas, sed ĝuste devas plifirmigi la rajtojn de la civitano estas jura konsultsistemo kiu klarigas la vojojn kaj regulojn de oficialaj decidproceduroj.

La lingva konekto al komputilaj sistemoj fariĝas pli kaj pli grava. Antaŭ ni estas grandega tasko.

The State of the Art in Machine Translation in the U.S.S.R.

Ivan I. Oubine and *Boris D. Tikhomirov*

Vsesojuznyj Centr Perevodov
naučno-techničeskoj literatury i dokumentacii
USSR Centre for Translation
of Scientific and Technical Literature and Documentation
ul. Kržižanovskogo 14, korp. 1
SU-117218 Moskva V-218
Soviet Union

Circulation of foreign scientific and technical literature in the U.S.S.R. is increasing at such a rate that translation organizations can not cope with the steadily growing stream of information. Therefore, the only way out of the existing situation seems to be full or at least partial automation of translation services. Automation of translation is also necessitated by the fact that an ever-growing stream of scientific and technical information is distributed directly on magnetic media or via communication channels.

The progress of machine translation (MT) in the U.S.S.R. has undergone the same phases as in the rest of the world. It was initially assumed that efforts should be concentrated on the development of powerful and fully automatic MT systems which would provide translation of such high quality that no post-editing be required; nowadays the difficulty of practical implementation of such systems in such a way that rate, quality, and cost are acceptable has been realized.

In the present state of the art, the necessity seems to have arisen for the development and employment of a complete range of text translation automation facilities (TTAF) with various degrees of human participation. These include:

- machine translation system,
- translation work stations,
- computer dictionaries and term banks,
- software utilities for natural language processing, i.e. standard or customized word processor facilities aimed at increasing the productivity of translators' labour.

Subject field and policy of language choice in developing TTAF must be based on a study of the information practice, particularly in traditional translation. The major languages of scientific and technical exchange are currently English, Japanese, German, French, and Russian, which is reflected in existing TTAF in the U.S.S.R.

The foregoing concept is confirmed in principle by the practice of development of TTAF in the U.S.S.R. The bulk of work aimed at developing and implementing multipurpose and specialized systems of machine translation, various automatic dictionaries and other means of automatic support for translators is concentrated in the U.S.S.R. Centre for Translation (VCP) and the Leningrad State pedagogical institute (LGPI).

At the present time, a modular system of machine translation from English and German into Russian (ANRAP) is in service in the VCP. The system is based on two earlier MT systems: AMPAR – from English into Russian, and NERPA – from German into Russian (Marčuk/Tikhomirov/Ščerbinin 1982; Tikhomirov 1984). ANRAP has the following basic modules: the English language module (English input dictionary and all kinds of analysis), the German language module (German input dictionary and all kinds of analysis), and unified Russian language module (Russian output dictionary and all kinds of synthesis). The system's software package is common for all the modules. ANRAP differs from AMPAR and NERPA in that it has a more advanced software and technology (Tikhomirov 1987), which facilitates adaptation of the system to concrete conditions of different users. ANRAP has several changeable dictionaries for different subject areas and can translate texts on computer technology, programming, radioelectronics, mechanical engineering, metallurgy and agriculture. The translation rate is 160 thousand characters per hour on EC-1035 computer (from the start of input till the end of output). The quality of translation is sufficient to use it as preliminary information. In 1986-1987 over 800 mln symbols were translated from English and German into Russian on a commercial basis. About 70% of all translated texts were on magnetic tape. Translations were handed back to the customers on printout and magnetic tape. Orders for both unedited MT and MT with lexical and grammatical post-editing were executed. The quality, price, and promptness of the output depended on the degree of post-editing required by the customer. A multi-split screen editing facility had been developed for ANRAP with a view to automatic and interactive post-editing (Tikhomirov 1987). The first mode affords only lexical editing by replacing certain words and phrases in the output text with lexical units from a topical or text-oriented vocabulary file. In the second mode the target text is shown on the screen sentence by sentence along with the source text, so that a human editor can edit it. The system is being reprogrammed for a personal computer.

Development of a French-into-Russian MT system FRAP is continuing at the VCP. The following sequence of steps has been accepted for the analysis: graphematics, accidence, syntax, and semantics. The linguistic components are separate and relatively independent, making it possible to operate the system in different modes. The decisive role in the system is played by the syntactic analysis, which determines the sentence structure, as well as to the semantic analysis, which provides its semantic interpretation. The syntactic structure is defined in terms of sentence members. The nodes of the grammar employed are meaningful words, which ensures liaison between the syntactic and semantic components. The system has been programmed for EC-type computers and is operated on an experimental basis (Leont´eva/Kudrjašëva 1983).

The SILOD universal system has been devised in the Leningrad State pedagogical institute for machine translation from English, French, and Spanish into Russian and vice versa. The SILOD system can solve the following problems: information back-up of technical staff (tentative translation); speeding up traditional translation of scientific and technical literature (lexical word-for-word translation); handling standardized documents (unedited lexical technical translation). The software package is designed for an analytical input language like English. A change-over to flexion-type language, like Russian, will require modifications in the linguistics and software. Output dictionary software facilities are intended for flexion-type morphological synthesis. Conversion to analytical languages will involve changes only in the linguistic components. At present two modules are operated on an industrial basis: English into Russian (social and political affairs and computer technology) and French into Russian (social and political affairs). Two more modules are operated on an experimental basis: Russian into English and Spanish into Russian (Piotrovskij 1987; Beljaeva/Kondrateva et al. 1985).

An English-into-Russian MT system for electrical engineering called ETAP-2 has been developed in the U.S.S.R. The system is aimed at obtaining translation of superior quality. Input texts are analyzed on morphological and syntactical levels. The syntactic analysis is single-path with back-tracking. Heuristic preference rules can be used in the process. The output text is synthesized while transforming the source sentence structure into into the target sentence structure. The transfer stage has about one thousand rules, of which 96 are general rules, 342 are local rules, and the other are lexical rules. The system has been tested on an experimental basis. The dictionary contains four thousand entries. In the experiment about half the sentences were translated with satisfactory quality. The translation rate was three to four minutes per sentence of an average length (Cinman 1986; Apresjan/Cinman 1982).

Great interest on the part of scientific and industrial organizations in rapid translation of scientific and technical documentation, produced on paper and especially on magnetic media, has led to the development of several monofunctional MT systems for narrow subject areas. Examples are found in such systems as an English-into-Russian MT system for titles of warehouse patents, an MT system on petrochemistry, and a word-for-word and phrase-for-phrase MT system on polymer chemistry. The MT system for titles of warehouse patents is linked to an automated system for handling scientific and technical information and allows prompt retrieval of information on patented inventions. The linguistic basis of the MT system is an English-Russian computer dictionary of word forms and phrases, a set of syntax patterns for titles, and sets of diagnostic features for determining title structures. Assessment of the results of the system's experimental operation has on the whole confirmed correctness of the linguistic algorithms and sufficiency of the dictionaries (Karpilovič/Deckina et al. 1986).

An interactive English-into-Russian MT system on petrochemistry has been developed in VNIIPKneftechim of Kiev. The linguistic framework of the system includes graphematic, lexical and syntactic analyses and a semantic component. Semantic analysis is based on finding intersections of semantic primitives in chains of syntactical classes obtained during syntactic analysis. Non-zero intersection of primitives either serves as a key to the translation equivalent reflecting the lexico-semantic variant of the word realized in the given semantic context, or specifies the syntactic representation by the semantic closeness of the elements. The system is programmed for EC computers using PL/I and Assembly languages. The system has been tested experimentally. At the present time (as of 1986) the system translates correctly about 50% of all sentences in scientific papers and patents and 75 to 80% in summaries. The system designers expect that on-line editing can ensure the 75% quality level of all texts, which in their opinion is sufficient for commercial operation (Gal'čenko/Miram 1986).

For a number of years a word-for-word and phrase-for-phrase MT system has been operating on an industrial basis in the Čimkent pedagogical institute. The system is based on an English-Russian computer dictionary of word forms and phrases, compiled on a corpus of 400 thousand words containing over 22 thousand different lexical units. Translation rate with post-editing is 2 to 2.5 hours for a text of 40,000 symbols (Bektaev 1983; Bektaev/Bektaev et al. 1985).

In the last few years an ever increasing amount of attention has been given to various automatic dictionaries based on "mainframe" computers and particularly on micro- and personal computers. A large automated lexicographic system has been developed in the VCP. The system is a multilanguage automatic dictionary (English, German, French and Russian languages) with versatile linguistic and software support. The dictionary includes common words and terms on computer technology, programming, and radioelectronics. The dictionary is reversible, i.e. it can be used for translation from foreign languages into Russian and from Russian into foreign languages in both dialogue and batch modes. Queries can be formulated in text form. If a requested phrase is not found in the dictionary, it is split into separate words and the user gets their translation equivalents. The volume of output information can be varied. The dictionary has dual software and can run on both EC and CM computers. The total volume of all dual-language lexical stocks is about 100 thousand items (Oubine 1987).

The VCP also develops a work station for translator and human editor which is an adaptable combination of five subsystems and is intended for automating and optimizing the labour of the following categories of information service workers: translators (editors), executive editors and translation service administrators, terminologists and lexicographers.

The nucleus of the work station is formed by three subsystems:

- translation text input, computer dictionary lookup and translation editing,
- dual-language two-way computer dictionary support,
- personal glossary of new terms.

The three subsystems ensure computer support for translators, editors, lexicographers, and terminologists. Two ancillary subsystems keep stock of completed translations for the administration and produce printed translations with high typographic quality. Translator's work station is built around the EC-1841 personal computer. Linguistic information and algorithms (dictionary items, lemmatization rules, etc.) are borrowed from the VCP computer dictionary running on the EC-1045 computer. The software package for the work station is original and provides an interactive link between the subsystems with response times acceptable for the operator (2 to 3 seconds). Depending on the computer configuration equipment, main and external memory size, and the user requirements, some subsystems can be expanded, curtailed, or completely excluded from a concrete work station (Voržev/Kikot′ et al. 1986).

A similar device is developed in the Minsk institute of foreign languages. Their English-Russian computer dictionary is meant primarily for professional translators. The dictionary has two interactive modes and runs on the EC-1840 and EC-1841 computers. In the first mode, a user refers to the dictionary by keying in a word or a phrase in the dictionary form. The dictionary responds with Russian equivalents. In the second mode, the microcomputer is used as a typewriter with sufficiently flexible editing capabilities. Searching for translation equivalents in dictionaries can be carried out at the same time as the keyboarding or editing a text on the screen (Karpilovič/Kavcevič 1987).

An English-Russian and Russian-English computer dictionary of colloquial remarks in dialogues has also been compiled in that institute. It contains 1235 English and Russian dictionary pairs in 19 very common subject areas divided into 53 typical situations involving city communication. Structurally, the linguistic support provided by the computer dictionary consists of the following modules:

1) English-Russian and Russian-English dictionary of colloquial remarks;

2) dual-language micro-dictionary of individual colloquial remarks;

3) dual-language topical dictionaries of remarks for different situations on a given topic;

4) common dual-language dictionary for all topics, situations and remarks. The dictionary is programmed for a micro-computer and has appeared on the market (Zubov/Nechaj et al. 1982).

Increased interest on the part of scientists and information workers as well as of designers of MT systems and computer dictionaries has been created by Japanese. A Japanese-into-Russian translation software package POJARAP has been developed in the VCP as the first step towards creating a polythematic MT system and/or a Japanese component of a computer dictionary or of a terminology data bank. Based on a linguistic model devised in the Institute of oriental studies of the U.S.S.R. Academy of Sciences (Šaljapina 1980), software, technological and linguistic tools have been designed which will make it possible for anyone who has no command of Japanese to key in Kanji texts and obtain a normalized word-for-word translation. The transfer grammar rules change the word order of Japanese sentences to suit the requirements of Russian, and the translation equivalents are presented not in dictionary form, but as context-motivated word forms wherever this is possible without complicated syntactic treatment. The software package, a specialized programming language for MT algorithms, and the Russian dictionary of the ANRAP system are employed in the project. A special technique has been devised enabling interactive keyboarding of Japanese texts by anyone who does not know Kanji.

A Japanese-into-Russian MT system is worked upon in the Institute for oriental studies of the U.S.S.R. Academy of sciences. Two operation modes are envisaged: normalized word-for-word translation and sentence-for-sentence translation with interlingual transfer and semantic and syntactic representation in terms of a dependency grammar.

The first mode involves segmentation of the source text into words, their morphological analysis, preliminary homonym resolution on the basis of close linear context, replacement of Japanese units by Russian equivalents and normalization of the word string obtained, i.e. changing the word order with regard to the most common rules of correspondence between Japanese and Russian word order patterns.

The second mode involves implementation in the system's linguistic support of all methodological principles worked out as part of research on the ARAP English-into-Russian automatic translation system (*Intellektual'nye sistemy. Praktičeskie priloženija.* 'Intelligent systems. Practical applications' [forthcoming]).

The VCP conducts R&D work aimed at improving the technological properties of MT systems and raising the quality of machine translation. It is here that the LINTRAN linguistic framework for machine translation belongs. The LINTRAN is a generating system designed for automatic construction of MT systems tuned to specific information requirements of users. The first version is based on English and Russian languages (Lovckij/Tikhomirov 1987).

Development of a unified meta-system for machine translation FLOREAT has begun, i.e. a language-independent translation model with no linguistic data (either lexical or grammatical) incorporated in the routines and oriented towards certain representation forms of dictionary and transformational information. It is expected that concrete reversible MT systems for different language pairs and specified subject areas can be built on the basis of the FLOREAT meta-system. Teaching the meta-system, i.e. the formation and input of linguistic data (dictionaries, parsing, transfer, and generation rules) will be conducted interactively. The result will be a copy of the meta-system, an initial version of a desired concrete MT system, and a set of teaching routines with a user's manual for further development of the system (Martemjanov 1983; Eliseev 1983).

The above notes briefly outline the state of the art in automating translation in the U.S.S.R. In our view, further development of automatic facilities will take the following course:

- development and extensive application of MT systems (multifunctional and polythematic systems in large translation and information organizations; monofunctional and narrow-subject-area systems in small translation bureaus and R&D organizations), and a wide range of translator's work stations and computer dictionaries on personal computers;

- setting up pools for linguistic and algoristic packages, as well as systems for generating and distributing MT systems adaptable to technical facilities and subject area requirements of specific users;

- cooperation of organizations dealing with scientific and technical information with organizations possessing lexical stockpiles in collecting and systematizing terminology for new subject areas;

- development of reversible MT systems for specified language pairs and subject areas on the basis of language-independent theories;

- construction of integrated systems, combining automated translation with information retrieval and expert systems.

Research already accomplished makes it possible to start such work even now.

References

Apresjan, Ju. D. / L. L. Cinman (1982): Ob ideologii sistemy ETAP-2.
In: *Formal'noe predstavlenie lingvističeskoj informacii*. Novosibirsk, pp. 3-19

Bektaev, K. B. (1983): Promyšlennyj MP v režime dialoga čelovek–ĖVM.
In: *Meždunarodnyj seminar po mašinnomu perevodu*. Moskva, pp. 35-36

Bektaev, K. B. / A. K. Bektaev / P. A. Abdullaeva / V. N. Bazarbaev / G. Nurmuchanbetova / E. P. Purputidi (1985): Realizacija mašinnogo perevoda v uslovijach primenenija sistemy razdelenija vremeni.
In: *Meždunarodnaja konferencija "Teorija i praktika naučno-techničeskogo perevoda"*. Moskva, pp. 8-9

Beljaeva, L. N. / A. A. Kondrateva et al. (1985): SILOD – sistema avtomatičeskoj obrabotki naučno-techničeskich tekstov.
In: *Meždunarodnaja konferencija "Teorija i praktika naučno-techničeskogo perevoda"*. Moskva, p. 130

Cinman, L. L. (1986): Razvitie logiko-algoritmičeskogo obespečenija.
In: *Predvaritel'nye publikacii Instituta russkogo jazyka AN SSSR. Problemnaja gruppa po ėksperimental'noj i prikladnoj lingvistike [174]*. Moskva, pp. 1-47

Eliseev, S. L. (1983): Realizacija transformacionnogo sinteza.
In: *Meždunarodnyj seminar po mašinnomu perevodu*. Moskva: VCP, pp. 130-132

Gal'čenko, O. N. / G. E. Miram (1986): Sistema mašinnogo perevoda "SIMPAR" – principy razrabotki i zadači ėksperimental'noj ėkspluatacii.
In: *Problemy avtomatičskogo i ėksperimental'no-fonetičeskogo analiza tekstov* (Sbornik naučnych statej). Minsk, pp. 141-146

Intellektual'nye sistemy. Praktičeskie priloženija.
Moskva: AN SSSR (forthcoming)

Karpilovič, T. P. / R. V. Deckina et al. (1986): O resul'tatach opitnoj ėkspluatacii SMP zagolovkov patentov.
In: *Problemy avtomatičeskogo i ėksperimental'no-fonetičeskogo analiza tekstov* (Sbornik naučnych statej). Minsk, pp. 157-162

Karpilovič, T. P. / A. I. Kavcevič (1987): Razrabotka avtomatizirovannogo rabočego mesta perevodčika na baze mikroĖVM.
In: *Informacionnyj i lingvodidaktičeskij aspekty naučno-techničeskogo perevoda.* Voronež, pp. 4-5

Leont'eva, N. N. / I. M. Kudrjašëva / S. L. Nikogosov / E. G. Sokolova / M. S. Suchanova (1983): Obščaja strategija lingvističeskogo analiza v sisteme FRAP-2.
In: *Meždunarodnyj seminar po mašinnomu perevodu* (Tezisy dokladov). Moskva, pp. 115-117

Lovckij, E. E. / B. D. Tikhomirov (1987): O distributivnych sistemach mašinnogo perevoda. In: *Perevod i avtomatičeskaja obrabotka teksta*. Moskva: Institut jazykoznanija AN SSSR / VCP / KŠI, pp. 29-30

Marčuk, Ju. N. / B. D. Tikhomirov / V. I. Ščerbinin (1982): Ein System zur maschinellen Übersetzung aus dem Englischen ins Russische. In: *Automatische Sprachübersetzung*. Darmstadt: Wissenschaftliche Buchgesellschaft, pp. 319-336

Martemjanov, Ju. S. (1983): Osobennosti sistemy FLOS i ich sledstvija dlja analiza. In: *Meždunarodnyj seminar po mašinnomu perevodu*. Moskva: VCP, pp. 80-81

Oubine, I. I. (1987): Perevodnye avtomatičeskie slovari. In: *Naučnotechničeskij perevod*. Moskva, pp. 105-134

Piotrovskij, R. H. (1987): Lingvističeskie avtomaty i mašinnyj fond russkogo jazyka. In: *Voprosy jazykoznanija* [4], pp. 69-73

Šaljapina, Z. M. (1980): *Maket lingvističeskogo obespečenija sistemy japonsko-russkogo avtomatičeskogo perevoda: obščaja struktura i osnovnye komponenty*. Moskva: IV AN SSSR

Tikhomirov, B. D. (1987): Promyšlennye sistemy mašinnogo perevoda. In: *Naučno-techničeskij perevod*. Moskva: pp. 92-105

Tikhomirov, B. D. (1984): Some specific Features of Software and Technology in the AMPAR and NERPA Systems of Machine Translation. In: *International Forum on Information and Documentation* 9 [2], pp. 9-11

Voržev, A. V. / A. I. Kikot′ / L. Ju. Korostel′ëv / B. D. Tikhomirov (1986): Razrabotka ARM perevodčika v VCP. In: *Vsesojuznaja konferencija "Podgotovka i ispol′zovanija naučno-techničeskich slovarej v sisteme informacionnogo obespečenija"* (Tezisy dokladov). Moskva, pp. 117-119

Zubov, A. V. / O. A. Nechaj / L. I. Tribis (1982): Ėkstralingvističeskie i lingvističeskie komponenty banka dannych mikrokomp′jutera-perevodčika. In: *Problemy vnutrennej dinamiki rečevych norm*. Minsk, pp. 191-198

Ivan I. Oubine *kaj* Boris D. Tikhomirov

La aktuala stato de perkomputila tradukado en Sovetunio

Resumo

La amasa fluo de scienca kaj teknika literaturo postulas almenaŭ partan aŭtomatigon de la tiucelaj tradukservoj en Sovetunio. La evoluo de perkomputila tradukado en Sovetunio disvolviĝis laŭ la samaj fazoj kiel en la cetera mondo. Oni nun konscias pri la neebleco de tutaŭtomata tradukado sen postkorekto. Tial ŝajnas nun necese strebi al gamo de diversspecaj tradukhelpiloj, nome komputilaj traduksistemoj, tradukistaj laborkomputiloj, komputilaj vortaroj kaj terminbankoj, komputilaj tekstprilaboriloj.

La ĉefaj lingvoj bezonataj en Sovetunio estas la angla, la japana, la germana, la franca kaj la rusa. La plejparto de la ĉi-rilata laboro okazas ĉe la Tutunia Tradukcentro (VCP) kaj la Leningrada Ŝtata Pedagogia Instituto (LGPI). Nuntempe VCP uzas la tradukistemon ANRAP (angla, germana → rusa). En 1986-87 oni tradukis 800 milionojn da simboloj. La mendintoj ricevis laŭmende ĉu krudan tradukon, ĉu korektitan, magnetbende aŭ surpapere. Por ANRAP ekzistas interaga redaktilo kun multoble dividita ekrano. VCP evoluigas franc-rusan sistemon (FRAP), kiu ĝis nun funkcias eksperimente. La leningrada instituto evoluigis la sistemon SILOD (angla, franca, hispana ⟷ rusa), el kies tradukdirektoj kelkaj jam funkcias industrinivele. Ĝi taŭgas por analizaj lingvoj kiel la angla, sed bezonas adaptojn por fleksiaj (rusa). ETAP-2 estas sistemo por altkvalita tradukado (angla → rusa) pri elektrotekniko. Ĝia vortaro nuntempe enhavas mil enskribaĵojn kaj ĝi tradukas duonon de la frazoj kontentige. Aro da sistemoj estis konstruita por tre specialigitaj fakterenoj, ekz. petrokemio (angla → rusa).

Lastatempe oni dediĉas pli da atento al apliko de malgrandaj komputiloj. VCP evoluigis aŭtomatan, inversigeblan vortaron por la angla, germana, franca kaj rusa. Ĝi ankaŭ konstruas komputilan laborĉirkaŭaĵon por tradukisto kaj korektisto, uzeblan ankaŭ por redaktoroj, leksikografoj kaj terminologoj. Similan sistemon oni havas en Minsk. Kreskas la intereso pri la japana. Instituto de la Akademio de Sciencoj laboras pri japan-rusa sistemo (POJARAP) kiu ankaŭ antaŭvidas uzon fare de neregantoj de la kanĵi-ideografaĵaro. Ĉe VCP oni krome laboras pri aro da metasistemoj por la kreado de traduksistemoj (LINTRAN, FLOREAT).

La estonta evoluo direktos sin al

- *pluevoluigo kaj grandskala apliko de perkomputila tradukado kaj komputile helpata tradukado,*
- *koncentrado de lingvistikaj kaj algoritmaj pakaĵoj por krei traduksistemojn,*
- *kunlaboro kun organizaĵoj kiuj posedas grandajn provizojn de fakvortenskriboj,*
- *evoluigo de inversigeblaj traduksistemoj por unuopaj lingvoparoj kaj temterenoj surbaze de lingvosendependaj teorioj,*
- *konstruado de kombinitaj sistemoj por tradukado kun informserĉo kaj ekspertsistemoj.*

MT Research in China

Dong Zhen Dong

China Software Technique Corporation
Language Engineering Lab.
P. O. Box 936
Beijing
China

I. A brief historical review

Machine translation research in China could date back to the mid-50s. In the course of its 30 year history, China's MT research has seen its ups and downs, just like MT in the rest of the world. The history of MT research in China can be divided into four periods: initiation, standstill, recovery and development.

1. Initiation (1957-1965)

MT Research and development in China is characteristically supported by the government. As early as in 1956, when the Chinese government made its first National Programme for Science Development, machine translation as well as NLP was initiated. The research subject was named "machine translation, the making of translation rules for natural languages and the mathematical theory of natural languages". In 1957, MT research in Russian-Chinese and English-Chinese began. In

1959, China demonstrated its first experimental MT system, and that was the fifth demonstration in the world. The system, Russian-to-Chinese, included 2030 words in the dictionary and 29 sets of grammar rules. During the initiation period, more than five institutes and universities were involved in the research, such as Institute of Linguistics Research, Institute of Computing Technology, Institute of Foreign Languages, University of Polytech, etc. After the first demonstration, most research was focused on linguistic scheme or conceptual design.

2. Standstill (1966-1975)

In terms of technical problems, the standstill of China's MT research was caused by insufficiency in linguistic studies, inadequacy of the computers available for MT systems, and the barrier of Chinese ideograms. As for the first two types of difficulty, most MT researchers have shared our bitter experience. However, the difference in language family between Chinese on the one hand and English, Russian, or other Indo-European languages on the other adds much to the difficulty in MT research, because deep level syntactic and semantic interpretation is required (Nagao 1987). And it is obvious that it would make no sense for an MT system with Chinese as its target language to output just some kinds of codes instead of Chinese-characters. Thus Chinese ideogram processing turned out to be a bottleneck for MT research, and even for popularization of computer applications in China. A satisfactory solution of this problem was not found until the early 1980s.

3. Recovery (1975-1982)

In 1975 MT research entered into China's fifth five-year plan as a part of intelligence simulation, and began its recovery. During this period, great achievements were made both in techniques and in the training of professionals. The most prominent achievements relevant to MT research could be enumerated as follows:

- Advances in syntactic analysis, especially for English. Special attention was paid to the disambiguation of homographs, in particular, those of multi-part-of-speech words, the treatment of co-ordinate structures, and the processing of English prepositions. And some effective algorithms were introduced into the English-Chinese MT systems developed during the period.

- Achievements in semantic studies and their effective application to MT research, with logical semantics as the outstanding example. The theory of logical semantics was first put forward in 1979 (Dong 1987) and then successfully applied to China's first English-Chinese system, MT-1178, which was developed into a commercial system called TRANSTAR.

- A breakthrough in Chinese character information processing. In the early 80's there were more than 400 methods for Chinese character input coding, among which about fifty have been commercially available and popular in China up to now (Chen 1987). In 1981, GB 2312-80 (Chinese Character Coding Set for Information Exchange, Basic Set, as the National Standard) was established, and a 32×32 Chinese ideogram generator was developed. The advance in Chinese character information processing was not only a great help but also a powerful stimulation for MT research in China. During the period of recovery, 6 English-Chinese systems, 2 Russian-Chinese systems, 1 French-Chinese system, and 1 Chinese-to-multi-languages system were in an experimental stage. The latter two were developed in GETA, as the first step to international cooperation in MT research.

II. The current status (1983 -)

Since 1983, China's MT research has entered a critical period of development, for Chinese MT researchers began to endeavour to build practical or commercial systems, on the basis of experiments in the recovery period.

1. Different types of R&D

Roughly speaking there are two types of MT research and development in China at present, namely experimental development and practical development. They are different in many respects, including the institutions involved, organizational schemes, funding source, ways of R&D, main features of systems, as well as the goals to be achieved.

2. Major institutions involved

The major institutions involved in MT in China are: the Language Engineering Laboratory (LEL) of CSTC, the Institutes of Linguistics Research of the Chinese Academy of Social Sciences, the Institute of Scientific and Technical Information of China (ISTIC), the Institute of Computing Technology, the Institute of Software, Qinghua University, Nanking University, Heilongjiang University, Huanan Polytechnical Institute, Harbin Polytechnical University, Huazhong Polytechnical Institute, etc.

Here we would like to give a brief introduction to LEL of CSTC in particular. CSTC (China Software Technique Corporation) is the first national high-tech enterprise concerned with administration of China's software industry, the development of software technologies, and the marketing of software products. LEL is one of the principal laboratories of CSTC. LEL is now responsible for conducting and organizing the MT projects approved by the Chinese government for its 7th five-year plan (1986-1990), in which English-Chinese and Japanese-Chinese MT R&D has been established as one of the major projects of science and technology. LEL is also the executor and organizer of China for an international cooperative MT project – Research Cooperation on MT Systems with Japan's Neighboring Countries (Tsuji 1987). In this project, more than ten institutes and universities have been engaged in various subjects of research. Among them are the Languages Institute of Beijing for basic dictionary, ISTIC for technical term dictionary, Northeast Polytechnical Institute for Chinese analysis, etc.

In addition, LEL is engaged in many other R&D projects relevant to NLP, such as a Chinese-English MT system, modern Chinese electronic dictionary compilation, terminology bank building, language understanding, knowledge description, etc. And late this year, LEL will be engaged in machine translation services. Its TRANSAR English-Chinese system and some of its by-products will be marketed. Currently, joint venture is under negotiation with some companies in Hongkong and the United States.

In China, there are several academic bodies which are closely related to MT research. They are: Scientific and Technical Information Society of China, Scientific and Technical Information Society of Beijing, and Chinese Information Processing Society of China. Under each of these societies a special MT committee has been formed, and it plays an important role in the academic exchange.

3. Introduction to major MT systems

The development period of MT research in China has been characterized by more efforts in developing operational systems rather than experimental ones. There are now three MT systems which have passed the technical assessment. This is an important official procedure for the authentication of research projects. A brief introduction to these systems is shown in Table 1.

It is also noteworthy that some experimental systems, though currently confined to laboratories, seem promising in view of their good conceptual designs, e.g. English-Chinese systems named JFY-IV and TECM, and an Esperanto-Chinese/English system named ECHA.

III. Some views on the future

1. Building of knowledge of the world

It is generally acknowledged that an MT system needs three kinds of linguistic knowledge: intra-linguistic, inter-linguistic and extra-linguistic. In the past 30 years of MT research, we have concentrated almost exclusively on employment of intra-linguistic and inter-linguistic knowledge, and these could no long contribute much to the research without powerful extra-linguistic knowledge, i.e., the knowledge of the world. Much effort has been made in the field, some of which, such as Schank's CD, is really of great significance. However, how to build up a powerful and practical world knowledge bank still remains as a formidable question. My answer to the question is to establish static knowledge of the world by building a concept feature description dictionary, and dynamic knowledge of the world by constructing a conceptual grammar for revealing the relationship among concept features. The dictionary and the grammar will form a concept information system (CIS). CIS is not limited by such subject fields as Schank's "script", but just controlled by the given features and the given relations between features. The preparatory research of this kind is presently being carried out by a team of EEE. The crux of our research is to find a proper way to a generalized description of knowledge. Special attention is paid to the work in the dictionary construction, for the quality of the dictionary is crucial to the system.

2. Aiming at effective interlingual architecture

We appreciate the efforts at interlingual architecture made by DLT researchers at BSO (Witkam 1987) and by the researchers of Japan's CICC and their partners in neighboring countries. It is known that the conceptual fundamentals of our TRANSTAR system is similar to the interlingua put forward by our Japanese partners in some respects (Dong 1987). Admittedly many pros and cons of interlingua and transfer approaches exist in the MT community. Thus an effective interlingual architecture is very important. And we have all come to know that an interlingua is necessary for multilingual MT systems.

3. Establishing international cooperation

Knowledge is created, possessed and employed by everyone. The barrier of language exists nearly among all the national languages of human beings. Hence it would be difficult to solve the problems without common efforts from all the nations. We are happy to see that many kinds of international cooperation have been established in MT and lexicology research, and China has already joined in a lot. We are looking forward to more international cooperation after this conference.

Table 1

System Names	TRANSTAR	ISTIC-I	MT-IR-EC system
Organizations	CSTC	ISTIC	Academy of Posts and Telecommunications
Current status	marketed and MT services	trial-operation	trial-operation
Language translated	English-Chinese	English-Chinese INSPEC titles	English-Chinese INSPEC titles
Dictionaries Structure/Size	basic English 40,000 basic bilingual technical terms 40,000	basic bilingual 20,000 technical terms 60,000	basic and technical terms 32,000
Approach	transfer	direct	direct
Linguistic features	Constituent Functional Relation Grammar; function-driven rules; word-driven rules; Logical semantics	phrase-structure	phrase-structure
Software tools	SCOMT: problem-oriented language COBOL	COBOL	COBOL
Equipments available and OS	Universe 68000 UNOS; IBM AT, CCDOS convergent S/1280, CTIX	VAX-11/750	ACOS 500 Laser-printer on ACOS 400
Facilities	bilingual editor OCR interface user's dictionary editor	bilingual editor	bilingual editor
Performance	1,200 words/hour on IBM AT	600 titles/hour	1,400 titles/hour

References

Chen Liwei (1987): Some Key Issues in Chinese Information Processing and their Prospective Development.
In: *ICCIP'87*. Beijing.

Dong Zhendong / Zhang Deling (1987): KY-I MT System and some Linguistic Aspect Concerned.
In: *ICCIP'87*. Beijing.

Nagao, M. (1987): Present and Future Machine Translation Systems.
In: *Machine Translation Summit* (Hakone 1987). Tokyo: Japan Electronic Industry Development Association

Tsuji, Y. (1987): Research and Development Project of Machine Translation System with Japan's Neighboring Countries.
In: *Machine Translation Summit* (Hakone 1987). Tokyo: Japan Electronic Industry Development Association

Witkam, T. (1987): Interlingual MT – An Industrial Initiative.
In: *Machine Translation Summit* (Hakone 1987). Tokyo: Japan Electronic Industry Development Association

Dong Zhen Dong

Komputtradukaj esploroj en Ĉinujo

Resumo

La historion de la esplorado pri perkomputila tradukado en Ĉinujo eblas priskribi laŭ kvar stadioj: iniciato, halto, resaniĝo kaj evoluo.

En la iniciata fazo ŝtataj institutoj engaĝiĝis en perkomputila tradukado ekde 1956. Jam la kvina demonstro en la mondo de eksperimenta traduksistemo okazis en Ĉinujo. Oni tiam laboris pri rusa-ĉina kaj angla-ĉina sistemoj.

La halton en la evoluo kaŭzis nesufiĉo de lingvistiko kaj komputiloj, kaj precipe la problemo de la ĉinaj ideogramoj. Traduki al ĉina lingvo skribita alie ol ideograme estus sensence. Oni trovis solvon ne antaŭ la 80-aj jaroj.

La resaniĝon de la kampo kaŭzis progreso en sintakso, semantiko kaj ideogramtraktado.

De 1983 la esplortereno pli vigle evoluas. Okazas nun kaj eksperimenta kaj praktika evoluiga laboro. Aro da institutoj kaj universitatoj partoprenas en la esploroj, kaj nun ankaŭ firmaoj. La intereso fokusiĝas nun al tradukado el la angla kaj la japana.

En Ĉinujo ĉiam estis forta akcento sur tuj aplikeblaj sistemoj. La tri nun disponeblajn priskribas tabelo 1. Krome oni laboras pri aro da eksperimentaj sistemoj, i.a. angla-ĉinaj kaj unu esperanta-ĉina/angla.

Komputa traduksistemo bezonas tri specojn de scio: enlingvan, interlingvan kaj eksterlingvan. Post multjara esploro de la unuaj du, oni nun turnas sin pli emfaze al la tria. Tiurilate estas konsiderataj precipe diversaj modeloj de scenaroj. Ankaŭ interlingva sistemstrukturo estas objekto de nuntempa esplorado.

Pros and Cons of the Pivot and Transfer Approaches in Multilingual Machine Translation

Christian Boitet

Groupe d'Etudes pour la Traduction Automatique (GETA)
Université Joseph Fourier (UJF)
Centre National de la Recherche Scientifique (CNRS)
BP 53X
F-38041 Grenoble
France

Introduction: Why is the pivot approach not universally used?

The pivot approach seems best suited to the construction of multilingual M(A)T systems, for obvious reasons of minimality and economy. The idea is to translate the input text into a pivot language, and then from this pivot into the target language. In a multilingual setting with n languages, only n analyzers and n generators have to be constructed, comprising 2n grammars and 2n dictionaries (which give monolingual information and translations into or from the pivot lexicon).

In the transfer approach, there is the same number of analyzers and generators, but n(n-1) transfers must be added. They transform source interface structures into target interface structures, using n(n-1) transfer grammars and transfer dictionaries. If the interface structures contain a deep enough level of linguistic description, the transfer grammars are very small: the transfer dictionaries represent the bulk of the cost of the n(n-1) transfers, they may be large, and they are more difficult to construct than monolingual dictionaries.

However, the pivot approach has been followed in very few systems until the eighties, when several new projects revived this design. Why was it almost abandoned for more than a decade, and why don't all modern MT systems rely on it? The answer can not be simplistic, because there are several kinds of pivots, several kinds of interface structures, and several kinds of situations, which we will call "1–>m" or "m–>1", if translation occurs from one language into the m (=n-1) others, or into one language only, and "n<–>n" if there are many language pairs (at least 2m, with m>1).

I. Pure pivot approaches

A pure pivot contains no information relative to the particuliarites of expression in the source and in the target language. This means that:

- there is an independent *pivot lexicon*, made of *pivot lexical symbols (terms and "semantic" features);*
- all grammatical information is replaced by *pivot grammatical symbols* : there is a universal notation for determination, quantification and its scope, actualisation (time/modality/aspect), thematisation (theme/pheme/rheme), abstract sex and quantity replace morphological gender and number, etc.;
- the *pivot structure* combines lexical symbols, annotated by grammatical symbols, by using *pivot relational symbols* like argument places or semantic relations ; their level of interpretation is at least that of Tesnière's *actants*, or of Fillmore's *deep cases*, which are thought to remain almost invariant across families of languages, whereas syntagmatic categories and syntactic functions (used in c-structures and f-structures) do not.

I.1 Pure pivot lexicons are challenging...

According to J.I. Tsujii (1987), there are three kinds of "pure pivots": *interpretation languages, standard languages, and conceptual decompositions*. This classification concerns the three aspects of lexical, grammatical and relational symbols, but we may concentrate on the pivot lexicon for the moment.

1.1 ... but specific of a domain (interpretation language)

If the texts to be translated refer to a fixed and restricted domain, and are of a well-defined type, it may be possible to define a completely artificial language to describe them. This is illustrated by the TITUS system (Ducrot 1982), which is still in use and evolving at the Institut Textile de France. The lexical symbols stand for concepts in the textile domain, and the input languages are controlled in such a way that there is a one-to-one correspondence between their vocabulary and the set of lexical symbols. In such situations, input of the texts is best done in an interactive way, and storing in the pivot form.

While this approach leads to excellent results in some situations, it is apparently not possible to use it without controlling the input language. Another problem is that the lexical symbols and the corresponding natural vocabulary must be reconstructed for each new situation: the pivot lexicon is not universal, while the grammatical and relational symbols may be.

1.2 ... or specific of a language group (standard language)

A standard language is an existing or artificial natural language, like English or Esperanto. Taking an existing natural language as pivot necessitates double translations for all pairs of languages which do not contain the pivot. In human translation, this leads notoriously to a decrease in quality, as ambiguities and misunderstandings (misanalyses and mistranslations, in our case) may increase. No experiments have been conducted yet in practice, with English or any other natural language.

If an artificial language is chosen, like Esperanto in the BSO project, all translations are double, and the difficulty is augmented by the lack of sufficient technical vocabulary. There is an accepted mean figure of 50,000 terms in any typical technical domain. But, then, there is a very interesting aspect to this choice: if the project succeeds on a large scale, the vocabulary of Esperanto will have been developed in such a way that the esperantist dream may finally come true, as Esperanto will become a transnational language really able to support all kinds of international communication, without any political prejudice.

In order to reduce the number of added ambiguities, the BSO project seems to bracket the Esperanto text with "invisible" parentheses. This amounts to using some kind of surface structure. It is not clear to the author whether those parentheses are labelled or not, and, if yes, how. In any case, this addition may be viewed as a first step towards the idea of using structural descriptors to compose two transfer-based systems (see III.2 below).

If a natural language is chosen, so goes Tsujii's argument, the approach is limited to the language group or the language family of the standard language (Germanic or Indo-european for English). The "idiosyncratic gap" between Indo-european languages and Japanese has been pointed out more than once by Japanese colleagues. In the case of Esperanto, the basic vocabulary has been taken from several language families, but the problem still exists, because a choice has been made in each case, making it unavoidable that many distinctions and ways of expression are left out.

It should perhaps be added that very simple concepts may be expressed with different degrees of precision by languages of the same group. For instance, *mur* in French has two translations in Italian, *muro* (the wall seen from outside) and *parete* (the wall seen from inside). With the same distinction, *wall* may be translated as *Mauer* or *Wand* in German. This is true of a considerable number of names for concrete objects or notions (like colour, kinship,...).

1.3 ... and always very difficult to construct (conceptual decomposition/enumeration)

It is always difficult to construct a vocabulary in a coherent way, even for a natural language. Institutional bodies labour to create or normalize terminology. In any technical domain, however, perhaps less than 10% of the terms are normalized. This difficulty appears obviously when using interpretation languages or standard languages for MT, but the effort is immediately beneficial for areas other than MT.

J.I. Tsujii calls the third kind of pivot lexicon "conceptual decomposition". This technique has been popularized by R. Shank and his school since the early seventies. The idea is to define a small set of *conceptual primitives* (about 20 in the first versions) and to decompose all lexical items of a language in terms of them, obtaining *conceptual dependency (CD) structures*.

Of course, while predicative elements are relatively easy to decompose in this way, this is not true of the vast majority of the vocabulary of a natural language. For example, how does one distinguish all types of natural noises, rocks, plants, or animals, with so few primitives? The associated CD graphs are certain to be enormous.

Even if neuropsychology some day comes up with a proven set of, say, 200 or 2000 basic primitives, the objection remains. The obvious solution used by natural languages and by some current Japanese MT projects (Fujitsu's ATLAS, NEC's PIVOT, ODA's CICC project on Asian languages) is to use *conceptual enumeration* on top of conceptual decomposition. In theory, this would amount to give names to some CD graphs, and to use them in the construction of other, more complex, CD graphs. In practice, it seems that the aforementioned projects simply give a name to any new concept encountered, like "wall-outside" and "wall-inside", together with a definition written in natural language, very much like in usual dictionaries.

Then, the notion of concept may be equated with that of "meaning" in usual dictionaries. Complex terms such as "road haulage" are identified as concepts when this is clear in the considered language, or when their translation into another language of the system is not considered language, or when their translation into another language of the system is not compositional ("camionnage" or "transport par route" for this example, in French).

There are at least three main difficulties in the construction of such conceptual lexicons:

- First, there is *the sheer size of the set of concepts* to be defined, for any reasonably general MT application. The Japanese CICC project is said to already use more than 250,000 concepts.
- Second, *the construction process is non-monotonic*. When a new concept is created from a term of some language, it is necessary to revise the dictionaries of all n-1 other languages. For example, "wall" is a unique concept when only English and French have been treated. When Italian or German comes in, it must be split.
- Third, *it is difficult to look for an existing concept* if its name is difficult to guess. For example, suppose one is adding a new complex term, like "pros and cons", in one of the dictionaries, and that no translation into another language is available (in a usual dictionary). The only solution seems to try tentative definitions and to ask some support system to perform an associative search based on partial matches to check whether the pivot lexicon already contains the appropriate concept or not.

It would be an oversimplification to think that this approach is a mere extension of the interpretation language approach, because one tries to take the union of many domains/situations: it is much more linguistic in spirit. A main difference is the possibility, and even the necessity, of ambiguity (see again the "wall" example). Also, there is no pretence to formalize all domains in which the MT system will work, as this would imply the explicit use of formal representations like the CD graphs, augmented by general and specific facts and inference rules, etc.

The ambition of the projects based on the conceptual decomposition/enumeration approach is enormous, but so are the human and financial resources allocated to them. Outside the field of MT, these projects may give two very important by-products:

- the international normalization of a considerable amount of technical terms;
- a kind a multilingual encyclopedia.

I.2 Pure pivot structure loses information...

It is extremely rare that two different terms or constructions of a language are completely synonymous. Using a pivot language makes it unavoidable that information useful for quality translation will be lost. But perhaps this is justified in view of the economic advantage in n<->n situations.

2.1 ... at the lexical level

Translating through an interpretation language certainly reduces distinctions between terms of the natural vocabulary, but, considering the situations in which this approach is used, this is of no importance. As a matter of fact, the overall process consists in creating an internal representation of the messages to be generated, through the use of a "quasi-natural" (strictly controlled) input language, or even menus, and then in expressing them in many languages. This is a problem of generation rather than of translation in the usual sense.

In the case of a standard language, the problem is real. Of course, it is always possible to translate a simple term of the source language by a compound term ("wall seen from outside") of the standard language, and then again by a simple term of the target language. But this must be done with care, as nothing prevents the input text from using the unmarked word for "wall" in an expression such as "wall seen from outside": this should be indicated in the pivot representation, or else the translation will be inexact. Also, the natural temptation for dictionary writers is to imitate usual bilingual dictionaries and to translate both "muro" and "parete" by "wall", making it impossible to recover the distinction if going from Italian to German through English.

Perhaps the only way not to lose in lexical precision is to reach the ideal state where a complete conceptual dictionary will have been constructed, for all the terms used in the class of texts to be translated. This certainly calls for active international cooperation.

2.2 ... at the lower interpretation levels (style)

With the pivot methods, one obtains paraphrases rather than translations, because it is impossible to produce the desired parallelism in style, as all trace of the surface expression is erased. For example, it is not possible to force the system to translate the English passive by the French reflexive, in some predetermined contexts *(many equations are solved by iteration ——> beaucoup d'équations se résolvent par itération),* and by the French impersonal in other cases.

This makes it impossible to aim at a rough translation of professional quality. Perhaps it is the price to pay for the automation of translation in n<-->n contexts. But this limitation might be alleviated by the construction of (monolingual) stylistic editors, with which it would be a simple matter to change a whole text, or selected portions of it, from imperative to subjunctive *(do this —> you/one should do this)* or from some tense to another, etc.

2.3 ... at non universal grammatical levels

Another severe problem with the pivot approaches is the "all-or-nothing" problem: no translation is possible if analysis has not produced a correct result in terms of semantic relationships, a very difficult task. If the size of the unit of translation becomes larger than one sentence, e.g. one or several paragraphs, it is almost certain that the result of analysis will not be complete, and hence that the majority of units will have to be translated as fragments.

II. Transfer approaches

The transfer approach is very frequently used, because of the difficulties mentioned above, and perhaps because 1–>m or m–>1 situations occur more frequently than n<–>n situations. This means that the source interface structure produced by the analyzer, usually a tree or a graph, contains lexical and grammatical information attached to the nodes and/or the arcs, and has to be submitted to a lexical and to a structural transfer, the latter incorporating some *contrastive knowledge* of the given language pair.

Structural transfer is simpler if the *level of interpretation* obtained is higher. These levels are, in ascending order, those of *syntactic classes* (noun, verb, adjective...), *syntagmatic classes* (nominal phrase, relative clause...), *syntactic functions* (subjet, object, attribute, circumstancial...), *logical relations* (predicate, first argument, second argument...), and *semantic relations* (possession, quantification, accompaniment, instrument, location, cause, consequence, agent, patient, beneficiary...), the last two being sometimes not distinguished.

II.1 The hybrid approaches may be worse, because the square problem remains...

In the hybrid approaches, the lexicon is that of the source or target language, while the grammatical and relational symbols are universal. To go from a source interface structure to a corresponding target interface structure, a unique phase of lexical transfer is used. This means that, for each pair of languages, a big transfer dictionary has to be constructed: the square problem remains.

The term "hybrid pivot" was coined by Shaumjan in the sixties. Perhaps "hybrid transfer" would be a better term, because the main difference between the two approaches lies in the presence or absence of transfer dictionaries, and not of transfer grammars. In honour of Shaumjan, we will however continue to use his term.

1.1 ... if the lexicons are only monolingual (CETA)

The hybrid pivot technique was first tried by the Grenoble group (CETA) between 1961 and 1970. It was then abandoned for the transfer approach. Until 1983, no n<->n situation appeared, so that the square problem was not really a hindrance. The results obtained seemed also to demonstrate that the quality limit was really higher than with the previous method.

B. Vauquois also recommended this approach for the Eurotra project, although the situation was clearly n<->n. There are three main reasons for that. First, the project was initially designed to be a development effort, starting from existing state-of-the-art techniques, and the construction of an adequate pivot language seemed too far-fetched. Second, it was clear that the pivot approach would necessitate a very strong discipline, and the centralized building of the linguistic components. Third, it was felt that the system should produce the best possible translations, in order to demonstrate the superiority of the second-generation (2G) architecture over the first generation's (1G), at a time when the EC was beginning to use SYSTRAN binary systems in Luxemburg.

1.2 ... and even if some part becomes universal (EUROTRA)

In 1983, when Eurotra was launched and became more research-oriented, the transfer approach was kept, no doubt for the second reason: as linguistic development was to be scattered in 9, then 11 countries (for 7, then 9 languages), the development of a common pivot lexicon was not envisaged.

Now, with 72 language pairs to consider, and some results to produce with 20,000 terms in each language by the end of phase 3, the square problem looks ominous. To alleviate it, S. Perschke has recently proposed to use a kind of conceptual lexicon for the technical terms. The idea is to associate a unique number (e.g., 19875545) to each such term, in the analysis and generation dictionaries. Then, the transfer dictionaries would not contain entries for these numbers, which would remain invariant through transfer.

Apart from the fact that using numbers is more difficult than to use mnemonic names, and that the square problem stays for the general vocabulary (up to 50,000 terms?), the problem of normalization and centralized control crops up again. The effort to assign those numbers in a reliable manner would be an enormous project in itself.

II.2 Transfer architectures using m-structures...

In all approaches, analysis may be sequential or integrated. In the first case, the unit of translation is analyzed at each level of interpretation, the result being the representation of the unit at the last level for which analysis was successful. In this case, several structural transfers must be provided, one for each level of interpretation, or else a certain percentage of the input will not be translated, or translated by default as unrelated fragments (the "all-or-nothing" problem again). Of course, transfer at the syntagmatic level may be quite complicated, while it is quite simple at the last two levels, even if the two languages considered pertain to very different families. For reasons of modularity of development, this technique has been chosen by the EUROTRA project, as it had been 20 years earlier by CETA.

The alternative to sequential analysis is *integrated analysis*. It consists in letting the levels of interpretation interact during analysis, and in producing a *multilevel structural descriptor* as a result. Such a technique has been proposed by B. Vauquois in 1974, and has since been used in all MT systems developed with GETA's methodology. All the computed levels are represented on the same graph, a "decorated tree" which geometry is obtained by a simple transformation from a (not necessarily projective) dependency structure. With this scheme, some semantic information may be used to disambiguate at the syntactic level, as in the following sentences:

John drank a bottle of beer.

John broke a bottle of beer.

When disambiguation is impossible on the basis of linguistic criteria, the ambiguity can be coded in the structure, as for:

John lost a bottle of beer.

Also, it becomes possible to treat large units of translation, several paragraphs long, without encountering the "all-or-nothing" problem. If analysis at the highest levels of interpretation does not give satisfactory results on some part of the unit, this part, and only it, is transferred on the basis of the lower levels, which act as *safety nets* (Vauquois & Boitet 1985).

2.1 ... allow to reach a higher quality

One must admit that our linguistic knowledge is very incomplete. For many years, for example, some renowned laboratories have been looking for a universal notation to represent the tense/aspect/modality triad. This goal has not yet been attained. Moreover, even if such a description were found, it is not at all certain that computational linguists would be able to *compute* it from the input texts. One example of this situation is given by semantic relationships, which even human experts can not assign in a reliable way on arguments (strong complements) of predicates (this has been experimentally proven several times, in particular in the Eurotra ETL-4 reports).

Hence, the fact that there are some "traces" of the source language expression in the source interface structure may be used by the structural transfers translating from this language to compute a good rendering in the target languages. The grammar writer incorporates here his general contrastive knowledge of a given language pair, plus, if possible, some "translator's tricks", thus improving the naturalness and idiomaticity of the rough translation.

2.2 ... may be preferable in 1->m situations

Finally, it must be emphasized that 1->m situations seem to be the most frequent when high quality translation is desired. This is the case for the majority of the big firms, which produce their documentation in one language and translate it into many others. The domains and typologies are fixed, and... going through a pivot would just add 1 lexical transfer to the m needed, and, of course, necessitate the construction of the pivot lexicon.

III. Both approaches for the future?

Because there are so many development efforts in many countries, with both approaches being used, it is not very risky to guess that they will both endure, with perhaps some evolution.

III.1 Pivot

1.1 Domain-specific pivots: new applications?

With the enormous development of CAD/CAM and expert systems, it is very probable that many situations will appear, in which some information or documentation could be directly generated from the knowledge base of the system. As techniques for the generation of natural language texts from a conceptual representation begin to be well known, the main problem will be to design efficient tools to construct a large variety of "quasi-natural" languages for the man-machine dialog.

1.2 Conceptual decomposition/enumeration: a challenge

The Japanese have embarked on a very ambitious multilingual and conceptual dictionary project, coordinated by the Electronic Dictionary Research Institute (EDR). Large scale work has begun on Japanese, English, Chinese, Korean, Thai and Malay.

This remarkable initiative is a challenge to other countries, in particular in the EC, to join in a common effort to develop an entirely new kind of ***multilingual conceptual data base***. In the far future, we may think of analogous efforts to develop multilingual textual and grammatical resources, with many potential applications.

III.2 Transfer

2.1 Conversion from first to second generation

We have mentioned some situations in which it may be advisable to develop new MT systems with the transfer approach. There are also situations in which one would like to improve existing MT systems (e.g., Systran) by converting them from first generation (1G) to second generation (2G), without losing the enormous amount of lexical and contrastive knowledge encoded in the bilingual dictionaries.

This effort could entail the development of neutral multilingual/multipurpose integrated dictionaries (Boitet & Nedobejkine 1986), which would be a first step toward the future integration in multilingual conceptual dictionaries, by the addition of references from terms to concepts.

2.2 Composition in n<->n situations: the structured standard language approach

Finally, the idea of composing transfer-based systems might give a solution to the square problem, without requiring the construction of a pivot lexicon. Let us explain this in more detail. The input to a generator is a *target interface structure* which is not in general the same as the *source interface structure* produced by an analyzer. This is because the final form of the text is not yet fixed (paraphrases are possible), because polysemies not reduced by the transfer may appear as a special type of enumeration, and because the transfer may transmit to the generator some advice or orders (relative to the possible paraphrases), by encoding them in the structure.

Our idea is simply to physically divide the structural generation phase into two successive steps, the first choosing a paraphrase and producing a *source interface structure for the target language,* and the second the surface tree passed to the morphological generator. Then, this intermediate result of the generation can be fed to any transfer from the generated language, and the number of transfer dictionaries and grammars in a multilingual transfer-based system can be drastically reduced. This approach might be called the ***structured standard language approach***.

For instance, consider the 9 languages of the European Community. They may be divided in three groups: 4 romance languages (French, Italian, Spanish, Portuguese), 4 germanic languages (English, German, Danish, Dutch), and Greek. Instead of constructing 72 transfers, it might be enough, for the beginning, to construct only 14 transfers, 6 between the groups, for example French <-> English, Greek <-> Italian, German -> Greek and Greek -> English, and 4 in each group, for example Portuguese -> Spanish -> French -> Italian -> Portuguese and Danish -> German -> English -> Dutch -> Danish (or any pragmatically better arrangement). To translate from Spanish to Dutch, one would then use the Spanish -> French -> English -> Dutch route.

If one were to insist on never having more than double translations, it would be possible to take one of the most important languages as "center" (we consciously avoid the term "pivot", which is already overloaded), and to get a complete multilingual system by constructing just 16 transfers.

Conclusion: m-structures with Esperanto or pivot lexicon?

Although perfectly pragmatic, this last solution might seem politically unacceptable. If so, why not take Esperanto as the central language? There would be obvious advantages, from the esperantist and political points of view, while the differences with the BSO design would not be very important:

- interface structures would be m-structures, which would increase the upper limit in quality, and perhaps help to offset the loss due to systematic double translation;
- the representation of a text transported by the network would contain the Esperanto text, as well as its m-structure. In uncompressed form, the size of an m-structure is slightly less than 4 times that of the corresponding text, in the author's experience.

Another suggestion for the future could be to use the m-structure approach with a pivot lexicon. With this ***true hybrid pivot approach***, there would be no transfer dictionaries, but there might be up to n(n-1) transfer grammars, to handle the contrastive phenomena. In case some transfer grammar were absent or incomplete, transfer would occur by default, on the basis of the universal grammatical and relational symbols produced by the analyzers.

Acknowledgments

I would like to thank the organizers of this Conference on the new directions in Machine Translation for having given me the occasion to prepare this communication. Also, thanks to Elizabeth White, who helped remove many grammatical errors from the first draft of this paper.

References

Boitet Christian (1976): Un essai de réponse à quelques questions théoriques et pratiques liées à la traduction automatique. Définition d'un système prototype. Thèse d'Etat, Grenoble.

Boitet Christian (1988): Software and lingware engineering in modem MAT systems. To appear in: *Handbook for Computational Linguistics*, Bátori, ed., Niemeyer, 1988.

Boitet Christian, Nedobejkine Nikolai (1981): Recent developments in Russian-French Machine Translation at Grenoble. In: *Linguistics 19*, 199-271.

Boitet Christian, Nedobejkine Nikolai (1986): Toward integrated dictionaries for M(a)T: motivations and linguistic organization. In: *Proc. COLING-86*, IKS, 423-428, Bonn.

Ducrot Jean-M. (1982): TITUS IV. In: Information research in Europe. Taylor, P.J., Cronin, P., eds., ASLIB, London. In: *Proc. of the EURIM 5 conf.*, Versailles.

Guilbaud Jean-Philippe (1984): Principles and results of a German-French MT system. Lugano tutorial on Machine Translation.

Guilbaud Jean-Philippe (1986): Variables et catégories grammaticales dans un modèle ARIANE. In: *Proc. COLING-86*, IKS, 405–407, Bonn.

Nomura Hirosato, Naito Shozo, Katagiri Yasuhiro, Shimazu Akira (1986): Translation by understanding: a Machine Translation system LUTE. In: *Proc. COLING-86*, IKS, 621-626, Bonn.

Slocum Jonathan (1984): METAL: the LRC Machine Translation system. In: *Lugano tutorial on Machine Translation.*

Tomita Masaru, Carbonell Jaime G. (1986): Another stride towards knowledge-based Machine Translation. In: *Proc. COLING-86*, IKS, 633-638, Bonn.

Tsujii Jun-Ichi (1987): What is pivot? In: *Proc. of the Machine Translation Summit*, p. 121, Hakone 1987.

Vauquois Bernard (1975): La traduction automatique à Grenoble. Document de linguistique quantitative n° 29, Dunod, Paris.

Vauquois Bernard (1979): Aspects of automatic translation in 1979. IBM-Japan, scientific program.

Vauquois Bernard (1983): Automatic translation.
In: Proc. of the summer school *"The computer and the arabic language"*, ch. 9, Rabat.

Vauquois Bernard, Boitet Christian (1985): Automated translation at GETA (Grenoble University).
In: *Computational Linguistics, 11:1, 28-36.*

Vauquois Bernard, Chappuy Sylviane (1985): Static grammars: a formalism for the description of linguistic models.
In: *Proc. of the Conf. on theoretical and methodological issues in Machine Translation of natural languages 298-322*, Colgate Univ., Hamilton, N.Y.

Veillon Gérard (1970): Modèles et algorithmes pour la traduction automatique.
Thèse d'Etat, Grenoble.

Witkam Toon (1987): Interlingual MT – an industrial initiative.
In: *Proc. of the Machine Translation Summit*, p. 135-140, Hakone 1987.
Proc. of the MTS, 135–140, Hakone.

Christian Boitet

Avantaĝoj kaj malavantaĝoj de la pivota kaj la transira aliroj al multilingva perkomputila tradukado

Resumo

La pivota aliro ŝajnas plej oportuna por multlingva perkomputila tradukado ĉar ĝi nur bezonas 2n tradukmodulojn por n lingvoj, dum la transira bezonas n(n-1). Tamen oni longe ne uzis la pivotan modelon, ĝis en okdekaj jaroj kelkaj sistemoj revivigis ĝin.

Vera pivota lingvo estas sendependa de la originaj kaj celaj lingvoj. Ekzistas pivota vortaro, pivotaj gramatikaj simboloj kaj pivotaj gramatikaj rilatiloj. Laŭ Tsujii (1987) ekzistas tri specoj de pivotoj. Ili havas tri tipojn de malavantaĝoj: Unue, ili ofte estas specifaj por mallarĝa temtereno. Due, homa lingvo kiel pivoto (ekz. la angla aŭ Esperanto) estas specifa por lingvofamilio. En Esperanto krome mankas sufiĉa terminaro. Trie, pivoto estas malfacile konstruebla. Shank k.a. provis iri la vojon de bazaj konceptoj konstruante strukturojn de koncepta dependeco. Tamen la serĉado de semantikaj atomoj funkcias bone nur pri propoziciantaj konceptoj, dum la plejparto de la nocioj, ekz. ĉiuspecaj bruoj, rokoj, plantoj k.s., estas malfacile alireblaj per tiu metodo. Tradukado per pivoto implicas informperdon unue pro nekongruantaj vortsignifoj, due ĉar ĝi produktas parafrazojn anstataŭ tradukoj, maltrafante la stilan kaj espriman nivelon, kaj trie, ĉar ĝi ne kaptas neuniversalajn, superfraznivelajn tekstfenomenojn.

La transira modelo estas pli ofte uzata ĉar ĝi estas pli simpla kaj ĉar la bezono traduki de n al n lingvoj okazas malpli ofte ol tiu traduki inter 1 lingvo kaj n aliaj. La hibridaj versioj (kun lingvospecifa vortaro kaj universalaj gramatikaj rilatoj) restas problemaj. Oni aplikis hibridan modelon ĉe CETA de 1961 ĝis 1970 kaj proponis ĝin por EUROTRA. Ĉar ĝi tamen premisas grandan disciplinon rilate al la universalaj gramatikaĵoj, oni decidis ne uzi ĝin en ties dislokitaj esplorejoj. EUROTRA evoluigas por naŭ lingvoj 72 tradukmodulojn, sed planas uzi centran numerkodon por terminoj. Tio ne forigas la problemon de kombina multobligo por la ĝenerala vortaro. GETA uzas multnivelajn strukturpriskribojn (m-strukturojn). Ili reprezentas ĉiun bezonatan informon en unusola dependoarbo kiu ebligas pli altan tradukkvaliton kaj estas preferinda por tradukado inter 1 lingvo kaj n aliaj.

Malfacilas antaŭdiri la estontan evoluon de la du modeloj. La forte disvastiĝantaj sistemoj por perkomputila fabrikado eble implicos plian uzon de temterenspecifaj pivotoj. Aliflanke en Japanujo oni komencis ambician projekton pri multlingva konceptaro, al kiu eble eŭropanoj devus aliĝi. Por ne perdi la laboron investitan en la dulingvajn vortarojn de transiraj sistemoj, necesas evoluigi multlingvajn, multaplikajn vortarojn, eble celante al multlingva konceptaro. La kombinproblemon povus solvi kunligado de transirmodelaj sistemoj. En EK oni povus kunigi la samfamiliajn lingvojn (ĝermanaj/latinidaj/greka) kaj traduki ekz. ne hispane→nederlande, sed hispane→france→angle→nederlande. Kvankam ĝi estas tre praktika, ĉi tia solvo eble estas politike malakceptebla. Kial do ne preni Esperanton kiel centran lingvon, anstataŭ aŭ en la m-strukturoj? Tia sistemo ne multe diferencus de DLT. Alternativa propono estus hibrida pivotmodelo kun n(n-1) transiraj gramatikoj kaj centra vortaro.

A Sublanguage Approach to Japanese-English Machine Translation

Michiko Kosaka
Dept. of Computer Science
Monmouth College
West Long Branch
New Jersey 07764
USA
kosaka@monatt.uucp

Virginia Teller
Dept. of Computer Science
Hunter College
The City University of New York
695 Park Avenue
New York
New York 10021
USA
vmthc@cunyvm.bitnet

Ralph Grishman
Dept. of Computer Science
New York University
251 Mercer Street
New York
New York 10012
USA
grishman@nyu.edu

1. Introduction

Most work in machine translation at present follows one of two paths. Transfer systems, which have a large syntactic component, are gradually adding more and more semantic constraints in order to improve the translation process, but in a rather *ad hoc* way. Knowledge-based systems aim to develop deep domain knowledge and a language-neutral interlingua. Such systems have been limited to very narrow, often artificial domains because knowledge representation techniques for complex domains are not sufficiently developed. The sublanguage approach uses text analysis techniques to identify the information patterns of a sublanguage and then uses these patterns as the basis for both disambiguation of input and translation. This approach provides an intermediate path between the transfer and interlingua approaches. More important, it provides a **principled** method for system development and refinement, which most current approaches seem to lack.

We describe below an approach to Japanese-English machine translation for technical text based on the following premises:

(1) There is a correspondence between the sublanguage categories and patterns in the source language (Japanese) and the target language (English);

(2) these categories and patterns are the appropriate units for lexical transfer rules; and

(3) the use of operator trees as an intermediate representation substantially reduces the amount of structural transfer needed in the system.

2. Sublanguage

A sublanguage is the specialized form of language used in discourse limited to a circumscribed domain. Sublanguages are typically used for communication between technical specialists in areas such as science or medicine, but there are also some sublanguages written by specialists for general consumption (e.g. summary weather reports). Sublanguages have lexical, syntactic, semantic, and discourse characteristics that distinguish them from standard language (Kittredge/Lehrberger 1982; Grishman/Kittredge 1986).

Harris's (1968) discussion of sublanguage focused on the co-occurrence properties of words in the sublanguage. The language as a whole contains selection constraints on what classes of subjects and objects can occur with particular verbs; *think* and *believe*, for example, take animate subjects. Within a sublanguage much finer and tighter constraints of this type can be stated. The language of biochemistry, for instance, accepts *The polypeptides were washed in hydrochloric acid.* but excludes *Hydrochloric acid was washed in polypeptides*. Such constraints can be captured in terms of detailed sublanguage word classes and co-occurrence patterns.

Sublanguage co-occurrence constraints may be viewed as a manifestation of the underlying semantic constraints of the domain. In fact, there is a close correlation between the sublanguage classes obtained from co-occurrence phenomena and the basic semantic categories perceived by a specialist in a particular field. An advantage of the sublanguage approach is that the co-occurrence patterns can be determined by a distributional analysis of a sample of sublanguage text. Although the linguistic analysis we carried out was done by hand, Hirschman (1986) describes some preliminary computer implementations that can partially automate the laborious and time-consuming process of discovering sublanguage linguistic patterns.

A machine translation system can take advantage of all the characteristics of a sublanguage. The specialized vocabulary limits the dictionary that must be constructed, and the specialized syntax reduces the complexity of the grammar that is required. The semantic constraints embodied in co-occurrence patterns play the dual role of reducing the ambiguity of the source language analysis and providing a principled basis for translating source language vocabulary into equivalent terms in the target language.

3. Operator-argument grammar

The operator-argument framework for grammatical description proposed by Harris (1982) further explicates the underlying relationships among sublanguage word classes. Harris's goal in developing this theoretical framework was to devise a grammatical means of regularizing the surface representations of equivalent sentences in a sublanguage in order to arrive at a canonical representation that accords with their information content. Operator-argument grammar provides a model of "syntax-driven semantics" in which a syntactic grammar yields the information content of a sentence while it assigns syntactic structure. In this approach there exists a set of base sublanguage sentences ("kernel sentences") that express the information content of the sublanguage and contain no paraphrases. All of the observed sublanguage sentences are derived from the base by a set of grammatical transformations called "reductions" that generate surface representations and paraphrases. The underlying representation of a sentence in this framework is an operator tree that reveals the operator-argument structure of the sentence.

The operator tree representations that we propose are not as abstract as those proposed by Harris because we do not undo all reductions, for example, morphological and some kinds of adjunct reductions. As a result our operator trees contain host-modifier as well as operator-operand relationships.

The operator-argument formalism simplifies the internal representation of input sentences by mapping different but equivalent forms (paraphrases) into a single semantic representation. This facilitates distributional analysis, which is used to extract word classes and kernel co-occurrence patterns from sample texts. Operator-argument grammar has the added advantage that the relations among component sentential structures within an utterance are much more directly represented than in previous sublanguage formalisms such as string grammar (Kosaka 1984).

4. Comparative linguistic analysis

In North America the sublanguage approach has found several computational applications, particularly in the work of the Linguistic String Project at New York University (Sager 1981; Sager/Friedman/Lyman 1987) and the TAUM group at the University of Montreal, where sublanguage grammars have been used in machine translation projects (Lehrberger 1982; Isabelle/Bourbeau 1985; Kittredge 1987). To date, however, these techniques have not been tested on languages as dissimilar as Japanese and English, and the correctness of the premises outlined above is far from assured. The close correspondence between French and English sublanguage patterns found by the TAUM group is not guaranteed to carry over to Japanese and English. The relationships could just as easily be one-to-many or many-to-one.

We investigated this question with the goal of determining if sublanguage categories and patterns would facilitate the computer analysis of source texts in Japanese in the sublanguage domain of computer manuals intended as instructional material. Our efforts have concentrated on the *FOCUS Query Language Primer*, which has been published in both Japanese and English.

4.1. Sublanguage patterns

Approximately 50 sentences were selected for analysis from a 20 page section of the *FOCUS* manual. Working independently, two linguists listed for each sentence all of the co-occurrence patterns (subject-verb-object relationships) and constructed an operator tree. Over 100 kernel sentences were extracted from each sample of text. (The numbers differed slightly but insignificantly for Japanese and English.) When the elements of these kernel sentences were classified and compared with their counterparts in the other language, we identified 15 word classes in Japanese and 15 corresponding English word classes. These word classes formed 18 matching kernel patterns in the two languages. This was an encouraging outcome given the possible number of combinations of 15 word classes that could appear in kernel patterns consisting of two, three, and even four elements. In addition, these 18 kernel patterns, together with matching higher order operator-argument structures (modals, conjunctions, paraphrastic operators, etc.) accounted for over 90% of the source and target language sample texts.

Within the subdomain of texts we have examined so far, the correspondences between Japanese and English are not limited to sublanguage word classes and co-occurrence patterns but extend to the overall structure of operator trees as well. For example, Japanese sentence (1a) and its matching English sentence (1b) are represented in our operator tree system as shown in Figures 1a and 1b, respectively:

(1)a. IN-GROUPS-OF to TOP-wa ACROSS-to issho-ni siyoo-suru koto-ga deki-masu.
b. IN-GROUPS-OF and TOP can be used with ACROSS.

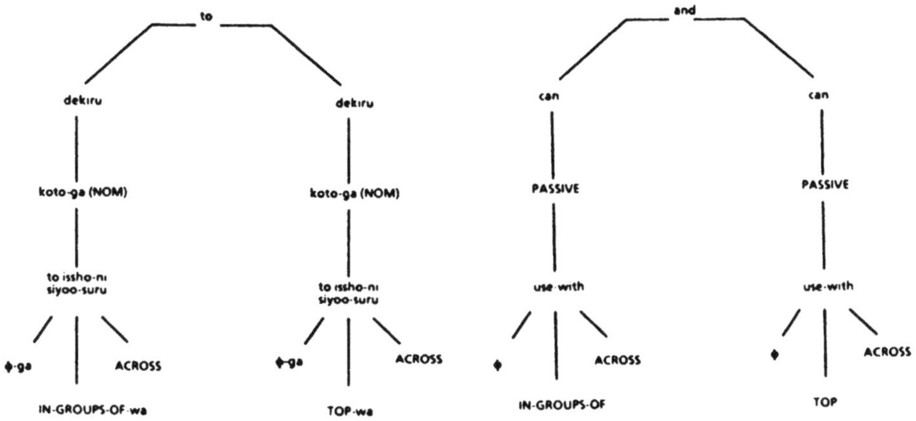

Figure 1. *Operator trees for sentences (1a) and (1b).*

Structurally the trees are identical, except that the nominalization operator *koto-ga* appears in Japanese where English uses passive. This difference reflects the syntactic fact that the Japanese predicate *dekiru* 'possible, possibility' requires a noun or nominalization as its complement but the English modal *can* must take a sentential complement. Although the sublanguage predicate 'use-with'/*to issho-ni siyoo-suru* allows three arguments (*x* uses *y* with *z*), the Ø's indicate that no argument appears in subject position in either Japanese or English.

In many cases the nearly one-to-one correspondence between Japanese and English operator-argument patterns extends not only to the paraphrastic operators such as nominalization and passive but also to other types of second-order operators such as coordination and subordination. An example of a perfect match of this type is the relativization shown in Figure 2, which gives the operator trees for the following

Japanese phrase and its English equivalent:

(2)a. keisan-ni kanren-sita futatu-no doosi
b. two verbs related to computation

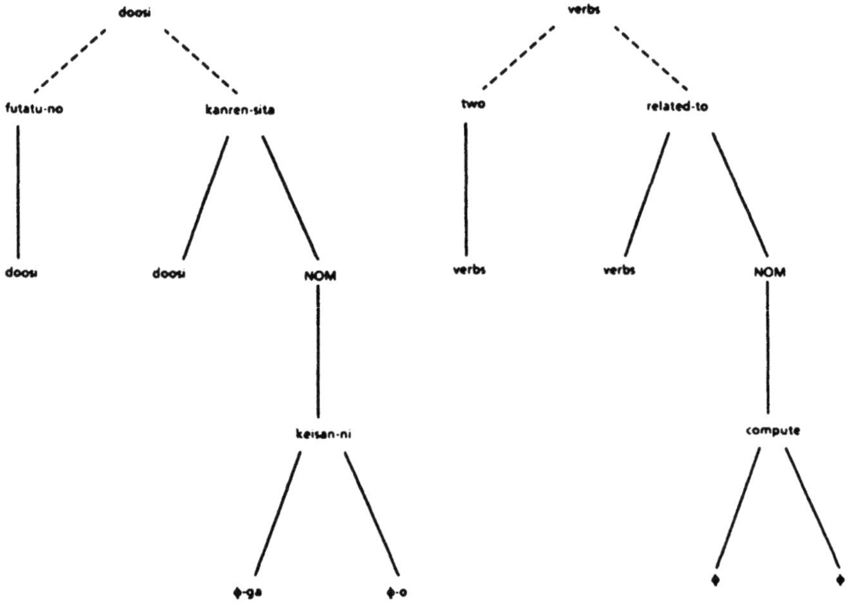

Figure 2. *Operator trees for sentences (2a) and (2b). Dashed lines indicate an adjunct relationship to the parent node. Solid lines indicate an operator-argument relationship.*

As for the roughly 10% of the text not accounted for by direct or near direct matches between Japanese and English operator trees, our strategy has been to assess whether an acceptable English sentence could, in principle, be produced from the Japanese operator tree. These sentences contain single instances of patterns, attributable at least in part to our relatively small sample of text, and about ten patterns with meta-operators. The meta-operators in our sample revealed a particularly interesting source of deviation between Japanese and English. In many cases sentences containing members of this class of operators express very different meanings in the two languages. Example (3a) below gives the literal rendering of a Japanese sentence, and (3b) its English equivalent from the *FOCUS* manual.

(3)a. By now we hope that you are able to understand each component of the following TABLE command.
b. At this point the following components of the TABLE command have been introduced.

Although devices could be introduced to map the Japanese meta-operators into different, and possibly more appropriate, English sentences, we prefer to maintain our strategy of avoiding such structural change as long as the Japanese operator tree can be used as the basis for a grammatical English sentence. The meta-operators appear to be one of the parameters that contribute to stylistic differences in expression between the two languages.

4.2. Resolution of ellipsis

A crucial aspect of analysis in the sublanguage approach is the resolution of ellipsis in the source language text. This is especially important in Japanese, where zeroing is far more widespread than in English. A grammatical sentence in Japanese may consist only of a verb or predicate, whereas in English a surface subject must be present as well. In the subdomain of discourse we have studied, null subjects are the most frequent type of ellipsis. Sentence (4) is a typical example; the topic phrase is followed by two clauses, a subordinate clause S1 and a main clause S2, both of which contain null subjects. S2 contains a null object as well:

(4) $[_{S_0}$ $[_{Topic}$ kono shori-no gijututeki-na naiyoo-wa$]_i$

$[_{S_1}$ Ø taN-itu doosi-ni-yoru TABLE command-o kanzen-ni syuutoku-sita ato-

de$]$ $[_{S_2}$ Ø $Ø_i$ setumei-site-imasu$]$ $]$

The initial problem is one of determining the proper role of the topic. Any of several relationships may hold between the topic and the missing arguments in subsequent clauses.

When there are multiple possibilities, as in (4), a correct decision about the role that the topic phrase plays in the rest of the sentence cannot be made without sublanguage analysis or other suitable knowledge-based techniques. Kameyama (1986) treats zero pronominalization in Japanese from the perspective of discourse analysis. Her preference rules for antecedents limit the possibilities by excluding some possible antecedents for zero pronominals, but more than one alternative may remain. This approach alone, therefore, is often not sufficient to resolve ellided material. Sublanguage patterns, however, rule out the topic phrase *kono shori-no gijututeki-na naiyoo-wa* 'the technical content of this process' as a possible subject for the verbs *syuutoku-sita* 'master' in S_1 and *setumei-site-imasu* 'explain' in S_2, thus leaving the missing object in S_2 as the only remaining possibility.

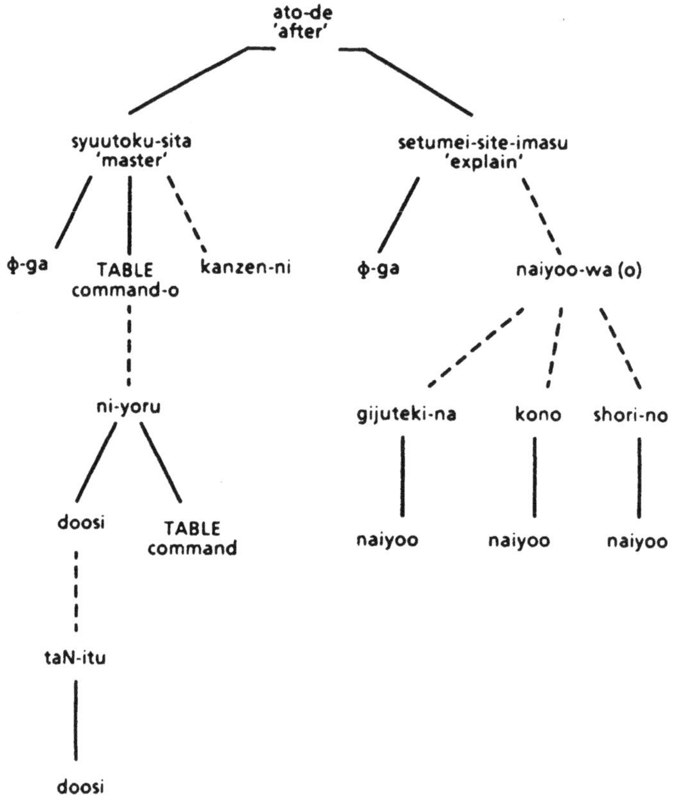

Figure 3. *Operator tree for sentence 4. Dashed lines indicate an adjunct relationship to the parent node. Solid lines indicate an operator-argument relationship.*

The resolution of ellipsis is essential to the high quality translation of source sentences with zeroed material. Consider the problem of generating an intelligible, accurate translation of (4), given the operator tree representation in Figure 3. If correct referents for the missing subjects have not been filled in, the possibilities for surface syntax are limited to constructions in English that allow null underlying subjects, among them nominalizations and agentless passives. Relying on these syntactic structures and using straightforward, quite literal lexical transfer, we can produce (5a) with a nominalization in the subordinate clause and a passive in the main clause or (5b) with passives in both clauses:

(5)a. After mastery of the TABLE command with a single verb, the technical content of this process is explained.
b. After the TABLE command with a single verb is mastered, the technical content of this process is explained.

Although these are awkward but at least marginally acceptable sentences, the sublanguage approach to translation offers a more felicitous alternative by permitting us to fill in the missing underlying subjects. In the domain of instructional material it is the reader who masters or learns the contents of a manual and the author or book that explains what is to be learned. Sublanguage word class patterns allow this information to be inferred and inserted into the operator tree, with the result that a sentence like (6) can be generated:

(6) After you learn the TABLE command with a single verb, we explain the technical content of this process.

A translation system capable of resolving ellipsis would be an advantage even if the target language did not require surface subjects. In generating Spanish, for example, information about the missing subjects in Figure 3 would be needed to determine the person and number for verbs. The operator-argument intermediate representation can thus handle problems of languages other than Japanese and English.

5. Design of an MT system

The strong similarities between operator trees for two languages as different as Japanese and English is an unexpected result that has implications for the design of a machine translation system. With operator trees as an intermediate representation, it may be possible to construct a system to translate Japanese into English without the structural transfer usually associated with such systems. Structural transfer is required when analysis of the source language produces intermediate representations that contain syntactic structures not found in the target language. The rules for structural transfer map the source intermediate representation into an underlying representation of target language syntactic structure. Since Japanese is strictly left branching, left-branching complements in Japanese, for instance, must be converted into right-branching structures in English. The operator tree intermediate representation that we propose, however, is sufficiently abstract that language specific surface syntactic properties such as left and right branching are eliminated. The remaining syntactic patterns in the data we have examined are in such close agreement at this level of representation that further restructuring in the form of syntactic transfer may no longer be necessary.

What we are arguing for is a redistribution of work among the components of a machine translation system based on the analysis-transfer-synthesis model. Extra effort is required to analyze source text into an intermediate representation as abstract as that of operator trees and to synthesize target text from this level of representation. This effort is balanced by eliminating the structural part of the transfer component, although lexical transfer from source to target language is still necessary. The production of surface syntax in the target language is viewed as a problem of generation, not of transfer. The basis for this conclusion is our analysis of two languages as different as Japanese and English. Should the need for structural transfer arise as a result of further data analysis, we hope that the sublanguage approach will offer a principled, systematic basis for building transfer rules.

The fact that lexical transfer requires restructuring at times is illustrated by the differences between the Japanese and English expressions for "ratio". In both languages this noun takes two arguments. The Japanese expression *x to y no wariai* 'the ratio of x and y' is equivalent to English *the ratio of x to y* (or, less commonly, *the ratio between x and y*) as in *The ratio of oil to vinegar is 3 to 1*. In this case the operator-argument structures for Japanese and English are identical, and lexical transfer consists of little more than a direct replacement of the Japanese words with their equivalents in English or a replacement of the entire Japanese kernel pattern with its English counterpart. In addition, Japanese often uses the form *x ni taisuru y no wariai* 'the ratio of y against x' when x and y express a part-whole relation, that is, when y is a total amount and x is a percentage or fraction of that total. In order to obtain a natural expression of this in English, the Japanese operator-argument subtree must be converted into an English equivalent using *percentage* or *fraction*. Structural changes of this type are strictly local and do not affect other parts of the operator tree.

The design of the system we propose is basically that of a transfer system without a component for structural transfer. In contrast to conventional analysis-transfer-synthesis systems (e.g. Nagao 1987), which convert source intermediate structures into target intermediate structures before synthesis, we propose a single structure in the form of operator trees. As a result a greater burden is placed on the analysis component to achieve this deeper level of abstraction and on the synthesis component to generate target text from it. After lexical transfer an operator tree contains information about **what** to say in the target language, but leaves open a great deal about **how** to say it. The greater level of grammatical abstraction formalized in operator trees is justified, we believe, by the problems standard transfer systems encounter when dealing with dissimilar language pairs and multi-language situations.

Compared to the interlingua model, our approach uses distributional analysis to lay a firm foundation for semantic representation. The basic idea of an interlingua system is to analyze source text into a universal, language independent representation of its meaning – an interlingua. Although proposals have been made, there is as yet no agreed-upon interlingua, and no one has suggested a way of arriving at one. The sublanguage approach has clear discovery procedures that lay down a route to follow (Grishman/Hirschman/Nhan 1986). The linguistic patterns uncovered during the sublanguage analysis of a domain define the classes of relationships found among word classes in the domain. These sublanguage structures are presumed to be the information structures of the subject matter. While not an interlingua in themselves, these semantic patterns provide a framework for a meaning representation and thus the first step toward an interlingua.

Unlike an interlingua, the operator tree system of intermediate representation retains a significant amount of syntactic as well as semantic information from the source text. Operators indicate major constructions such as nominalization, passive, relative clauses, etc. It becomes the task of the synthesis component to decide if such information should be used in generating a particular sentence or should be ignored. In many cases lexical constraints dictate the complement and case frame structures that must appear in the target text.

6. Scope and limits

The operator-argument formalism is capable of producing a linguistic analysis of input that accounts for significant aspects of sentence grammar. The functional structure of operator-argument representation, foi example, allows the semantic case frames for verbs to be expressed directly in kernel patterns. Although paraphrases are mapped into a single semantic representation, the paraphrase operators themselves are retained in operator trees. Thus, differences in interpretation and subsequent translation due to such operators can be taken into account (e.g. in the focus assigned to the target sentence). An additional strength of the sublanguage approach lies in its ability to resolve ellipsis in source language text. This is especially important for Japanese because of the prevalence of zeroing. In many cases the expectations about subjects and objects encoded in kernel patterns allow correct inferences to be made when these elements are missing and, as we have shown, can assign the correct role to topic phrases as well.

Sentence grammar as we define it, however, is incapable of inferring properties that are not implicitly present in source language sentences. Part of the problem in translating Japanese into English is that there are linguistic features such as number and definiteness for nouns that are overtly required in English but may be completely absent in Japanese. The noun phrase *doosi* 'verb' is not inherently singular or plural, definite or indefinite. In a given discourse context it may be possible to construct appropriate attributes for it and convey these in English, but this is a problem of extrasentential analysis rather than intrasentential syntax or semantics and consequently lies beyond the scope of our project at present. Noun phrases that contain the necessary indicators (e.g. *futatu-no doosi* 'two verbs') pose no problems in this regard. In the remaining cases our solutions may be *ad hoc* initially.

References

Grishman, Ralph / Lynette Hirschman / Ngo Nhan (1986): Discovery procedures for sublanguage selectional patterns: Initial experiments. In: *Computational Linguistics* 12, pp. 205-215.

Grishman, Ralph / Richard Kittredge (eds.) (1986): *Analyzing language in restricted domains: Sublanguage description and processing.* Hillsdale, NJ: Erlbaum.

Harris, Zellig (1968): *Mathematical structures of language.* New York: Wiley Interscience.

Harris, Zellig (1982): *A grammar of English on mathematical principles.* New York: Wiley.

Hirschman, Lynette (1986): Discovering sublanguage structures. In: Grishman/Kittredge (eds.), pp. 211-234.

Isabelle, Pierre / Laurent Bourbeau (1985): TAUM-AVIATION: Its technical features and some experimental results. In: *Computational Linguistics* 11, pp. 18-27.

Kameyama, Megumi (1986): A property-sharing constraint in centering. In: *Proceedings of the 24th Annual Meeting of the Association for Computational Linguistics*, pp. 200-206.

Kittredge, Richard (1987): The significance of sublanguage for automatic translation. In: Nirenburg (ed.), pp. 59-67.

Kittredge, Richard / John Lehrberger (eds.) (1982): *Sublanguage: Studies of language in restricted semantic domains.* Berlin/New York: Walter de Gruyter.

Kosaka, Michiko (1984): An operator-argument grammar of quantity expressions. New York University doctoral dissertation.

Lehrberger, John (1982): Automatic translation and the concept of sublanguage. In: Kittredge/Lehrberger (eds.), pp. 81-107.

Nagao, Makoto (1987): Role of structural transformation in a machine translation system. In: Nirenburg (ed.), pp. 262-277.

Nirenburg, Sergei, Ed. (1987): *Machine translation: Theoretical and methodological issues.* Cambridge: Cambridge University Press.

Sager, Naomi (1981): *Natural language information processing: A computer grammar of English and its applications.* Reading, MA: Addison-Wesley.

Sager, Naomi / Carol Friedman / Margaret Lyman (1987): *Medical language processing: Computer management of narrative data.* Reading, MA: Addison-Wesley.

Michiko Kosaka, Virginia Teller *kaj* Ralph Grishman

Lingvofrakcia aliro al japan-angla perkomputila tradukado

Resumo

La lingvofrakcia aliro staras meze inter transira kaj interlingva perkomputila tradukado. Ĝi uzas por malambiguigo tekstanalizadon en lingvofrakcio (t.e. la speciala lingvoformo uzata en difinita temtereno). En lingvofrakcio la eblaj kuntekstoj de vortoj estas pli precize difineblaj, kio rezultas el profundaj semantikaj limigoj de la temtereno. Kaj la sintakso kaj la gamo de eblaj vortsignifoj estas pli precizaj. Tio helpas malambiguigon.

La priskribata japan-angla traduksistemo baziĝas sur gramatiko de operatoroj kaj argumentoj, "sintakse stirata semantiko" kun bazaj frazoj, laŭ la modelo de Harris (1982). La sistemo estas konstruita sur kvindeko da frazoj el gvidlibro de komputila sistemo, eldonitaj paralele en la japana kaj la angla. Oni analizis la vortspecojn kaj ties apudeckondiĉojn en ambaŭ lingvoj kaj trovis strukturrilatojn, esprimatajn en operatoraj arboj.

Grava kaj ofta fenomeno estas elipsaj konstruoj, precipe en la japana. Oni solvas ĝin per enkonduko de malplenaj kategorioj kaj klopodas ligi la frontelementon de la frazo al unu el la malplenaj lokoj. La diskutata aliro ĉi-rilate ebligas kontentigajn rezultojn.

La altgrada simileco de la operatoraj arboj por tiel malsamaj lingvoj estas agrabla trovaĵo, ĉar ĝi povus permesi uzi tiajn arbojn kiel interan reprezentaĵon, malnecesigante la kutimajn strukturajn transirregulojn. Tial estas proponata redisdono de la taskoj de la moduloj en traduksistemo. Oni investu pli en analizon de la origina teksto ĝis al operatorarboj, regajnante la investon per multe pli facila transiro inter la lingvoj. La poste necesa generado de la cellingva strukturo estas plia unulingva proceso, ne rekte rilatita al la transiro mem. Estas proponata sistemo kiu ne havas la tradician strukturon analizo-transiro-sintezo, sed iru de originlingva interstrukturo al cellingva interstrukturo. Tiel en la transira fazo oni ĉefe esprimas **kion** *diri, sed ne* **kiel** *diri ĝin.*

La aliro funkcias bone por grava parto de la frazgramatiko en la elektita lingvofrakcio, sed havas limigojn kie certaj trajtoj bezonataj en unu lingvo tute mankas en la alia.

ATAMIRI – Interlingual MT Using the Aymara Language

Iván Guzmán de Rojas

Casilla 5838
La Paz
Bolivia

1. Introduction

The ATAMIRI System has been developed by the author in La Paz, from 1980 to 1985 on a hobby-basis, from 1985 to 1987 on a semi-professional basis. Since 1987 this small-scale MT project has continued with the collaboration of a lexicographic team consisting of 3 persons and a privately owned computer, supported by its first users.

ATAMIRI is operational at the Translation Office of the Panamá Canal Commission, assisting in legal and technical document translation from English into Spanish. The Wang International Translation Center in Panamá also uses this system. This year, ATAMIRI is being tested at the European Wang ITCs, in a pilot operation to translate technical handbooks written in English simultaneously into German, Dutch and French. Plans are being made to expand the number of operational target languages to Italian and Swedish for 1989. At testing level, the system also supports Spanish as source Language and Aymara, Portuguese and Hungarian as target languages.

The current ATAMIRI version runs in a Wang VS computer. Most subroutines were written in BASIC and are now being converted to PLI. The system requires a multi-user installation, with at least 2 MB memory and a dedicated disk of at least 60 MB and WP software

2. Matricial language representation

The fact that the ATAMIRI project, in spite of its very limited resources, has been able to deliver practical results working in a multilingual environment, has to do with the interlingua concept underlying this system's design.

The language representation used is formally defined as follows:

| M >	called **CONCEPTOR** is an invariant entity in a rank-three tensorial space of N dimensions.
< i,j,k,l |	called **UNITOR** is a three-subindex unit sensor of the l-reference frame substanding the tensorial space.
< i,j,k,l | M >	called **EXPRESOR** is the matrix obtained by the scalar product of the two entities given above, thus conforming the corresponding component of | M > in the l-reference frame.

N is always finite, but may be very big depending on the volume of the text universe considered.

The ordered union U < i,j,k,l | M > of all expressors for a certain conceptor | M >, fully represents the written sentence in language l of the message M expressed in that language.

In this mathematical model we are not interested in quantitative results, but we rather want to ensure that tensorial transformation will reflect translations from one language into another. Thus we are compelled to restrict the class of transformation groups to be allowed. We adopt two types of restrictions:

TOPOLOGICAL	restrictions to ensure one to one correspondence of components in any two language reference frames (point to point transformations avoiding addition of components).
METRICAL	restrictions to avoid multiplying factors other than ones or zeros; e.g. no changes in "size" of components is allowed.

In a true natural language representation we have to deal with transformations where "distortion", "creation" and "destruction" of components are allowed. In fact, the current version of ATAMIRI is based on an extended tensorial language representation using such nonlinear operators. Here we only discuss matricial components in order to illustrate they way in which ATAMIRI uses a formal syntactical representation of Aymara as interlingua.

Bearing in mind the above restrictions, it is now valid to view a sentence translation from source language l1 to target language l2 as the matrix transformation:

$$< i2,j2,k2,l2 \mid M > = S\ (i2,j2,k2,l2,l1,k1,j1,i1) < i1,j1,k1,l1 \mid M >$$

Here the sum **S** runs over both sets of indices i,j,k for each pair of languages l1 and l2.

For simplicity, we write this transformation as follows:

$$< 2 \mid M > = (l2 \mid l1) < 1 \mid M >$$

The corresponding inverse transformation is written:

$$< 1 \mid M > = [l1 \mid l2] < 2 \mid M >$$

These formulas provide us with the representation of the two sentences, in languages l1 and l2, expressing the same message M. The transformation coefficients build the matrix (l2 | l1) and the inverse matrix [l1 | l2] which represent the corresponding syntactical reordering rule of that class of sentence for the translation in that pair of languages.

The tensor components < l | M > represent each of the sentence elements of the message expressed in a given language l. Their "values" are the symbols adopted to codify the syntactical categories to be used by the three level parser operating under a specific representation model.

Obviously we require that the set of syntactical categories adopted in a given representation model, has to deliver consistent descriptions of all parsing operations undertaken on sentences expressed in any of the languages included in the model. We call **canonical** language the natural language or the formal language whose syntactical categories are adopted as the codifying base.

The ATAMIRI system is capable of operating under any user defined canonical languages. The current version operates under a representation model in which Aymara is the canonical language. This suffix structured language, thanks to its positionally defined syntactical categories, is very well suited for this purpose, since suffix positions can be directly related to matrix subindices. There are also other algorithmic properties in Aymara, which do not need to be discussed here, which make this old Andean human communication tool into an ideal canonical language.

The matricial language representation here succinctly explained, produces three enormous advantages:

EXTERNAL SYNTAX	defined by the transformation matrices, whose coefficient values can be stored in a syntactical data base, externally to the parser subroutine. It is thus possible to enrich the system's syntactical knowledge by using the experience with previously translated texts and without touching the program. This gives ATAMIRI a powerful syntax learning capability.
MULTILINGUAL	simultaneous translation capability, since now the user may choose which set and direction of transformation coefficients to use for a source and for a target language. The user can also decide whether to load in memory one or more sets corresponding to various target languages.
INTERLINGUA	transformation bridge designed to minimize costs in the development of the multilingual syntactic data base.

The concept of interlingua as used in the ATAMIRI system needs further explanation: we call **interlingua** one of the languages in the representation model, which is always used as the common reference frame for all other languages.

For example, if our representation model covers 21 languages, we only need to store 20 transformation matrix sets, one set for each language transformed relative to the interlingua. The transformations among any two languages can be immediately defined by a matrix product:

A	is the interlingua,
X and Y	are any two languages,
(A I X)	transformation matrix X to A,
(A I Y)	transformation matrix Y to A,
(Y I X) = [Y I A] (A I X)	is the resultant transformation from X to Y.

Otherwise we would have needed to generate and work with 400 matrix transformation sets!

Our first implementation of ATAMIRI uses a representation model where **Aymara** is both the canonical language and the interlingua. Nevertheless the system gives the user an unrestricted choice of the language to be used as interlingua, provided it is a well defined language in the representation model, e.g. it possesses a complete and consistent set of syntactical categories with respect to the rest of the languages in the model (interlingua cannot be a subset language). From this explanation we see that ATAMIRI does not use a semantical interlingua. The Aymara lexicon is not used at all, unless the user asks for a translation into Aymara (as target language).

3. Confrontation with the praxis

The syntactical analyzer subroutine reserves a maximum memory area of half a MB to store the transformation coefficients foreseen for simultaneous translation from the source language to five target languages. After three years experience, both in test runs and in normal operation in production environment, the number of transformation sets stored has not yet pushed up that maximum value. This fact shows how few elementary structures are needed to describe real life sentences when using three-level symbolic descriptors of the syntactical categories.

We have found a few frequently occurring cases, where the canonical language had to be extended beyond Aymara, introducing empty categories for this language. For example, the use of auxiliary verbs for the future tense in some languages like English, has no equivalent in Aymara. Such categories, which are empty in some languages, compelled us to introduce deviant algorithms using "creation" and "destruction" operators. This deviation from linear transformations caused quite an increase in code for the syntax handling algorithms. Nevertheless, the additional execution time was not more than 5%.

Another difficulty encountered in the praxis, while translating from English into German or Dutch, was the need to store too many redundant transformation matrices for handling "Gliedsätze". For example the compound sentence:

In English:	*If K1, I1.* has its equivalent in
German:	*Wenn K2, I2.*

But I2 is not the "normal" translation from I1, when taken as a single sentence, it is a "distorted" form.

Therefore the system would have to forget that the transformation coefficients for the compound sentence can be built from the corresponding coefficients for the component sentences and it must ask for a new matrix (redundant for English and other languages where such distortions are not present) for the compound sentence.

Here again, with the help of deviant "distortion" operators, even though at the cost of developing a highly intricated logic code, the syntactical data base size can be reduced, making the language "teaching" task easier.

Since syntactical errors in the translated draft have a strong negative effect on the post-editing work, the system's performance for German and Dutch has been significantly improved by extending the representation model to include the capability to handle transformations with "distortion".

The ATAMIRI system experience shows that the matricial language representation with its Aymara interlingua, when complemented with deviant nonlinear operators, can become a very powerful and economical syntax handling tool in a multilingual environment.

Iván Guzmán de Rojas

ATAMIRI – interlingva perkomputila tradukado per la ajmara lingvo

Resumo

La malgrandskala komputila traduksistemo ATAMIRI estas de 1980 evoluigata en La Paz en Bolivio. Ĝi nun funkcias en la tradukejo de la Komisiono de la Panama Kanalo por helpi en jura kaj teknika tradukado el la angla en la hispanan. Ĝi krome funkcias ĉe la Internaciaj Tradukcentroj de Wang en Panamá kaj Eŭropo. Pilotprojekte oni tradukis teknikajn manlibrojn el la angla samtempe al la germana, la nederlanda kaj la franca. Testversio de la sistemo krome havas la hispanan kiel originan lingvon kaj la ajmaran, la portugalan kaj la hungaran kiel cellingvojn.

ATAMIRI baziĝas sur interlingva sistemplano kun matematika matricmodelo por la reprezentado de tekstoj. La interlingvo estas formala sintaksa reprezentaĵo de la ajmara lingvo. Principe la sistemo povas same bone funkcii per alia interlingvo, difinita de la uzanto. Tamen la ajmara, homa lingvo el la Andoj, havas strukturon, kiu igas ĝin aparte taŭga por ĉi tiu funkcio.

Kune kun la matrica reprezento, la elektita interlingvo havigas al la sistemo gravajn avantaĝojn: Unue, la sintakso estas kodita en matricoj ekster la parsalgoritmo, tiel ke la sistemo povas lerni el jam tradukitaj tekstoj sen ke tio necesigus ŝanĝon en la parsilo. Due, la sistemo kapablas samtempe traduki al pluraj lingvoj. Trie, la interlingvo minimumigas la kostojn por evoluigi multlingvan sintaksan regularon.

En la ĝis nun trijara testado la parsilo neniam bezonis pli ol duonan megabajton da storo. Necesis adapti la ajmaran kelkagrade por taŭgigi ĝin por difinitaj kategorioj de unuopaj lingvoj, kiel ekzemple helpverbaj konstruoj en la angla. Similan diferencon prezentas kompleksaj subpropozicioj en la germana kaj la nederlanda.

La sperto gajnita kun ATAMIRI pruvas, ke matrica tekstreprezento kun la ajmara kiel interlingvo povas fariĝi potenca kaj ŝpara sintaksprilaborilo por multlingva apliko.

The Architecture of DLT – Interlingual or Double Direct?

Klaus Schubert

BSO/Research
Postbus 8348
NL-3503 RH Utrecht
The Netherlands

schubert@dlt1.uucp

1. Practical design and a theoretical classification

The architectures of machine translation systems are often classified in a triple division: **direct, transfer** or **interlingual** (cf. Hauenschild in this volume). In this contribution I try to assign a place in this classification to the set-up chosen for a machine translation system that is known to be built on unconventional ideas, the DLT system. Of course it may be objected that filling a design conception into a slot in a classification has no importance for the developer of the system, but only for the observer. It seems to me, however, that this is so only at first sight. Considerations about this classification may shed a clearer light on the functionality brought about by the basic design decisions of a machine translation system, and they may help to assess how the decisions already made condition those to be made in future development steps. Before I take a closer look at the DLT system, a few words of general background information are in order.

2. Distributed Language Translation

Distributed Language Translation (**DLT**) is the name of a large-scale research and development project for multilingual semi-automatic high-quality machine translation. It is carried out at the software house Buro voor Systeemontwikkeling (BSO/Research) in Utrecht (Netherlands). It was started around 1980 by Toon Witkam. After a number of years of preparatory study, the project received a subsidy from the Commission of the European Communities for a detailed feasibility study (Witkam 1983). Implementation started in the beginning of 1985. Since then the DLT project has been in a seven-year research and development period, jointly funded by BSO and the Netherlands Ministry of Economic Affairs. The budget for 1985-1991 is 17 million guilders.

Since 1985 the DLT system has been built up at a fast pace. Allen Tucker, to cite an external observer, is impressed with "the progress that has been made in the last three years" (Tucker 1988: 85), but he does not know that the book he reviews (Papegaaij 1986) is an account of only one and a half year of development (January 1985 to July 1986) with a preceding period of fund raising. The progress of the DLT project is accounted for in a series of publications. The major ones are the feasibility study (Witkam 1983, summarised in Witkam 1985), the definition of DLT's syntactic model (Schubert 1986a), a detailed account for DLT's semantic-pragmatic word expert system with its lexical knowledge bank (Papegaaij 1986), a description of a syntactic translation mechanism (Schubert 1987) and a first approach to text grammar (Papegaaij/Schubert 1988).

3. Direct, transfer, interlingual

The pros and cons of the three types of machine translation systems are well known:

- **Direct** systems make maximum use of the similarity of the source and the target language, but they are only suited for a single language pair (and, normally, a single translation direction) and cannot without entirely giving up the design be extended to form a multilingual system.

- **Transfer** systems perform a deeper analysis of the source language before the translation step proper towards the target language is taken, and they take this step at a more abstract level, in some analysed, labelled, tagged or otherwise decorated representation. Transfer systems require more effort in analysis and synthesis, but in return they allow for multilingual translation. The intermediate steps are carried out in source or target language-dependent representations, so that adding a new language to the system requires interfaces to be established with each of the already included languages separately. Alternatively or in addition, adaptations of the translation grammars may be needed.

- **Interlingual** systems translate from all source languages into an intermediate representation and from there on to the target languages. If the intermediate representation is truly autonomous, a text in the intermediate form does not carry any source language features and is thus ready for translation into an arbitrary target language no matter from which source language it comes. An interlingual system requires the highest degree of analysis and synthesis, which pays in the form of straightforward extensibility.

The DLT machine translation system has an intermediate language. Therefore, its place in the triple distinction appears to be obvious: interlingual. But however clear the situation seems to be, it is so only due to an unclear use of terms. The term intermediate language (or interlingua) is used for rather different symbol systems. The features that distinguish these systems do not only mark gradual differences, but at least one of them marks an essential and decisive difference in the quality of intermediate representations. It is the difference between an artificial symbol system and a human language in the function of an intermediate representation. This distinction, veiled by undifferentiated use of the term intermediate language, makes all the difference.

Reviewing systems and system designs that are labelled interlingual, one finds a number of intermediate representations that are more or less artificial systems of symbols. These symbols are called predicators with arguments, semantic units, entities, operators, objects etc. In various accounts sometimes also the idea is encountered that a normal human language might function as an intermediate representation, at least in theory (Tucker/Nirenburg 1984: 132). It is often overlooked that there is a fundamental difference between a human language and an artificial symbol system, as a consequence of which the one cannot replace the other in a machine translation system without far-reaching repercussions in the entire set-up of the system.

A machine translation process can only profit from the interlingual architecture to the full extent, if the intermediate representation meets two requirements: It should be **autonomous** and **expressive**. An intermediate representation is in this sense autonomous, if both the form and the content of its elements are independent from source and target languages. It is expressive enough for its function, if it is as expressive as the source and target languages. These two requirements are brought about by the fact that straightforward extensibility to a multilingual system (the main effect of the interlingual design) is only achieved if the intermediate representation indeed is the only link between any two periphery languages of the system.

As I argue in more detail elsewhere (Schubert 1988a,b), an artificial symbol system is inherently insufficient as for both requirements. It is never truly autonomous, but always relies on one or more human reference languages, and its expressiveness cannot be more than a subset of its reference language(s). Artificial intermediate representations can come close to, but cannot ultimately attain the full functionality of an intermediate language. Therefore, when an intermediate representation is artificial, the difference from transfer systems is only gradual, however big it is.

In the DLT system the intermediate language is a **human language**, which, in addition to autonomy and expressiveness, has to meet a third requirement: **regularity**. DLT is interactive in the first half of the translation process, but the second half, from the intermediate into the target language, has to be fully automatic. This requires the intermediate language to be semantically over-clear and syntactically extraordinarily regular. In view of these three requirements, DLT opts for Esperanto. Esperanto is extremely regular because it was made as a special type of an artificial symbol system. It is autonomous, because it has come into communicative use in a (second-) language community and is now a human language (cf. Kuznecov forthc.: 92), so that the meaning of its elements is maintained by convention in the community as it is in ethnic languages. And finally, through communicative use and as a consequence of its autonomy, Esperanto has obtained the required expressiveness. A few minor modifications were performed for the use in DLT, so that DLT's intermediate language contrasts from common Esperanto by being syntactically unambiguous.

This is not the place for a more explicit justification of the choice of Esperanto as an intermediate language in machine translation (cf. Schubert 1988a). My main interest in this contribution is to investigate in which way the architecture of the DLT machine translation system, which is based on a human intermediate language, differs from designs currently labelled interlingual, which are based on artificial intermediate representations.

4. The DLT translation process

In the DLT system, the intermediate language is a tightly defined interface to every source or target language. The system owes its name *Distributed* to the fact that the translation process is split up into two independent halfs: a module for translating from the source into the intermediate language and another module for the step from the intermediate to a target language. The two halfs are not only independent, they are designed to work at different locations, even in different countries, since the DLT system is designed as a software component that makes data communication services in international computer networks multilingual. Texts are passed through the network in the intermediate language, that is, in a coded version of the linear text string. For the linguistic architecture of the system this has an obvious consequence: The intermediate language is the only means to convey meaning from the source text into its translations. Everything has to be expressed with linguistic means only. The intermediate form of the text has to be ready for being translated into arbitrary target languages, so that it must not carry any source language-specific features. The translation step into the target language is in DLT fully automatic, whereas in the first half the operator is prompted for disambiguating decisions in an interactive dialogue. The intermediate text is therefore "enriched" in that it carries not only the information contained in the original source text, but renders the text's content in a version disambiguated by the joint efforts of the system and the user.

As a consequence of this distributed design, a text being translated from a source into a target language passes two complete translation processes underway. Hence the question I chose as the title of this contribution: Isn't the DLT translation process actually double direct, rather than interlingual? The answer is neither yes nor no, so that it is necessary to have a closer look at the two translation processes.

The translation method applied in the two halfs of the DLT system is based on two principles which help to assess the nature of the process. Firstly, grammatical and extragrammatical features of the source text that are directly **translation-relevant** are wherever possible separated from features that only function as traces or indicators of other, translation-relevant, features. Extra work load in the translation step proper is avoided by keeping the not directly translation-relevant features in the monolingual analysis and synthesis steps and including into translation proper only those characteristics that are essential to the process (cf. Schubert 1987: 152ff.; Papegaaij/Schubert 1988: 160ff.). Secondly, syntax on the one hand and semantics and pragmatics on the other hand are kept apart as much as possible.

Guided by these two principles, the DLT translation process in the first half of the system (source language → intermediate language) runs as follows.

Step 1. **Source language parser**: The current DLT prototype contains such a parser for English. It recognises English words and their syntactic features (including morphology). Not directly translation-relevant features, such as the case of pronouns and nouns, are recognised and used to identify translation-relevant syntactic relations, that is dependency relations such as subject, object, attribute etc. The result is a dependency tree. In the case of syntactic ambiguities, the parser delivers alternative dependency trees. No semantics is applied.

Step 2. **Metataxis: Monolingual tree transformations** in the source language ("source language filters", cf. Schubert 1987: 167ff.): Not directly translation-relevant syntactic variants are reduced to a common form. These may be minor measures, e.g. *can not, cannot, can't → can not*, but also major tree transformations, such as the reduction of auxiliary-verb constructions to a single verb stem with appropriate features (*has been eaten → eat* [present perfect, passive]).

Step 3. **Metataxis: Bilingual tree transformations** ("translation proper"): The words in the English dependency trees are replaced by their Esperanto correspondences; English syntactic dependency labels are replaced by Esperanto ones, which may entail major rearrangements of the tree, insertion of function words etc. Especially due to the ambiguities in lexical transfer (several translation alternatives for a single entry word in the bilingual dictionary), for each English tree an enormous amount of translation alternatives into Esperanto is generated. No semantic-pragmatic choice whatsoever is performed as yet.

Step 4. **Semantic-pragmatic word choice**: From the abundance of syntactically correct translation alternatives in the intermediate language, DLT's Semantic Word Expert System for the Intermediate Language ("SWESIL") on the basis of the knowledge encoded in its Lexical Knowledge Bank chooses that alternative which is most likely to fit in with the given context. At the time of writing the accessible context in the DLT prototype is still basically limited to the syntagma, as described by Papegaaij (1986: 108). Future developments will extend the scope of the context beyond the sentence boundary (Papegaaij/Schubert 1988).

Step 5. **The disambiguation dialogue**: Choices which cannot be made by SWESIL with sufficient confidence are presented to the operator in an interactive, system-initiated dialogue. At the end of steps 4 and 5 there is only a single intermediate translation for each input sentence.

Step 6. **Metataxis: Monolingual tree transformations** in the intermediate language ("intermediate-language filters"): The translation step proper may produce syntactically incorrect trees within certain well-defined limits, which highly enhances its regularity and prevents unnecessary complications. ("Incorrect" means that the linearised form of these trees, made for temporary use, would be ill-formed; the "incorrect" trees are, however, well defined in terms of metatactic tree manipulation.) These are removed in this step. In addition, not directly translation-relevant features of the intermediate language are inserted into the tree. Hereby first of all the requirements of form government and agreement are met. This information is superfluous as long as the sentence stays in tree form, with explicit syntactic labels, but it becomes essential as soon as the tree is linearised and extralinguistic elements are removed.

Step 7. **Tree linearisation**: The intermediate-language tree is linearised. The words are arranged in a correct word order and all labels, feature lists etc. are removed. The output is a plain Esperanto text, ready to be read by humans, to be compared with text corpora etc.

Step 8. **Correctness check**: As a security measure, each sentence is passed through a recogniser for the intermediate language, which analyses the sentences read in string form and rejects syntactically incorrect ones. They are returned to the metataxis module for correction.

Step 9. **Coding and network transmission**: When it has been made sure that no incorrect output can leave the source language module, the accepted sentences are coded and transmitted through the network.

In step 3 the number of alternative Esperanto trees becomes extraordinarily high. If a sentence of ten or fifteen words contains five content words with, say, five translation alternatives each, no less than 5x5x5x5x5 = 3125 trees are received. Longer sentences easily produce hundreds of thousands of trees. For the sake of the discussion it is simplest to imagine that all these trees are generated and handled separately in the subsequent steps. Practical considerations of processing speed and computer capacity, however, suggest another solution for the actual implementation. In the DLT prototype version of March 1988 – the most recent one at the time of writing – Step 3 generates compact Esperanto trees which have at their nodes not single words (as is supposed above), but lists of all the alternative words given at the Esperanto side of the English-Esperanto dictionary in DLT. Separate trees are only generated when dictionary entries bring about structural differences in the generated Esperanto trees, which is possible in the case of multi-word entries. The compact trees allow for fast processing in SWESIL with computing work loads that are substantially reduced as compared to what would be needed in the case of separate trees with one-word nodes. Nevertheless SWESIL does take into account all alternatives. The situation as described above may thus be taken as a valid theoretical picture of the process. In connection with this implementational rearrangement, the place of SWESIL in the overall process has been modified as compared to earlier accounts where it was not applied before the entire metataxis process was done (e.g. Schubert 1986b: 145). The present sequence allows for carrying out the monolingual steps, which have no consequences for the semantic-pragmatic processing, only in a single tree, the one selected as the right translation. The processes for form government and agreement etc. are thus not carried out for all the alternative Esperanto trees, but only for one.

The second half of the DLT translation process, in the present prototype from Esperanto into French, is similar to the first half:

Step 10. **Decoding.**

Step 11. **Esperanto parser**: The Esperanto string is parsed into a dependency tree. The process is fast since DLT's intermediate language is unambiguous at all levels of syntax.

Step 12. **Metataxis: Monolingual tree transformations** in the intermediate language.

Step 13. **Metataxis: Bilingual tree transformations**: Esperanto to French. Here, again, many alternative trees are generated (but represented and processed in a small number of complex trees).

Step 14. **Semantic-pragmatic word choice**: Again the SWESIL system performs the required semantic and pragmatic choices. The process is this time fully automatic. No interaction with the user is possible, since this half of the overall translation process takes place far removed in time and space from the author of the text, who assisted the system in step 5. As a consequence, the intermediate version of the text being translated has to be so good that the second half can rely entirely on its methods of Artificial Intelligence.

Step 15. **Metataxis: Monolingual tree transformations** in the target language. Both adjustments of deliberately incorrect French trees and the not directly translation-relevant processes of form government and agreement are carried out here.

Step 16. **Tree linearisation with contraction and elision**. The chosen French tree structure is linearised and thereafter those adjustments are carried out, which rely on the position in the string, such as in French contraction and elision (*à le* → *au*, *je ai* → *j'ai*). The output is a French text.

5. Copy or mirror image?

The DLT translation process is carried out in two clearly distinct translation modules, each linking two human languages. In the present DLT prototype, besides Esperanto, English and French are involved. Looking not at the entire process, but at the two halfs separately, one might draw the following scheme:

	Source language	Target language
First half	**English**	**Esperanto**
Second half	**Esperanto**	**French**

This scheme suggests a functional equivalence between English in the first and Esperanto in the second half on the one hand and between Esperanto in the first and French in the second half on the other hand, which does not hold. As the sixteen-step close-up above shows, the two halfs are not copies of each other. They are closer to being each other's mirror image. On the syntactic side of the process the picture of two congruent direct translation processes is still more or less true. An essential difference between English (and other source languages) and DLT's intermediate language is, however, that the latter is syntactically unambiguous.

On the semantic side the functions fulfilled by the different languages are still much less congruent, in that no semantic or pragmatic processings are carried out in English or French at all. All content-related translation steps are performed in the Esperanto kernel of the DLT system. In other words, in the first half of the overall process the heavy load of semantic-pragmatic treatment is in the target language (of that half), whereas in the second half it is in the source language. The reason for this design is obvious: In both halfs the most difficult part of machine translation, the content-related treatment, is carried out in the intermediate language Esperanto. As a consequence, the modules developed for these function can be applied to translation between arbitrary source and target languages, because these languages play no role in them.

This may sound surprising. Of course DLT does not translate without reference to the source and the target language. But the DLT design provides a technique for carrying out exclusively in the intermediate language the **reasoning** about the content that is expressed in the source language and is to be rendered in the target language. A few more details about this characteristic trait of DLT can help to get a clearer view on the question of interlingual versus double direct design as well.

The semantic-pragmatic kernel of the DLT system consists of highly complex software to perform an intricate process of meaning-related decision making. Leaving aside most of its particulars, one can for the sake of the argument describe the process in a few plain words: Syntactically correct alternative translations of the same source language sentence are in the word expert system ranked as to the semantic-pragmatic probability with which they fit into the given context. In the first half of the DLT translation process, the parser produces all syntactically possible analyses of the English input sentence, and for each of them the metataxis rule system delivers all syntactically possible alternatives in Esperanto obtained by inserting all alternative word translations from the bilingual dictionary.

The SWESIL module then works entirely on Esperanto tree structures. In its basic function, the word expert system ranks the alternative Esperanto translations of a given English word by comparing their context with typical contexts given in the lexical knowledge bank. This method has been described as the comparison of *ist* and *soll* contexts (Papegaaij 1986: 95ff.; Papegaaij/Schubert 1988: 191). The ist context is the one actually present in a given tree structure, whereas the soll context is relevant information from the entry in the lexical knowledge bank. Contexts are described in terms of surrounding words with their semantic relations to the entry word. The knowledge bank is entirely in Esperanto and uses no extralinguistic or metalingual means, that is, both the entry words and the context words are Esperanto, and the semantic relators are function words or morphemes from Esperanto.

It is important to realise that SWESIL compares contexts. The alternative Esperanto translations of a given English word (the entry words) play, as it were, the role of a "name" of a bundle of context descriptions, but they do not themselves have any function in the comparison. The contexts are compared and the entry words are ranked on a probability scale according to the degree of conceptual proximity their ist context has with the soll contexts.

That the context descriptions rather than the entry words themselves are used in the semantic-pragmatic comparisons does not seem to be an essential fact in the first half of the DLT process, but it turns out to be of utmost importance to the second half. When translating from Esperanto into a given target language, say French, one can apply the same system. From the Esperanto sentence all syntactically possible alternative French translations are generated and then the required semantic-pragmatic choices are performed. If the two halfs of the DLT translation system were designed as copies of each other, one would generate all the alternative translations in French and than have a French semantic word expert system with a French knowledge bank assess the contextual probabilities and perform word choices on that basis. However, building up and maintaining a knowledge bank and a word expert system that works on it is such an intricate, complex and voluminous task, that it is highly desirable to find a way out which does not require to repeat these labour-intensive pieces of work for each new target language.

It would highly enhance the extensibility of the system, if it could be made possible to use the same lexical knowledge bank and the same word expert system for all languages involved. As is shown above, this is indeed possible as far as source languages are concerned. The discussion of the function of SWESIL in the source language half of DLT also contains a hint at the possible solution for the target language half: The SWESIL system performs its comparisons entirely on the basis of contexts and does not use the words themselves that are decided upon, since the usage of those words is taken to be defined in terms of their typical contexts. The contexts in question are of a semantic-pragmatic nature, that is, they have to do with meaning and with extralinguistic reference, but not with form-related peculiarities of a particular language. (Those are catered for in syntactic valency information in the dictionaries.) As a consequence, it is perfectly possible that the typical contexts of French words are formulated in Esperanto, and the same holds of course for other target languages.

This is the solution adopted for DLT: It is inevitable to formulate **target language-specific semantic information** in a lexicographic work process, but it can be formulated in Esperanto. The differences in meaning among the alternative French translations of a given Esperanto entry word are expressed by means of contexts formulated in the intermediate language. When this is done, the same Esperanto-based word expert system SWESIL that functions in the first half of the DLT translation process can compute probability scores for the alternative French words by matching their typical (soll) contexts, given in Esperanto, with the actual (ist) context in the Esperanto sentence to be translated. Its calculations about the semantic proximity of various Esperanto words found in these contexts are based on the same Esperanto knowledge bank that functions in the first half.

The work needed for adding a new target language to DLT thus cannot be reduced to the syntactic requirements alone, but the semantic-pragmatic work load does not by far attain the size that was necessary for translating into the intermediate language. To illustrate the lexicographic work that has to be done, I give an extract from a sample entry in DLT's Esperanto-French dictionary. It contains some of the French alternative translations of *akr'a* 'sharp'.

In an impressionistic wording, a dictionary entry of this kind should be read as follows: The word *akr'a* is to be translated as *vif* if it is related with an *a* relator (attributive relation, marked with the Esperanto adjective marker *a*) to a noun that is conceptually closer to *dolor'o, mal'varm'o, riproĉ'o'j, vort'o'j, romp'o* or *eĝ'o* than to any of *naz'o, orel'o'j, tur'o, spic'o, pipr'o, brand'o, disput'o, batal'o, kriz'o, vent'o, ŝtorm'o, ironi'o*. The required semantic proximity calculation does not involve the French word and can thus make use of the huge Esperanto knowledge bank. The entry shown here is a relatively simple example, and it has been simplified for this paper by leaving out some ten more French translations of *akr'a*. In more complex cases, there might be different semantic relators which connect the entry word to either its syntactic governor or some of its dependents. In addition, neither the Esperanto contexts nor the French translations have to consist of single words, but may each be made up of several, syntactically related words (a syntagma), which are in that case represented as a syntactic dependency tree with appropriate labels etc.

A sample entry from DLT's Esperanto-French dictionary			
Esperanto entry word	Semantic relator (an Esperanto morpheme)	Disambiguating contexts: Esperanto words (with morpheme tokens), here illustrated with approximative English glosses	French word with syntactic word class
akr'a	*a*	*dolor'o, mal'varm'o, riproĉ'o'j, vort'o'j, romp'o, eĝ'o* 'pain', 'cold', 'blames', 'words', 'break', 'edge'	**vif/ADJ**
akr'a	*a*	*naz'o, orel'o'j, tur'o* 'nose', 'ears', 'tower'	**pointu/ADJ**
akr'a	*a*	*spic'o, pipr'o, brand'o* 'spice', 'pepper', 'brandy'	**fort/ADJ**
akr'a	*a*	*disput'o, batal'o, kriz'o, vent'o, ŝtorm'o* 'dispute', 'fight', 'crisis', 'wind', 'storm'	**violent/ADJ**
akr'a	*a*	*ironi'o* 'irony'	**mordant/ADJ**

In a target language module of the DLT system there are two sources of word-related knowledge: the general Esperanto knowledge bank and this smaller collection of typical contexts which in Esperanto **disambiguate** alternative target language words.

6. Direct *and* interlingual

After a brief assessment of both the form-related and the content-related procedures in DLT, the argument can now be concluded. The syntactic side of the DLT design is indeed a double direct translation process. (I do not take up the question here whether it is double direct or rather double transfer.) The two halfs do not influence each other in any other way than via the intermediate text itself. The syntactic translation method makes use of similarities between Esperanto on the one hand and the source or target language on the other hand. However, the semantic and pragmatic part of the overall design is clearly heavily biassed towards the intermediate language and may in this sense be called interlingual. It is the special nature of the intermediate language that makes DLT difficult to classify in the traditional scheme. The content-related part of the process renders it interlingual, but since the intermediate language is a human language, albeit an especially translation-friendly one, it is possible to translate **completely** into it. DLT's intermediate representation is not an artificial symbol system through which source language features would have to effect on the target language, as it were, directly. A full-fledged language in the function of an intermediate language has an interesting effect on the design of the system: The extremes of the triple scale meet. Because DLT's intermediate language is a complete human language the difference to transfer systems is no longer a gradual one, but is a true difference in quality, and because of the same reason the intermediate language has the regularness, expressiveness and autonomy required for taking over the entire semantic-pragmatic processing.

The attempt to find a place in the triple division of machine translation designs for the DLT system leads to the finding that the nature of the intermediate language has an essential influence on the set-up and the functioning of the entire system. The DLT solution makes the processings carried out in the intermediate language truly independent from the particulars of the source and target languages. In this way it provides for a high degree of modularity and thereby for multilingual extensibility of the system. In addition it is the ambition of the DLT designers that Esperanto as intermediate language allow for representing the complete content of a source text, enriched through disambiguation answers given by the user, and thereby for fully automatic translation from the intermediate into the target languages.

References

Kuznecov, Sergej N. (forthc.): Interlinguistics: a branch of applied linguistics?
In: *Interlinguistics – aspects of the science of planned languages*. Klaus Schubert (with Dan Maxwell) (eds.). Berlin/New York/Amsterdam: Mouton de Gruyter, pp. 89-98

Papegaaij, B. C. (1986): *Word expert semantics. An interlingual knowledge-based approach.* V. Sadler / A. P. M. Witkam (eds.). Dordrecht/Riverton: Foris

Papegaaij, B. C. / Klaus Schubert (1988): *Text coherence in translation.* Dordrecht/Providence: Foris

Schubert, Klaus (1986a): *Syntactic tree structures in DLT.* Utrecht: BSO/Research

Schubert, Klaus (1986b): Linguistic and extra-linguistic knowledge.
In: *Computers and Translation* 1, pp. 125-152

Schubert, Klaus (1987): *Metataxis. Contrastive dependency syntax for machine translation.* Dordrecht/Providence: Foris

Schubert, Klaus (1988a): Ausdruckskraft und Regelmäßigkeit. Was Esperanto für automatische Übersetzung geeignet macht.
In: *Language Problems and Language Planning* 12, pp. 130-147

Schubert, Klaus (1988b): Implicitness as a guiding principle in machine translation.
In: *Coling Budapest. Proceedings of the International Conference on Computational Linguistics* (Budapest 1988).
Dénes Vargha (ed.). Budapest: John von Neumann Society for Computing Sciences, pp. 599-601

Tucker, Allen B. (1988): [Review of Papegaaij 1986]
In: *Computers and Translation* 3, pp. 83-86

Tucker, Allen B. / Sergei Nirenburg (1984): Machine translation: a contemporary view.
In: *Annual Review of Information Science and Technology* 19, pp. 129-160

Witkam, A. P. M. (1983): *Distributed Language Translation. Feasibility study of a multilingual facility for videotex information networks.* Utrecht: BSO

Witkam, A. P. M. (1985): Distribuita Lingvo-Tradukado.
In: *Perkomputila tekstoprilaboro.* Ilona Kounty (ed.). Budapest: Scienca Eldona Centro, pp. 207-228

Klaus Schubert

La arkitekturo de DLT – ĉu interlingva aŭ duoble rekta?

Resumo

Oni ĝenerale klasas komputilajn traduksistemojn laŭ iliaj sistemplanoj en rektajn, transirajn kaj interlingvajn. Kiun lokon en tiu skalo okupas DLT? La demando estas interesa ne nur por konvene klasi plian sistemon, sed ĉefe ĉar ĝia respondo donas pli klaran komprenon de la interdependeco de faritaj kaj farendaj plandecidoj en konstruata traduksistemo.

DLT havas interlingvon, pro kio ĝia loko en la triobla distingo ŝajnas evidenta. Tamen la esprimo "interlingvo" kutime celas ne kompletan homan lingvon, sed interan reprezentaĵon de ia artefarita speco, bazitan sur ekzistanta lingvo. La fakto, ke DLT ja uzas homan lingvon – eĉ se tre specialan, Esperanton – grave ŝanĝas la situacion. Traduksistemo povas profiti sian interlingvecon plene nur se la interlingvo estas aŭtonoma, esprimiva kaj regula. Nur la plena esprimivo de homa lingvo permesas uzi la interlingvon kiel la solan interfacon inter origina kaj celaj lingvoj.

La tradukproceso en DLT povas esti priskribita en 16 paŝoj. La ĉefa konkludo estas, ke la semantikaj kaj pragmatikaj prilaboradoj okazas senescepte per la interlingvo (Esperanto), dum la originan kaj celan lingvojn oni prilaboras nur sintakse (kio inkluzivas morfologion). La ŝanĝo de unu lingvo al alia okazas sur sintaksa nivelo (metatakso) rekte al kaj el Esperanto. Estas generataj sintakse eblaj tradukalternativoj, el kiuj la semantika-pragmatika ekspertsistemo elektas la kontekste plej verŝajnan solvon.

DLT tial devas esti konsiderata kaj duoble rekta (aŭ eble duoble transira) pro la dufoja sintaksa tradukpaŝo, kaj interlingva pro la fakto ke la interlingvo portas la tutan enhavrilatan parton de la tradukproceso. Elekti homan lingvon kiel interlingvon signifas esencan paŝon for de la tradiciaj traduksistemoj.

Discourse Structure – Some Implications for Machine Translation*

Christa Hauenschild

Technische Universität Berlin
Institut für Software und Theoretische Informatik
Projektgruppe KIT
Sekretariat FR 5-12
Franklinstraße 28/29
D-1000 Berlin 10

0. Abstract

In this paper, my main perspective will be that of translation theory. I want to discuss the importance of discourse structure for translation in general and for machine translation, regarded as a special case of translation, as well as some consequences that might or should be drawn from this. After some general remarks on the role of discourse structure for human and machine translation, where I concentrate on the aspect of the thematic structuring of the text to be translated (section 1), I want to examine the interrelation between the stipulation of invariants in translation and the interlingual approach to translation theory, as well as machine translation (section 2). As a kind of counter-evidence to the interlingual approach, section 3 introduces some language-particular ways of expressing the thematic structuring of a text, which is partially manifested by different as well as analogous forms of thematic sentence structuring. Such idiosyncrasies and analogies lead us to an argumentation in favour of the transfer approach to translation (section 4). The conclusion is given in section 5 – both aspects of translation ought to be considered in machine translation, i.e. the fact that something has to remain unchanged during translation, which might be captured by an interlingual component of a machine translation system, as well as the fact that something has to be changed in the process of translation, which might be realized by a transfer component.

1. The Role of Discourse Structure in (Machine) Translation

Although there has been a long and still unsettled debate among translation theorists about the role of "equivalence" in translation (it is neither clear which aspects of equivalence ought to be captured by a theoretical model of translation nor is it agreed upon whether the concept of equivalence is at all relevant for translation, see e.g. Koller 1979: 176ff. and Snell-Hornby 1988), it is more or less accepted that something has to remain constant during the process of translating. Obviously, this is necessary in order to find at least some sort of relation between two texts that would justify their classification as an original and as a translation thereof. What this constant or invariant aspect or aspects of the text amount(s) to is essentially dependent on the type of text to be translated.

There is a way of modelling the translation process (as e.g. in Pause 1983: 394) that yields the following result with respect to the question of what has to be preserved during translation; first of all, we have to decide which aspect of the text to be translated is most important (be it formal value, semantic content or communicative function or any subclass of these); this aspect has to remain constant. Then we have to try and preserve the other aspects as well - as far as this is possible with the expressive means of the target language, but never sacrificing more important aspects for less important ones. This approach is sometimes debated on the basis of examples where translation is hardly possible at all (e.g. poems, advertising texts). In my view, these are interesting borderline cases of translation, but they are not suitable as a starting-point for a theory of translation that is to include machine translation as well (incidentally, even in those extreme cases there seems to be something that is to remain unchanged in translation, namely the communicative function, which is essentially esthetic in the case of many poems and commercial in the case of advertising).

These different aspects of texts and their translations, which may be considered as a criterion of translation quality, are often modelled as different kinds of structuring; the formal aspect corresponds to phonetic, morphological and syntactic structuring, the semantic aspect might correspond to isotopies and lexical coherence; the pragmatic aspect might be modelled as information structure among other things. Even the aspect of the communicative function may be regarded as a structured (rather than a monolithic) phenomenon; e.g. in the case of advertising there is normally the final goal of making somebody buy something, but there are sub-goals, namely the esthetic attractiveness, the novelty of the message and so on. All these structurings may interfere and overlap in very complex ways (as has been shown e.g. by Van Dijk/Kintsch 1983). Thus it is often not easy for the human translator to find out which aspects are most relevant. Moreover, for a really good translation, it is not enough to preserve just the most relevant aspects per se, but it is desirable to preserve all the relatively important aspects as far as possible.

In the case of machine translation, it seems to be unrealistic to burden the machine with the task of finding out the most relevant aspects of the texts in their proper ordering without human aid. For those texts that are most suitable for machine translation, we can fix the relevance order in advance – in the case of "informative" texts (i.e. texts that are to inform the reader of something he had not known before, on the background of something he already knows) it is primarily the information structure that has to be preserved in the process of translation. All the other aspects of the translated text may be changed if necessary, but the safest approach to a correct translation is still to preserve the syntactic and semantic structuring as well, provided that this is possible (the morphological and phonological levels are considered as irrelevant in the case of informative texts, while they may well be relevant for poems or advertising texts).

For translation theory as well as for machine translation, the information structure of a text may be represented in different ways. It is mainly in the field of Artificial Intelligence that one finds proposals for the representation of whole texts with their content structure. "Text models" of different kinds have been suggested that serve interesting additional purposes – one of the most fruitful fields of AI research in natural-language processing has been that of "anaphora resolution", i.e. the interpretation of anaphoric expressions on the basis of explicitly establishing the referential relation between the anaphor and its antecedent (see Hirst 1981 for a survey). Grosz (1981) describes a way of resolving anaphoric pronouns with the aid of a thematic structuring of the input text. It is plausible to assume that the most thematic expression in the preceding text (i.e. the expression referring to the most prominent object, which Grosz calls "focused") is best suited as an antecedent for an anaphoric pronoun.

From a text-linguistic point of view it is, of course, not surprising that the different aspects of the structure of a text should be interrelated: the thematic structure and the referential structure of a text can be regarded as two perspectives of text coherence, namely coherence on the level of propositions and coherence on the level of objects (see Van Dijk 1977). It is obvious that a coherent text has to be translated into a coherent text, which means that the manifestations of coherence in the target language have to correspond to their manifestations in the source language.

There are other interrelations between the different structuring aspects to be found; e.g. the interrelation between the thematic structure and the isotopic structure, which may serve to determine the proper reading of an ambiguous lexeme in a special context and thus makes it possible to choose the correct translation equivalent from the different possible candidates.

After all, it should be obvious that the thematic structure of an informative text has to be preserved in the process of translation in order to give the reader of the target text the desired information and, in addition, in order to enable the intended interpretation of anaphoric expressions as well as the correct translation of ambiguous lexemes to be selected. Whether these requirements are relevant for machine translation, too, is dependent on the standard that is to be attained. If we look at machine translation from a theoretical point of view, with the question in mind of how far it is possible to simulate the human process of translation with a machine (this is the view point I take in this paper, and incidentally, I hope that we can find out something more precise about human translation by trying to make machines translate, even if "fully automatic high quality translation" turns out to be impossible), we have to simulate (at least) the preservation of the thematic structure of a text as the most important aspect of discourse structure during translation by the machine.

2. Invariants of Translation and the Interlingual Approach

If we accept this argumentation, it must, of course, be asked whether such a goal for machine translation is at all realistic. The final answer to this question can only be given as a result of further research; it will be linked to the answer to the fundamental question of whether a true simulation of the human translation process is in general possible. As far as I can see, there is some hope for a partially positive answer to both questions if we take into account the results of Artificial Intelligence research as well as some relevant results of psycholinguistics and text-linguistics. We find converging approaches in these fields to the representation of whole texts with their coherence aspects, which might serve as a tertium comparationis for the translation of informative texts, provided that they are combined in a way that allows all the relevant aspects to be represented.

In the light of these considerations it seems plausible that some kind of an "interlingual" approach to machine translation has to be chosen in order to account for the invariants that have to remain untouched by the translation process. Such an interlingual component might be conceived of as an augmented form of a semantic network with an explicit indication of referential relations and of the hierarchical as well as systematic interrelations between the themes and sub-themes of a text. Several proposals have been made in this direction in recent machine translation projects (e.g. Nirenburg/Raskin/Tucker 1987: 99ff or Hauenschild/Pause 1983: 110ff).

Perhaps, this is a revival of the old dream of a universal language in a modern guise, and we are sure to find the old problems of this ideal – the problem of defining an interlingua that is suitable for any source or target language (which seems hardly solvable even in cases where the number of languages is limited as e.g. in EUROTRA, King/Perschke 1987, where the tertium comparationis need not be universal, but only "euroversal"), as well as the difficulty of very "expensive" analysis and synthesis components. This can be seen from figure 1 which shows the different possibilities for constructing a machine translation system.

In Tsujii (1986: 657) such figures have been called misleading; and they may indeed be misleading if interpreted not as a systematic overview over different classes of machine translation systems, but as pictures of the translation process. For the interlingual approach, it is not just the almost insurmountable difficulty involved in defining the interlingua in the first place, and then analyzing into and generating from that level of representation, but there is the danger that we end up with a paraphrase of the source text and not a proper translation. The difference between a paraphrase and a translation may be seen in the fact that a good translation preserves not just those aspects at the top of the relevance scale, but all aspects of relative importance (as far as possible).

Figure 1: Systematic Relations Between Different Approaches to Machine Translation

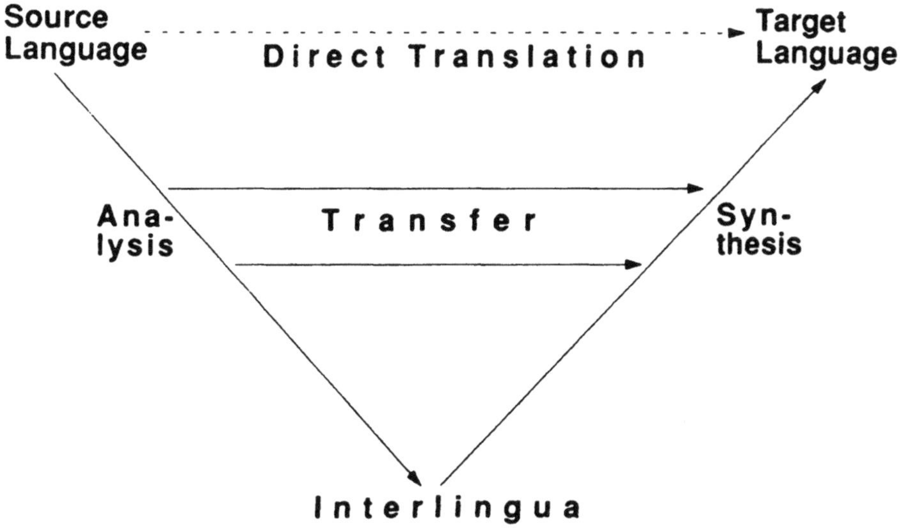

3. Thematic Structuring of Texts vs. Sentences

If we accept that the thematic structuring is one of the most relevant aspects of an informative text and must therefore be preserved in translation, we have to solve the problem of how to analyze it effectively, starting from the sequence of sentences that constitutes the source text. Even if we suppose that the main theme of the text is given by its title (which is not always the case!) or by supplementary information, we cannot be sure of finding the sub-themes, which may be essential for e.g. the referential interpretation of some anaphoric pronouns or the choice of translation equivalents for ambiguous words. The favourite approach of AI researchers, namely the strategy of assigning suitable frames to parts of the source text, ends up in the well-known "frame selection problem", in almost every case involving different frames that are not directly connected with one another (for a discussion of this problem see Charniak 1978 and Shann 1978: 83).

One possible way out of this dilemma might be found by taking the linguistic structure of the text more seriously than has often been done by AI researchers. We can find thematic structurings not only at the level of the whole text, but also at the level of the sentences constituting it (that these structurings are not simply analogous, is shown in Hajičová/Sgall 1984, an overview of my own conception of sentence themes and textual themes can be found in Hauenschild 1985: 377 and 1988: 425ff). Although I admit that we are far from having solved all the problems of analyzing the thematic text structure by linguistic methods, I want to propagate the idea that some of them might be solvable. Let us look at a very simple example:

(1) There was a bird flying in the sky.
It was blue.

The pronoun in the second sentence is normally interpreted as referring to the bird and not to the sky. Why should this be so? The first sentence makes it very clear by its structuring that it is rather about the bird than about the sky, and therefore the bird is a much better candidate for an antecedent than is the sky. Even if the second sentence contained a predicate that is very unlikely for birds, say "cloudy", we should hesitate to interpret the pronoun as referring to the sky. If we want to refer to the sky, we need to choose an alternative expression:

(2) There was a bird flying in the sky.
The sky was blue.

or

(3) There was a bird flying in the blue sky.

These examples suggest that the thematic structuring of a sentence may have an influence on the thematic structuring of the entire text.

Of course, the interrelation between the thematic structuring of sentences and of texts is not as simple as might be inferred from these simple examples, but it appears at least that there are structural positions in sentences where we can expect to find relatively prominent discourse subjects and thus very probable candidates for text themes. These positions have to be described in a language-particular way in the first place. However, there may be generalizations to be found across different languages, e.g. the position of a subject following the inflected verb in its sentence seems to be predetermined as a place for a newly introduced discourse subject which is likely to become a theme. If we translate (1) into Russian (which is normally regarded as rather different from English with respect to word order regularities, English being essentially a language with fixed word order and Russian being a language with relatively free word order), we find a similar structure with respect to subject position.

(4) Na nebe letela ptica.
'in sky (LOC.) flew (IMPERFECTIVE) bird (NOM.)'

Ona byla golubaja.
'it (FEM.) was blue (FEM.)'

In the first sentence of the Russian text, the locative phrase *na nebe* is placed in front of the inflected verb (which is not obligatory, but seems to be the most natural position), while the subject *ptica* is placed on the right-hand side of the inflected verb (the imperfective aspect of the Russian verb corresponds to the progressive form of the English verb in this case). The position behind the verb is typical for newly introduced discourse subjects in Russian. In the above case, it yields an indefinite interpretation of the subject (the indefiniteness of *ptica* need not be explicitly indicated in such a "rhematic" position). The anaphoric pronoun in the second sentence of (4) is not ambiguous. There is a difference in gender between *nebo* (neutral) and *ptica* (feminine), which is reflected in the form of the personal pronoun. This means that we need the information about the actual reference of the pronoun in order to choose the correct form in the Russian text (it would have to be *ono* instead of *ona*, if it was to refer to the sky). In our example, it is necessary to determine the most probable antecedent on the basis of facts about the thematic structuring of the text, which can be inferred from the structure of the sentences in this case. In the general case, all sorts of (linguistic and extra-linguistic) information about the text may be necessary in order to determine the actual antecedent of an anaphoric pronoun (see Hauenschild/Pause 1983: 106f).

What I wanted to show with the aid of these simplistic examples is that there are similarities as well as differences between particular languages in expressing the thematic structuring of sentences and whole texts. For an optimal (i.e. also: safe!) translation strategy, it is desirable to preserve as much as possible of the structuring of the source text.

4. Idiosyncrasies of Languages and the Transfer Approach

One of the consequences of the foregoing argumentation seems to be that for the task of translation we have to take the linguistic structures (and their pragmatic impact!) seriously, and thus we have to represent them explicitly in an adequate model of the translation process. This means, however, that we also need access to this kind of linguistic information for a machine translation system. In principle, the structural information might be made available by enriching the interlingua, but this would probably lead to a very clumsy form of a "universal" language because it would have to contain divergent structural information for any source or target language. Obviously, such an approach is hardly feasible.

If this is so, however, we need a transfer component for machine translation. In translation theory, too, there has been a shift, so to speak, from interlingual models to transfer models (Koller 1979: 114ff). This shift is due to the claim that meaning is language-particular. One need not be convinced of the Sapir-Whorf hypothesis of linguistic relativity (for a discussion of its relevance for translation theory see Koller 1979: 139ff) to assume that the semantic structuring of the world is – at least in part – specific to different languages. According to our argumentation in the preceding section, the same holds for the means by which different languages express the thematic structuring of sentences and whole texts.

However, if we want to treat seriously the claim that a good translation is characterized by the maximally possible preservation of relevant aspects of the source text, it does not suffice to simply account for the facts of thematic structuring. We also have to represent the (sentence) semantic and the syntactic structuring of the source and target texts in order to preserve them as far as possible. As was already pointed out, this is the safest strategy of translation because the danger of errors is minimized, given the fact that in a good text the structuring at all levels is not arbitrary, but serves specific purposes of information transport. This can be seen from the fact that the analysis of these different levels of linguistic structure is often necessary for the interpretation of anaphoric expressions.

This leads to a concept of different transfer components, each of which accounts for another aspect of the structuring. My favourite idea is that of a multi-level transfer model. Such a model would correspond to considerations in translation theory, most precisely expressed in the concept of "levels of equivalence" ("urovni ėkvivalentnosti") in Komissarov (1973: 72). A machine translation system organized according to this model would allow the representation and usage of structural information (in the sense of syntactic, semantic and pragmatic structure). Of course, it would have to be supplemented by further information about the domain of the text and about the communication situation (these are types of information that every translator needs for a correct translation). A further advantage of such a system would consist in the possibility of splitting up the highly complex task of translation into different, though interacting, components.

5. Conclusion – in Favour of a "Mixed" Approach

The conclusion of the foregoing argumentation is obvious – we have to account for both fundamental aspects of translation: the invariants and the different ways of expressing them. The tension between same and different seems to be the essence of translation (which is one of the most challenging linguistic tasks I can think of). An ideal machine translation system ought to represent this principal tension. To this end, we have to combine the interlingual approach with the transfer approach in a suitable way. That this is not a contradiction, can be seen from several recent approaches to machine translation; e.g. EUROTRA, where transfer takes place at the level of "interface structure" (King/Perschke 1987: 385ff), has developed a kind of "quasi-interlingua" by combining language-particular aspects of the interface structure with

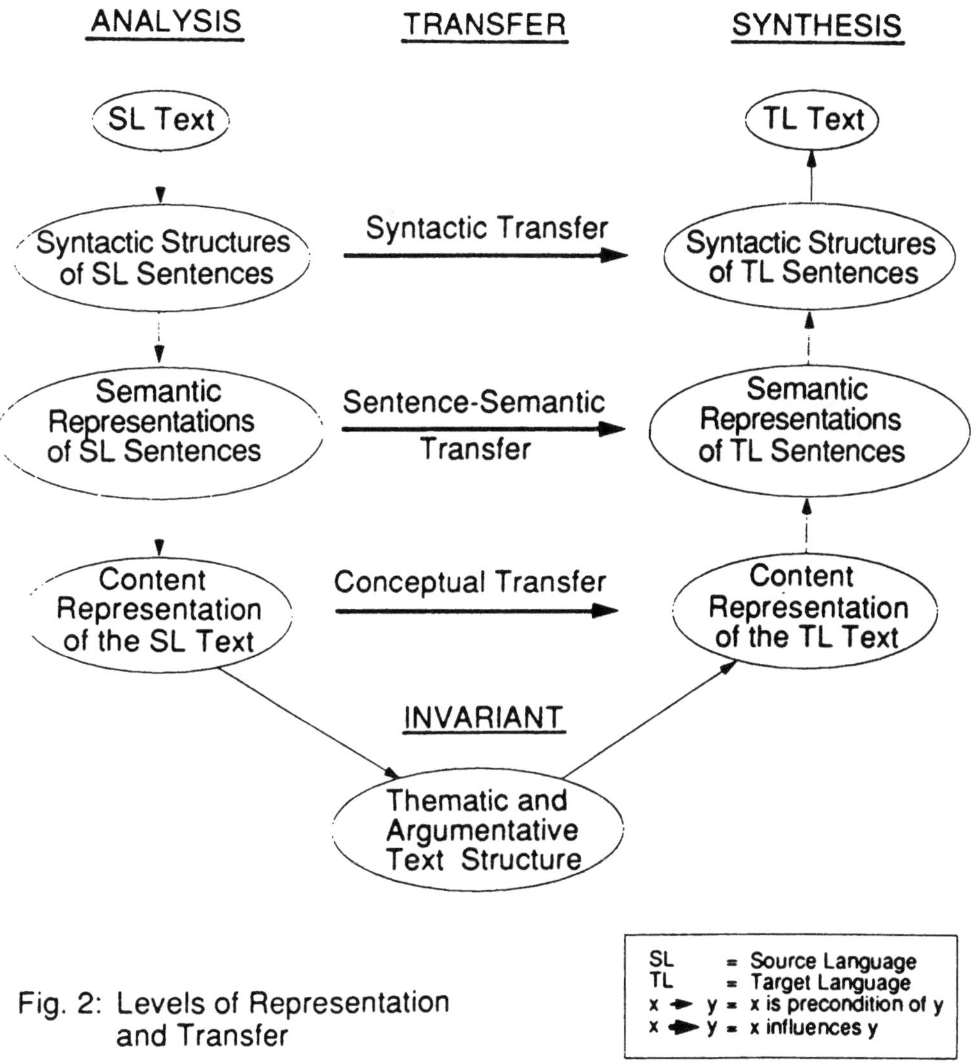

Fig. 2: Levels of Representation and Transfer

"euroversal" aspects (the semantic relations as well as the representations of time and modality are the same for every language within the EUROTRA community).

Figure 2 is to show how the interlingual approach might be combined with a multi-level transfer approach (for a more thorough argumentation in favour of such a model see Hauenschild 1986).

Constructing a working machine translation system corresponding to this model is, of course, a very ambitious enterprise. Whether it is at all possible to reach the ideal of machine translation as described above, is an open question which may be in the end impossible to answer. Still I am optimistic with respect to the insights about the nature of (human and machine) translation that one might gain in trying to construct such a system.

Note

* This work has been developed in the project KIT-FAST (KIT = Künstliche Intelligenz und Textverstehen = Artificial Intelligence and Text Understanding; FAST = Functor-Argument Structure for Translation), which constitutes the Berlin component of the complementary research project of EUROTRA-D and receives grants by the Federal Minister for Research and Technology under contract 1013211. I am obliged to my colleague Stephan Busemann, to Peter E. Pause and to Klaus Mudersbach for critical as well as encouraging comments, and to Margaret Garry for carefully reading and correcting my English.

References

Charniak, Eugene (1978): With Spoon in Hand This Must Be the Eating Frame. In: *TINLAP-2* (Theoretical Issues in Natural Language Processing). D. L. Waltz (ed.). New York: Association for Computing Machinery, pp. 187-193

Grosz, Barbara J. (1981): Focusing and Description in Natural Language Dialogues. In: *Elements of Discourse Understanding*. A. K. Joshi / B. L. Webber / I. A. Sag (eds.). Cambridge/London/New York: Cambridge University Press, pp. 84-105

Hajičová, Eva / Petr Sgall (1984): From Topic and Focus of a Sentence to Linking in a Text. In: *Computational Models of Natural Language Processing*. B. G. Bara / G. Guida (eds.). Amsterdam/New York/Oxford: Elsevier (North-Holland), pp. 151-163

Hauenschild, Christa / Peter E. Pause (1983): Faktoren-Analyse zur Modellierung des Textverstehens. In: *Linguistische Berichte* [88], pp. 101-120

Hauenschild, Christa (1985): Definite vs. Indefinite Interpretation of Russian Noun Phrases: A Proposal of a Format for Complex Evaluation Rules. In: *Journal of Semantics* 4, pp. 371-387

Hauenschild, Christa (1986): KIT/NASEV oder die Problematik des Transfers bei der maschinellen Übersetzung.
In: *Neue Ansätze in maschineller Sprachübersetzung: Wissensrepräsentation und Textbezug.* I. S. Bátori / H. J. Weber (eds.). Tübingen: Niemeyer, pp. 167-195

Hauenschild, Christa (1988): GPSG and German Word Order.
In: *Natural Language Parsing and Linguistic Theories.* U. Reyle / C. Rohrer (eds.). Dordrecht/Boston/Lancaster/Tokyo: Reidel, pp. 411-431

Hirst, Graeme (1981): *Anaphora in Natural Language Understanding. A Survey.* Berlin/Heidelberg/New York: Springer

King, Margaret / Sergei Perschke (1987): EUROTRA.
In: *Machine Translation Today: The State of the Art.* M. King (ed.). Edinburgh: Edinburgh University Press, pp. 373-391

Koller, Werner (1979): *Einführung in die Übersetzungswissenschaft.* Heidelberg: Quelle & Meyer (UTB 819)

Komissarov, V. N. (1973): *Slovo o perevode.* Moskva: Izdatel'stvo "Meždunarodnye otnošenija"

Nirenburg, Sergei / Victor Raskin / Allen B. Tucker (1987): The Structure of Interlingua in TRANSLATOR.
In: *Machine Translation. Theoretical and Methodological Issues.* S. Nirenburg (ed.). Cambridge/London/New York: Cambridge University Press, pp. 90-103

Pause, Peter E. (1983): Context and Translation.
In: *Meaning, Use, and Interpretation of Language.* R. Bäuerle / C. Schwarze / A. v. Stechow (eds.). Berlin/New York: de Gruyter, pp. 384-399

Shann, Patrick (1987): Machine Translation: A Problem of Linguistic Engineering or of Cognitive Modelling?
In: *Machine Translation Today: The State of the Art.* M. King (ed.). Edinburgh: Edinburgh University Press, pp. 71-90

Snell-Hornby, Mary (1988): The Role of Text-Linguistics in a Theory of Literary Translation.
To appear in: *Textlinguistik und Fachsprache – Akten des Internationalen Übersetzungswissenschaftlichen AILA-Symposions* (Hildesheim 1987). R. Arntz (ed.). Hildesheim: Olms

Tsujii, Jun-ichi (1986): Future Directions of Machine Translation.
In: *11th International Conference on Computational Linguistics, Proceedings of Coling '86.* Bonn: Institut für angewandte Kommunikations- und Sprachforschung, pp. 655-668

Van Dijk, Teun A. (1977): Sentence Topic and Discourse Topic.
In: *Papers in Slavic Philology* [1], pp. 49-61

Van Dijk, Teun A. / Walter Kintsch (1983): *Strategies of Discourse Comprehension.* New York: Academic Press

Christa Hauenschild

Tekststrukturo – kelkaj implicoj por perkomputila tradukado

Resumo

Mia ĉefa perspektivo en ĉi tiu artikolo estas lingvoteoria. Mi ŝatus diskuti la gravecon de tekststrukturo por tradukado ĝenerale, kaj por perkomputila tradukado, kiun mi konsideras speciala kazo de tradukado, samkiel kelkajn konsekvencojn kiujn oni povus aŭ devus derivi el tio. Post kelkaj ĝeneralaj rimarkoj pri la rolo de tekststrukturo en homa kaj perkomputila tradukado, en kiuj mi koncentriĝas al la aspekto de tema strukturigo de tradukota teksto (sekcio 1), mi esploras la interrilaton inter la supozo pri nevarieblaĵoj en tradukado kaj la interlingva aliro al tradukteorio kaj al perkomputila tradukado (sekcio 2). Kiel iuspecan kontraŭpruvon al la interlingva aliro sekcio 3 enkondukas kelkajn lingvospecifajn manierojn esprimi la teman strukturitecon de teksto, kio realiĝas parte en malsamaj kaj analogaj formoj de tema frazstrukturigo. Tiaj specifaĵoj kaj analogaĵoj kondukas nin al pledo favore al la transira aliro al tradukado (sekcio 4). La konkludo sekvas en sekcio 5: Necesas en perkomputila tradukado zorgi pri ambaŭ aspektoj de tradukado, t.e. kaj pri tio ke io restu senŝanĝa dum tradukado, kion oni povus prizorgi per interlingva ero de komputila traduksistemo, kaj pri tio ke io ja estu ŝanĝata dum la tradukproceso, kion eblus realigi per transira ero.

What Is a Cross-Linguistically Valid Interpretation of Discourse?

Jun-ichi Tsujii

Dept. of Electrical Engineering
Kyoto University
Yoshida-honmachi
Sakyo
Kyoto 606
Japan

tsujii%nagao.kuee.kyoto-u.junet%utokyo-relay.csnet@uunet.uu.net

1. Introduction

The pivot or interlingual approach has obvious advantages over the transfer approach, such as multi-linguality, high quality of translation, etc. However, there still remain many hard problems to be solved in designing a **true** interlingua. I discuss some of the problems in this paper, especially the problems concerning discourse representation.

2. Definitions of interlingua – different views

The crucial point in designing an **interlingua** is how to define it in a way which allows lexicographers and linguists to systematically relate expressions of individual languages to expressions of the **interlingua** and vice versa.

Researchers in the interlingual approach have already proposed various methods of defining the interlingua. The methods proposed so far can be roughly divided into three categories, each of which puts emphasis on different aspects of interlinguas.

One approach for defining an **interlingua** is to define the meanings of interlingual expressions in relation with a predetermined extra-linguistic domain. Concepts in a restricted domain, for example, physics, computer science etc., can be defined in the domain itself. That is, the concepts are defined by the **knowledge** of the domain. In some cases, the concepts are exactly the same as the concepts which are used in extra-linguistic processes such as problem-solving, deduction, inferences, etc. The technical terms of individual languages can be taken as mere labels denoting the concepts in the domain.

This approach defines an interlingua in a top-down fashion. It defines the concepts in a restricted domain, and then relates them to the words or expressions of individual languages.

On the other hand, the second approach functions rather in a bottom-up way. In this approach, one examines usages of words or expressions in an individual language and speculatively creates denoted concepts. In such a way, one will be able to establish **disambiguated** lexical items for the individual language. By comparing such disambiguated lexical items (or expressions) of various individual languages and merging equivalent ones, we will obtain a set of concepts in relation with the set of individual languages.

The **interlingual** concepts in this approach lack explicit definitions and are defined implicitly by usages of words or expressions of the individual languages. This makes it very hard for lexicographers to compare the concepts derived from different languages and find equivalent ones to merge them.

In order to judge the equivalence of concepts derived from different languages, they have to examine the usages of the words or expressions of individual languages which are related to the concepts. Lexicographers and linguists are required to have enough knowledge of each individual language in the set.

To avoid this difficulty, one can take a specific individual language as a **standard language** and use the disambiguated lexical items or expressions as the concepts to which words or expressions of other languages should be related.

This approach can be used as a design methodology of multi-lingual MT systems (More detailed discussions in this direction are found in Boitet, 1988). However, this approach can be seen as a two stage transfer approach and does not by itself contribute to the improvement of the quality of translations. In fact, a transfer based system can surely produce better translations than the systems in this approach.

So the third approach, the decomposition approach, comes in. The researchers in this approach first try to establish a relatively small set of **primitives** whose definitions are explicitly given or are supposed to be intuitively understandable by speakers of any language. Then, they try to give the definitions to the disambiguated lexical items by combining the primitives. We can also introduce certain kinds of **understanding processes** to improve translations by preparing inference rules based on these **primitives.**

If the set of **primitives** is complete, that is, if one can express all aspects of meaning by the combination of **primitives,** then we do not need the disambiguated lexical items at all. We need not compare and merge them on the basis of **primitives** but we can use the **primitives** directly as the basic items of the interlingua. This approach also recognizes the importance of structures organizing **primitives.**

I distinguished the following three kinds of **interlinguas,** which roughly corresponds to the above three approaches (Tsujii 1987).

- Interlingua as **Interpretation Results**
- Interlingua as a **Standard Language**
- Interlingua as a set of **Semantic Primitives**

None of the above three approaches has led us to the **true** interlingua. Furthermore, I doubt that such a **true** interlingua, at least one which can be used in some MT systems, exists at all.

In the meantime, we have to consider the problems of designing an **interlingua** from the engineering point of view. This means that we have to determine first what types of MT systems we want to design and then we can design an interlingua appropriate for the objectives. At least, from the point of view, the two main objectives of the interlingual approach, **multi-lingual translation** and **high quality translation,** should be discussed separately.

More specifically, if one wants to develop multi-lingual MT systems of a reasonable scale, the **Standard Language Approach** or the **Multi-Stage Transfer Approach** (Boitet 1988) might be a good idea to follow.

However, in order to realize a system based on this approach, one has to abandon the goal of **high quality translation.** One has to concentrate on the design methodologies of how to systematically establish a set of **neutral concepts** for a given set of individual languages, dictionaries, etc. Meanwhile, one has to ignore the quality of translations, or at least, one has to be ready to accept worse translation results than those produced by transfer based systems.

The research in this framework should concentrate on developing the methodologies which speed up and systemize the development of multi-lingual MT systems, etc.

On the other hand, the first and the third approach produce better translation results. The first approach, by its nature, can be applied only to a very restricted domain. We cannot expect that systems based on this approach will replace the currently available MT systems which aim to cover wide ranges of domains. However, the approach can be applied to the other types of MT systems which are pursued by various research groups such as CMU (Tomita/Carbonell 1986), ATR (Kurematsu 1987), etc.

In the following, I will discuss the possibility of the mixed approach of the first and the third in order to obtain better translation results.

3. Linguistic expressions and discourse understanding

In the last section, I briefly describes three different approaches to **interlingua**. The second and the third approaches stick to **linguistic meanings**. They aim to establish a set of **concepts** derived from individual languages or to establish a set of **primitives** to specify meanings of linguistic expressions.

On the other hand, the first approach tries explicitly to introduce **extra-linguistic knowledge** to define the meanings of interlingual expressions. That is, the interlingua in this approach can also be a framework for expressing **extra-linguistic** knowledge of the domain.

I believe that the first approach is inevitable for **high quality** MT systems, translation through **understanding** (Tsujii 1986), though it can be applied only to very restricted subject domains.

Though the decomposition approach captures certain aspects of **understanding**, I cannot believe that the approach can be applied to the meaning descriptions of concepts which are both highly specific to certain subject domains and can be used in knowledge-based processing in the domains.

On the other hand, we can also divide the three approaches into two groups. The first and second approaches try to define their interlinguas by **denoted concepts**, but the third approach does not.

The third approach presupposes that the relationships between linguistic expressions and the things expressed are not so straightforward as is supposed in the other approaches. It presupposes that we have to have a certain dynamic mechanism which relates the understanding results and the linguistic expressions.

In fact, though the first approach can capture the domain specific meanings of lexical items or expressions, there also exist words or expressions which cannot be directly related to **concepts** in restricted domains. In other words, we have to treat the other aspects of **understanding** which cannot be directly related to the knowledge of specific domains.

Straightforward examples are pronouns. Because they do not have fixed denoted concepts at all, it is obvious that we cannot replace them in interlingual expressions by predetermined **denoted concepts.**

They should be expressed structurally in the interlingual representation as reference relationships. Language dependent rules in the generation phase specify what kinds of reference relationships can be expressed by which pronouns. That is, we need a dynamic mechanism which relates understanding results and linguistic expressions.

In order to have such a dynamic mechanism, the understanding results should be properly structured to prepare sufficient information for choosing appropriate expressions. Simple reference relationships, for example, are not sufficient for appropriate generation of pronouns in discourse oriented languages such as Japanese, Chinese, etc.

For example, Takubo (1988) indicates that the usage of Japanese pronoun *kare*, which roughly corresponds to *he* in English, follows rules quite different from those of *he*. *Kare* can be used to refer to a man, only when the speaker judges that both the speaker and the hearer know him. Therefore, the two occurrences of *he* in the following examples should not be translated by *kare*. They should be translated into *Mr. Smith* or *Mr. Smith toiu hito* 'the man called Mr. Smith' (Takubo 1988).

A: I had to talk with Mr. Smith.
B: Who is **he**?
A: Oh, **he** is the lawyer who ...

Note also that, as Takubo (1988) shows, *Mr. Smith* should be translated in Japanese as *Mr. Smith toiu hito* 'the man called Mr. Smith' when the speaker judges that the hearer does not know him.

This example shows that the *interlingual* representation, from which we can generate appropriate referring expressions in Japanese, should not only express simple reference relationships but also be properly structured to represent **territory of information among the speaker and the hearer.**

Such a representaion is obviously far beyond the interlingua of the second approach which aims to design another **ideal** language. What we should do here is to design a language universal framework for expressing the understanding results of texts and to formulate language dependent rules relating understanding results and the linguistic expressions.

If we call the framework the interlingual representation, the interlingual representation should be structured to express the reference relationships, the territory of information, etc. The meanings of Japanese pronouns will be described in the lexicons or grammars by referring this structured interlingual representations.

The first approach is promising in the sense that it tries to **understand** texts in certain ways. However, it is insufficient in the sense that the degree of **understanding** required in MT is achieved only to a small extent.

We can escape in a very restricted subject domain from many serious problems caused by flexible relationships between words (nouns, verbs etc.) and the denoted concepts.

However, there appear a lot of words or expressions which cannot be directly related to concepts, even if we restrict our domain to a very narrow subject field. Pronouns are typical examples of such words. Other examples are shown in the following, most of which seem to require a suitable **discourse**-based treatment.

- adverbs: *even, only, certainly, probably,* etc.,
- conjunctions: *therefore, however, on the other hand, for examples,* etc.
- modal auxiliaries: *can, may, must,* etc.
- extended modal expressions: *it seems that, what I would like to say is,* etc.
- etc.

4. Text structure and translation

Our analysis of referring expressions in newspaper articles (Nagata 1987) shows that the appropriateness of Japanese referring expressions are highly dependent on text structures. The referring expressions here include pronouns, definite noun phrases, ellipses (zero pronouns) etc.

Ellipsis, for example, is appropriate when it refers to the focussed element in the immediately preceding sentence and the element remains focussed in the current sentence. If such an element is referred to by the other referring expressions, the text cohesion is destroyed.

Furthermore, even if the focussed element continues to be focussed in the succeeding sentence, the use of ellipsis is inadequate when a paragraph boundary exists between the two sentences. This fact indicates that, to generate ellipsis (zero pronoun) in Japanese, we have to refer to a certain structure beyond sentences. The same is true for the usages of the other kinds of referring expressions.

In the context of MT, the interlingual representation should express explicitly the structures of the source text, from which the language dependent rules for Japanese can generate appropriate referring expressions. The text structure here means something similar to the structures among **Discourse Segment** by B. Grosz or *Rhetorical Structures – RS* by the USC research group.

In Section 3, I indicated that the proper usage of Japanese pronouns requires a certain structure to express the territory of information. Here, we need another structure concerned with text organization.

In fact, we applied the RS to Japanese text (newspaper articles) and found that the structures given by the RST (Rhetorical Structure Theory) are useful for explaining the choices of referring expressions. That is, it seems possible, if not easy, to specify language (Japanese) dependent rules for choosing appropriate referring expressions based on the RSs of texts and the reference relationships among elements.

However, the problem in applying RST to MT is that the RSs of one language are not always the adequate RSs of other languages. That is, the RS of source texts cannot always be used as the RS of the target texts. Human translators often translate English texts into Japanese by splitting a sentence into several sentences, re-odering sentences, inserting appropriate sentential conjunctions which do not appear in English texts, etc. This means they often produce Japanese translations by using different RSs appropriate for Japanese.

We can say in short that RSs are language dependent structures and that we have to have more abstract structure representation of texts from which we can generate language dependent RSs. In fact, even in a mono-lingual mode of thinking, we can generate texts with different RSs whose **effects** are almost unchanged, by re-ordering sentences, inserting appropriate sentential conjunctions, using different modal expressions, etc.

Because RSs express the ways the writers organize texts to communicate their ideas, the abstract structures from which individual RSs can be generated should be the structures which express the writers' goals of communication. The abstract structure would be useful to express the **meanings** of not only referring expressions but also sentence connectives, speaker-related modal expressions and adverbs, etc.

Of course, we do not know the exact formalisms for this, but we can borrow various ideas from recent results of research in AI-based NLU and NLG where the researchers are highly interested in similar topics.

5. Conclusion

In this paper, I discussed some problems in designing an **interlingua** which are related to discourse representation.

In order to obtain **high quality translations**, we have to introduce various aspects of **understanding** texts. One possible way is to restrict the domain of translation to a very narrow field and introduce explicitly domain specific extra-linguistic knowledge.

However, even if we fix the domain, many words or expressions appear which cannot be related to the concepts in the domain. Most of them are related to the discourse structures or context in a broad sense, and should be treated dynamically in relation with abstract structures of texts. In order to solve these problems, we have to bridge the two different streams of research, the **MT** researches and the **AI** based NLU and NLG research.

References

Boitet, Christian (1988): Hybrid Pivot using M-structures for Multilingual Transfer-based MT Systems.
In: *SIG on Natural Language Processing and Communication*, Society of Electronic Engineers in Japan

Kurematsu, A. (1987): Natural Language Processing for Automatic Telephone Interpretation.
In: National Convention of the Society of Electronic Engineers in Japan [in Japanese]

Takubo, M. (1988): Management of Knowledge in Dialogue.
In: Report on Discourse, Semantics and Pragmatics, Kobe: Kobe University [in Japanese]

Tomita, Masaru / Jaime Carbonell (1986): Another Stride Towards Knowledge-based Machine Translation.
In: *11th International Conference on Computational Linguistics, Proceedings of Coling '86*. Bonn: Institut für angewandte Kommunikations- und Sprachforschung, pp. 633-638

Tsujii, Jun-ichi (1986): Future Directions of Machine Translation.
In: *11th International Conference on Computational Linguistics, Proceedings of Coling '86*. Bonn: Institut für angewandte Kommunikations- und Sprachforschung, pp. 655-668

Tsujii, Jun-ichi (1987): What is PIVOT?
In: *Machine Translation Summit* (Hakone 1987). Tokyo: Japan Electronic Industry Development Association

Jun-ichi Tsujii

Kio estas translingve valida interpreto de teksto?

Resumo

La pivota aŭ interlingva modelo havas evidentajn avantaĝojn kompare al la transira, sed restas multaj malfacilaj problemoj pri konstruado de vera interlingvo. La esenca malfacilaĵo estas kiel difini interlingvon tiel, ke leksikografoj kaj gramatikistoj povu per tiu difino interrilatigi la esprimojn de la interlingvo kun tiuj de aliaj lingvoj.

Oni proponis tri malsamajn metodojn. Unue, eblas difini interlingvon "desupre" per la scio pri limigita temtereno. Due, eblas difini "demalsupre", esplorante la uzon de vortoj en diversaj lingvoj, konjektante pri la signifataj konceptoj kaj konstatante kongruojn inter la lingvoj. Oni tiel ricevas malambiguigitan konceptaron, specifan por la elektita aro da lingvoj. La interlingvaj konceptoj ne havas eksplicitajn difinojn, do la lingvistoj devas sufiĉe regi ĉiun el la lingvoj en la aro. Por tion eviti eblas igi unu el la lingvoj norma, malambiguigante ĉion per ĝiaj konceptoj. Ĉi tiu metodo uzeblas por multlingva perkomputila tradukado, tamen tio estas dufaza transiro kaj malaltigas la tradukkvaliton. Trie, eblas difini interlingvon per malgranda aro da bazunuoj, eksplicite difinitaj aŭ senpere evidentaj. Se la bazunuaro estas kompleta, ĝiaj elementoj povas rekte funkcii en la interlingvo. Al la tri metodoj proksimume apartenas la tri specoj de interlingvoj, **rezulto de interpreto**, **norma lingvo** *kaj* **semantika bazunuaro**. *Neniu el ili estas vera interlingvo, kaj mi dubas ke tia ekzistas.*

Se oni tamen volas konstrui interlingvon, por multlingva tradukado kiel eble plej taŭgan el inĝeniera vidpunkto, necesas aboli la postulon pri altkvalita traduko kaj koncentriĝi al la difino de aro de konceptoj, neŭtralaj en difinita aro da lingvoj. La dua kaj tria metodoj baziĝas sur lingva signifo, dum la unua uzas eksterlingvan scion. Por altkvalita, perkomprena tradukado la unua metodo estas neevitebla, kvankam ĝi uzeblas nur pri tre mallarĝaj temterenoj. La bazunuara metodo ja ampleksas iom da kompreno, sed malhavas sufiĉan temspecifan precizecon.

Eblas alia grupigo: La unua kaj dua difinas per signifataj konceptoj. La tria tion ne faras, agnoskante ke kompreno ne funkcias nur per evidentaj rilatoj inter vortoj kaj konceptoj: Japan-angla komparo montras, ke por ĝuste traduki pronomojn necesas reprezenti la komunan scion de la interparolantoj. Tio grandskale transiras la eblecojn de interlingvokonstruado. En tre limigita temtereno eblas eviti tiujn problemojn. Sed ekzistas aro da vortoj kiuj ne rekte rilatas la konceptoj, sed strukturigas la tekston (ekz. adverboj, konunkcioj, modalaj helpverboj kaj esprimoj). Analizo de japanaj ĵurnalartikoloj montras ke referencaj esprimoj povas esti komprenataj nur per la tekststrukturo. Rolas tekstporcioj aŭ retorikaj strukturoj. Ili tamen estas lingvospecifaj, do necesas pli abstraktaj reprezentaĵoj por ebligi la tradukpaŝon inter lingvoj.

Por atingi altkvalitan tradukon necesas uzi tekstkomprenon. Eĉ se oni tre limigas la temterenon kaj aplikas eksplicitan terenspecifan eksterlingvan scion, necesas povi trakti tekststrukturigilojn. Por tio ni devas interligi la du esplordirektojn **perkomputila tradukado** *unuflanke kaj tekstkompreno kaj tekstgenero per* **artefarita inteligento** *aliflanke.*

Advanced Terminology Banks Supporting Knowledge-Based MT

Some reflections on the costs for setting-up and operating a terminological data bank (TDB)

Christian Galinski

Infoterm
affiliated to
Österreichisches Normungsinstitut
Postfach 130
A-1021 Wien
Austria

1. Introduction

TDB systems are a particular type of information system, handling terminological information, i.e. a special type of factual information on concepts and terms (or other symbols representing the concepts) as well as bibliographic information on the sources of the terminological information.

Advanced TDB systems therefore actually are computerized terminology documentation systems, combining computerized terminography at a high level with a specialized documentation system, thus becoming terminological knowledge data banks (TKDB) processing knowledge at the level of first order logic (i.e. conceptual logic) (Budin et al. 1988).

This study tries to evaluate the costs for the establishment of a TDB and for the input of terminological data in relation to the costs for the maintenance and updating of the terminological data.

2. The types of information handled by TDBs

Concepts of scientific and technical subject fields do not exist as such, but are created by man. New concepts – if they are **appropriate** – always rely on existing knowledge, i.e. on other concepts. After the creation of the concept, an existing or newly formed symbol (i.e. term or other symbol) is assigned to it in order to make it communicable in spoken or written form or by graphical or other representation. Terminologies (concepts and concept systems and the terms and other symbols assigned to them), therefore, can be regarded as artificial languages governed by principles of their own, which to a large extent differ from those of natural language. This is also the reason why particular methods and tools are needed for the handling and processing of terminologies – the so-called terminological data banks.

Concepts are the primary objects of data administration in a TDB. They can be represented in many ways by terms in various lexical forms within a text and/or by any kind of symbol (e.g. notation, graph, etc.). The link between all these representations is **the concept**. Since terms and other symbols develop at a pace and in a way different from that of concepts, which evolve within the framework of knowledge, the dynamics of conceptual change can only be controlled by recording the data on the systems of concepts, too. Only in this way it is possible to reduce the variety of representations of one concept and to disambiguate this concept during searches in the system. The biggest problem, however, is how to obtain sufficiently complete and reliable data for each concept record from subject specialists and to have these data regularly updated and automatically restructured.

At present the human mind is needed to discriminate concepts by conscious efforts. As for the computer, quite a comprehensive and sophisticated terminological data bank is needed to identify terms (representing concepts already contained in the bank) in a text as well as to extract "new" terms, which are encountered by the system for the first time.

2.1. Diverging development of concepts and terms

Undoubtedly the development of knowledge is much faster and its changes are more fundamental than that of language. In spite of all "creativity of language", de Saussure's "langue" at all its grammatical levels is very much governed by the linguistic norm, which is probably not so true for specialized languages than for the common language. The formation of new terms is impeded first of all by the very limited number of term elements to name new concepts. The number of concepts, on the other hand, increases more or less at the same pace as knowledge grows.

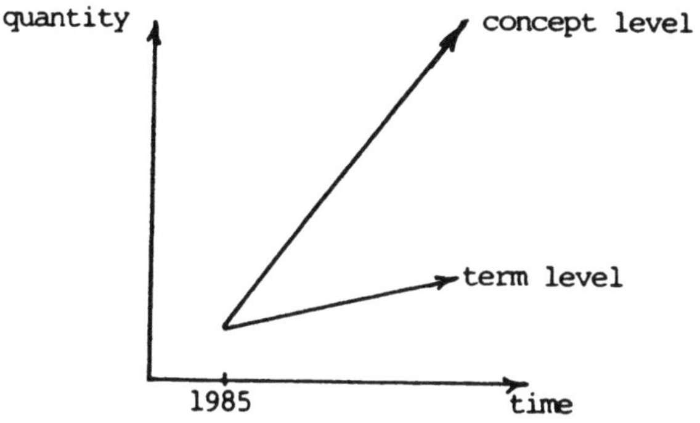

Fig. 1

Therefore, the quantitative development of concepts diverges considerably from that of terms. Some concepts vanish while most of the new concepts undergo changes and often become the genus of entire new concept systems, sometimes with and sometimes without a preceding change of meaning. These concept dynamics are not reflected and represented by the terms, which – as linguistic symbols – show much more stability than the concepts for which they stand. This could also be the reason why an automatic acquisition of knowledge by means of a reliable recognition of terms within specialized texts has failed so far.

Several arguments are usually voiced in favour of dictionary-type TDBs (see 3.) or the even less complex lexicographical term banks. It is argued that they do not necessarily require the special experience of neither the terminologist and terminographer (for running the TDB system) nor that of the subject specialist (concerning the quality of the terminological data prepared for input). But here one must accept the inevitable consequence of the renunciation of the expertise of both kinds of experts, namely a correspondingly low level of performance and reliability.

At present, the number of linguistic-lexicographical data categories of a term record in machine translation dictionaries is larger than the number of terminological data categories of a concept record. Machine translation experts tend to be absorbed by the problems encountered at the linguistic surface, i.e. the term level of specialized texts to be analyzed and translated by the computer. Since, however, the dynamics of concept development cannot be controlled by means of terms, it is advisable also to developers of machine translation systems to learn from the experience made at the beginning of this century in the field of conventional terminography. In the first quarter of the century several large scale projects for technical dictionaries failed because only lexicographical methods were applied. Terminological methods, starting from the concept as the basic unit of knowledge, however, proved feasible and yielded results which can be regarded as models still today.

Most probably machine translation oriented vocabulary-type TDBs (see 3.) are bound to come. Since they will contain also most of the conceptual data (maybe even more) being the result of conventional terminology work by subject specialists, it seems to be advisable to join forces instead of duplicating efforts for the preparation of high-quality terminological data, which can be applied in machine translation, in specialized lexicography as well as in so-called terminological knowledge systems for various purposes.

2.2. General language concepts and scientific-technical concepts

For the sake of completeness, it has to be mentioned that a type of concept for concrete objects or phenomena of man's environment such as sun, moon, ocean, lake, mountain, male, female, etc. exists, which is an integral part of the common language. These concepts differ from those of science and technology. They can be described, but not strictly defined and delimited. They can be grouped rather semantically than into systems of concepts.

There are probably other types of concepts, particularly in the humanities and social sciences, which carry already some characteristics of scientific-technical terminology and at the same time retain some of the ambiguities of common language. It has been proved recently that the principles and methods of scientific-technical terminology and terminography do also apply, with the methodology being adapted, to these terminologies (Infoterm/CEDEFOP 1987). Neither scientific-technical terminologies nor those of the humanities and social sciences can be controlled by linguistic-lexicographical means alone.

The majority of concepts in natural science and technology constitute the "semantic antipodes" of the above-mentioned common language concepts for which the application of computational linguistic methods may be sufficient. Of course linguistic-lexicographical methods can also be applied to the terms representing scientific-technical concepts, but do not suffice if it comes to concept systems and other means of representation of concepts.

2.3. Combination of terminographical and documentational data

Terminographical data are multifunctional in principle. They are structured according to the order of knowledge. This structure compares to the indexing language of information systems.

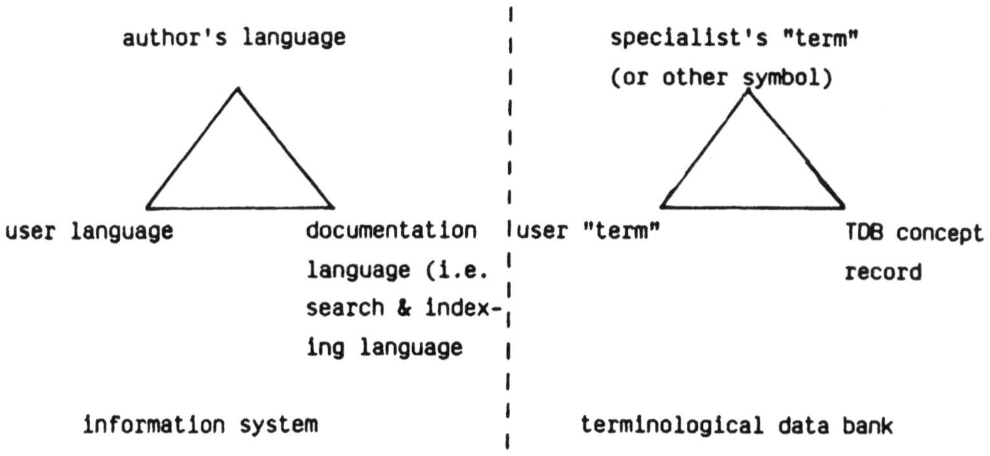

Fig. 2

The concepts (represented by terms and/or other symbols) as well as the systems of concepts can also be used for the structuring of all other types of factual or bibliographic information. If TDBs and information systems are well combined in an upgraded form, the concepts (within the conceptual systems) represent the microstructure of knowledge (a large part of which is laid down e.g. in specialized texts), while the documentation languages of the information system, which can also be applied to the terminological records, represent the macrostructure of that knowledge.

For the sake of

- high precision in the updating and maintenance of terminological data;
- diachronic control of the dynamics of concept development;
- control of the contents of texts and parts of texts;
- accurate retrieval from the terminological files;

it is necessary to

- apply the methods of conventional and computerized terminography (which can well be used in combination with computerized lexicographical methods);

- implement the conceptual relationships in addition to the information only referring to the concept as an isolated unit of knowledge which can be covered by one record each;

- provide the necessary formal links between the records representing conceptual relationships as well as other relationships and cross-references;

- foresee n-dimensional terminological record structures as well as n-dimensional file structures in principle (so that records and file structures can become more sophisticated, if necessary, at a later stage);

- design easy-to-handle man-machine interfaces necessary for a fast performance without restricting the complexity of the terminological data bank by those interfaces;

and to

- combine the methods of terminography and documentation in order to maintain control of all sources of terminological information.

This is true regardless of which technical aids are used, which computer programmes are implemented and which applications are intended.

3. Types of terminological data banks

The first large TDBs were systems to back-up translation in translation departments or services of large companies or public institutions. They handled a more or less limited number of data categories in a terminological format designed for translation purposes. Since the terminological records, which they contain, are not linked reflecting the conceptual relationships between the concepts, they represent so-called dictionary-type terminological data banks (TDB/DT) (Felber 1983).

3.1. Vocabulary-type TDBs

Towards the beginning of the eighties these "grand old systems" proved to be inappropriate for application by subject specialists, requiring computer assistance for research and development activities as well as tools of a higher degree of precision to access scientific-technical information at the workplace and from external information sources. This requires TDB systems of a higher degree of complexity and sophistication on the basis of

- an extended terminological format accommodating more data categories;
- a record structure of high complexity, allowing for various kinds of combinations of data categories and data elements, besides the wellknown repeatability by language and repeatability within language (ISO 6156-1987);
- a complex terminology file structure, allowing to represent conceptual relationships by means of links between related concept records.

Such TDB systems are called vocabulary-type terminology data banks (TDB/VT) (Felber 1983). In the course of the organization of the first International Congress on Terminology and Knowledge Engineering (Czap/Galinski 1987) a new type of TDB system was conceived for the purpose of a comprehensive information and knowledge management (Galinski/Nedobity 1987). Such systems are now in the process of implementation under the heading of knowledge logistics (Ericsson 1987) and can be called terminological knowledge data banks (TKDB) (Budin et al. 1988).

3.2. Dictionary-type TDBs

Computer technology and software development have opened new paths for the design and use of terminological data banks. In the past, for instance, it was hardly possible to implement TDB/VT for various reasons, such as:

- **limitation of hardware and software configurations**
  Some of the first term banks were developed from software designed for documentation purposes, which lacked the capacity to process the repeatability as well as multiple combinability of many data elements of a terminological record;
- **limitation with respect to user needs, retrieval and output requirements**
  Others were developed for terminological purposes, however, data categories were limited in order to increase the retrieval speed and to satisfy the user needs (mostly translators) at the time of their establishment;
- **lack of experience and theoretical foundation**
  Many data categories, particularly those for the handling of conceptual relationships, were not yet investigated sufficiently;

- **lack of appropriate terminological data**
  Systematically prepared terminological data were either not readily available or did not exist for those fields in which they were needed; even high-quality terminological data in machine-readable form for testing hardware and software were not available;

- **lack of qualified, properly trained terminologists and terminographers**
  Terminologists or terminographers aware of the necessity and able to record terminological data of high complexity had not yet been trained.

In general it was not considered necessary to develop highly sophisticated TDB/VT for purposes which – at the surface – required only a limited number of data categories and functions. Besides that it was hoped to save costs and to avoid time-consuming terminology work by subject specialists. Therefore, TDB/DT systems of reduced complexity and sophistication had been designed particularly satisfying the limited needs of human translators as presumed.

This is one of the reasons why the existing large TDB systems proved incompatible or inappropriate to machine translation systems, too.

3.3. Terminological knowledge data banks

Terminological knowledge systems are developed as the core components of a comprehensive information and knowledge management not only because they are just good for storage and retrieval purposes, but also because our natural, technical and colloquial languages are poorly suited to the task of ordering knowledge items (including terminological and other factual information) in a systematic way as well as of retrieving stored texts and other representations of complex knowledge. If such a system is to continue to perform in an adequate manner after the set-up and start-up phase, particularly in a multifunctional environment with a high increase in the total amount of information, it needs a minimum degree of complexity and sophistication from the very beginning.

Advanced terminological data banks of the kind described above are multifunctional in principle like the terminographical data they contain. They can be used for various purposes in the framework of information/knowledge management and transfer. Machine translation obviously would benefit from the existence of such advanced terminological data banks which – as knowledge data banks – could supplement the electronic dictionary necessary in machine translation systems with those data necessary to translate specialized texts with a high degree of reliability.

4. The costs for setting-up and operating a TDB

In the case of some large TDB/DT systems developed for the purpose of supporting human translation, it was assumed that a terminological data bank of a simple structure and low complexity would serve the "limited" needs of the users (i.e. the translators) best. This, however, applies only under very special conditions. If, for instance, the number of synonyms is drastically reduced by terminological regulation of one kind or other before the data input, if the variety of text types is limited and the texts themselves are of a highly homogene or even quasi-standardized nature as well as if the terminological data bank as a whole is more or less monofunctional, simple or even primitive TDBs may prove quite successful and highly satisfying in their results.

In all other cases where TDBs are applied multifunctionally as well as in an environment of unrestricted development of knowledge and its semiotic representation, the decision on a simple TDB system of low sophistication will be recognized as wrong at a certain stage, where it hardly can be corrected any more. This results in a situation where one has either to put up with a steady decline of system performance and rising cost for the maintenance and updating of data or to redesign the whole TDB system completely. In most cases, when the system is redesigned only a small number of records or terminological data contained therein can be transferred by conversion programmes from the old system to the new one without human intervention.

If one tries to save on the input side during the development and implementation of the TDB, one should be aware of the fact that this sum must be paid back at a much higher rate eventually during the operation of the TDB. It will also become necessary to regulate user-system interaction in order to keep it from becoming intolerably expensive. In the course of time such a TDB system largely fails to fulfill the purpose for which it was conceived and to accomplish what had been expected initially.

Only a TDB designed without built-in limitations, so that its structure can be further developed in order to meet future requirements, can increase its holdings, adapt to new developments and control the dynamics of conceptual development.

4.1. The relationship between the degree of complexity and sophistication and the costs for the establishment and operation of a TDB

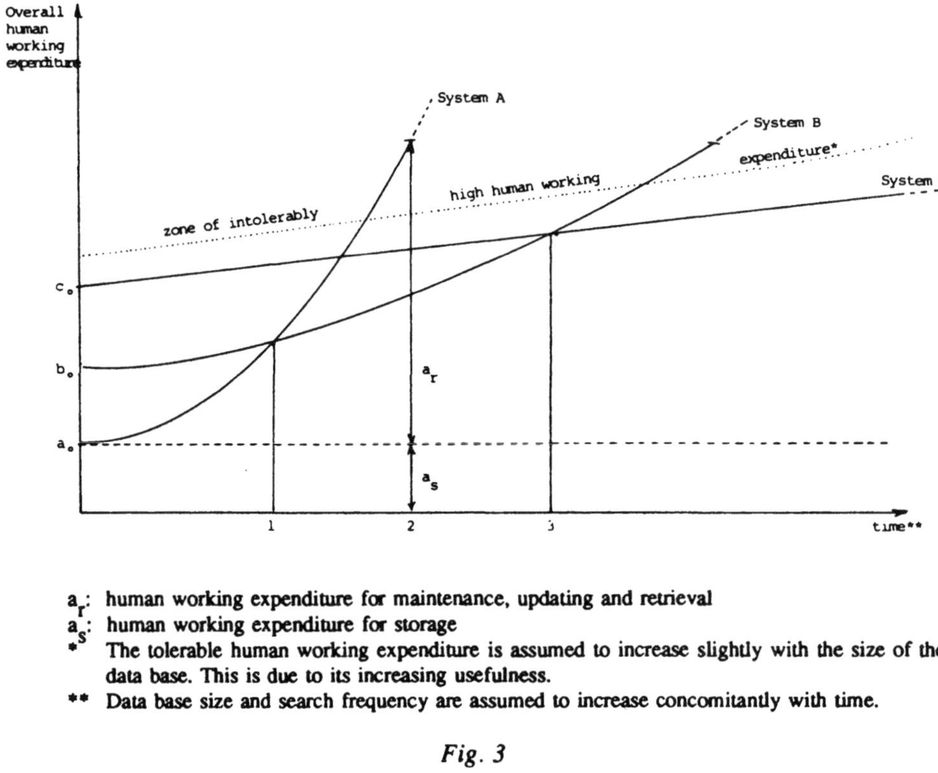

a_r: human working expenditure for maintenance, updating and retrieval
a_s: human working expenditure for storage
* The tolerable human working expenditure is assumed to increase slightly with the size of the data base. This is due to its increasing usefulness.
** Data base size and search frequency are assumed to increase concomitantly with time.

Fig. 3

Three terminological data bank systems, "A", "B" and "C", are depicted in this figure.

"A" is a system of low complexity and sophistication with low initial human working expenditure a and little investment in hardware and software, because at the time the system is initiated, no search costs and only relatively low input costs are incurred. But this system has a steep cost increase when it begins to be used and hence a low survival rate.

"B" is a system of a medium degree of complexity and sophistication involving more initial human working expenditure b and more investment in hardware and software than "A". At the beginning of being used, the system cost curve resembles very much that of "A". Then it shows its advantage over "A" in terms of costs for storage, maintenance, updating and retrieval. In spite of the capacity for many more records than in the case of TDB "A", its survival strength is limited, too.

By contrast to "A" and "B", the TDB system "C" is much more expensive at its initial stage, but its overall operation costs, which include those for the recording, input, updating, maintenance and retrieval of terminological data, which are largely determined by the amount of human work involved, will be lower after a number of years and will not rise exponentially. It does, however, have the handicap of a costly start-up period, and only shows its benefits afterwards and particularly in a multifunctional environment and/or with very large holdings.

The costs for system "C" must, therefore, be seen as the minimum investment to achieve the objectives of a reliable, multifunctional, large and stable high-performance TDB system.

TDB system "C" represents a terminological knowledge databank (TKDB), handling all types of information in written or other graphical representation as units of knowledge or parts of texts by using a combination of advanced terminographical methods (to control the "microstructure" of knowledge by means of the concepts and concept systems) and up-graded documentational methods (to control the "macrostructure" of knowledge, by means of the so-called documentation languages, subdividing the documents, including terminological and other records, bibliographic data, abstracts or any parts of a document into manageable sets of items).

4.2. The advantages of TDB/VT and TKDB

Conceptual relationships implemented in TDBs make it possible to

- clarify the equivalency between terms of different languages, which should represent the same concept, with a higher degree of reliability;

- find unknown terms for concepts of which only the position within the system of concepts is known;

- control synonymy as well as homonymy (particularly horizontal and vertical series homonyms);

and

- allow for at least semi-automatic updating/revision of related records after the revision of any of the records.

Via the concept and its conceptual relationships to other concepts the user is guided to the individual units of knowledge and information which he is looking for. Thus, information loss is kept at a low level. At the same time "noise" (i.e. false or ambiguous information resulting in irrelevant or even misleading responses) can be kept at a controllable level.

In contrast to this, an ever increasing human effort is needed in TDB/DT systems to suppress noise under an intolerable level.

Every new record or revision of an existing record necessitates the checking of other – particularly conceptually related – records. If the system does not provide any indication as to which record(s) should be looked at, the time and efforts needed for checking and cross-checking records will increase exponentially, if a high degree of reliability is to be preserved while the efficiency of the checking process is bound to decrease.

4.3. User-acceptance and staff qualification requirements

Low-complexity TDB may appear markedly user-friendly at the first glance, because they obviate the necessity of time-consuming training for the application of the system. But its disadvantages in form of a steep increase of the level of noise as well as its decrease in the reliability of individual items of information, resulting in a loss of reliability of the system as a whole, soon become obvious. Besides that, information specialists are still required to use these systems effectively. Nevertheless, the kind and extent of the information loss on the one hand and the increase in noise on the other hand, will develop in a way uncontrollable by the user as well as by the system operator.

4.4. Maintaining the reliability of the data

A TDB of a low degree of complexity and sophistication only allows for **formal** methods in carrying out the maintenance and updating of terminological information. This inevitably results in the **exponential** increase of human efforts and therefore of costs for maintaining a constant level of reliability, even in the case of a **linear** increase in the amount of terminological information.

In order to allow for an automatic or at least semi-automatic data maintenance and updating the number of data categories of the terminological format, the complexity of the file structure and the number of files as well as links between files have to be upgraded in the course of a constant increase in the amount of terminological data. This suggests the design of TDB systems with

- an n-dimensional record structure, allowing for an unrestricted increase in data categories;

- an n-dimensional file structure;

- no restrictions concerning the number of files and kind of links between files

in principle – in practice one will have to compromise.

If not, the reliability of individual items of terminological information constituting the overall reliability of the TDB system is at stake. The more data categories, data elements and records are interlinked under formal **and** conceptual aspects, the more the system allows for an at least semi-automatic **systematic** updating and maintenance of its holdings. The terminological information of new records as well as changes in existing records are then immediately matched with information in other conceptually or formally related interlinked records. Thus "noise" and loss of information is kept at a low level, while maintaining a high level of reliability of the system as a whole.

5. Conclusions

If knowledge is compared to a large storehouse with many partitions and shelves accommodating many containers full of parts or components for products, the documentation languages represent the order of the partitions, shelves and containers, while terminology represents the order within the containers. In the course of the development of new models and products, the degree of change within the containers is higher than that of the containers, shelves and partitions and ultimately of the whole storehouse.

The most widespread and oldest style of leadership is "management by ignorance". The occasionally disastrous consequences of this style have been obvious for a long time. Information management today has been recognized to be of vital importance to every kind of institution and organization. Nevertheless astonishingly little effort is being made in the information field to acquire the basic knowledge of and experience with the principles and methods of terminology as well as documentation languages crucial to information management (comp. GfK-SIG/IS 1985).

"Management by ignorance" in the information management of any institution or organization inevitably leads to a "management of ignorance" of the institution or organization as a whole resulting in "noise", communication losses, loss of time in search for information, etc. translating into high operational costs. This also holds true for the utilization of TDB systems of low complexity and sophistication in machine translation.

Note

This contribution has been triggered by the Recommendations for Classification "Free text in information systems. Capabilities and Limitations" (GfK/SIG-IS 1985). The similarities in the problems incurring during operation between free text information systems and low complexity TDB are so striking that whole parts of the recommendations just needed to be slightly adapted.

References

Budin, G. et al. (1988): Terminology and knowledge data processing.
In: *Terminology and knowledge engineering. Supplement.* Proceedings of the International Congress on Terminology and Knowledge Engineering, 29 Sept.-1 Oct. 1987, Trier (FRG). Frankfurt: Indeks, pp. 50-60

CEDEFOP / Infoterm (1987): *Tools for mutlilingual institutional work in the field of vocational training.*
A CEDEFOP-Infoterm publication. Berlin: CEDEFOP, 1st ed.

Czap, H. / C. Galinski (eds.) (1987): *Terminology and knowledge engineering.* Proceedings of the International Congress on Terminology and Knowledge Engineering, 29 Sept.-1 Oct. 1987, Trier (FRG).
Frankfurt: Indeks

Ericsson (1987): *Beiträge zur Wissenslogistik. CAT – Computer aided translation. 1. Anwendertreffen // Contributions to knowledge logistics. CAT – Computer aided translation. First user group meeting.*
Stuttgart: Ericsson

Felber, H. (1983): Computerized terminography in TermNet: the role of terminological data banks.
In: *Term banks for tomorrow's world.* Translating and the Computer 4. Proceedings of a conference, 11-12 Nov. 1982, London. London: Aslib, pp. 8-20

Galinski, C. / W. Nedobity (1986): *A terminological data bank as a management tool.*
(Infoterm 3-86 en) Wien: Infoterm

Gesellschaft für Klassifikation. Spezielle Interessensgruppe Indexierungssprachen (SIG-IS) (1985): Recommendations for Classification. EK-03 (en) Free text in information systems. Capabilities and Limitations (GfK/SIG-IS 1985).
In: *International Classification* 12 [2], pp. 95-98

International Organization for Standardization (ISO) (1987): *Magnetic tape exchange format for terminological/lexicographical records (MATER).*
(International Standard ISO 6156-1987) Genève: ISO

Christian Galinski

Altkvalitaj terminologiaj bankoj por perkomprena aŭtomata tradukado
Kelkaj ideoj pri la kostoj de starigo kaj funkciigado de terminologiaj informbankoj

Resumo

Terminologiaj bankoj estas specialaj informsistemoj, kiuj enhavas indikojn pri konceptoj kaj terminoj samkiel bibliografiajn referencojn al la fontoj de tiuj informoj. En ili kombiniĝas perkomputila terminografio kaj faka dokumentado, tiel ke ili fakte estas terminologiaj sciobankoj.

Terminoj ĉiam etikedas jam ekzistantan scion pri faktoj, tiel ke la ĉefa ligilo de ĉiuj ĉirkaŭaj informoj estas la koncepto mem. Tamen la disdividiĝo de konceptoj progresas pli rapide ol la donado de terminoj. Homa cerbo kapablas identigi konceptojn kaj iliajn terminojn, sed komputilo bezonas por tiu malfacila tasko ampleksan kaj kompleksan terminan informbankon.

En la ĉiutaga vivo kaj ankaŭ en la sociaj sciencoj multaj konceptoj povas esti priskribitaj, sed ne precize limigitaj. Natursciencaj kaj teknikaj terminoj havas malan karakteron.

Pro la multfunkcieco de terminologiaj informoj necesas kombini la metodojn kaj ilojn de dokumentado kaj terminografio, kio validas sendepende de la uzataj helpiloj kaj sistemoj.

En la okdekaj jaroj oni komencis forlasi la unuajn, grandajn terminbankojn destinitajn al perkomputila tradukado kaj nun strebas al pli fajnaj sistemaranĝoj, la t.n. vortlistecaj terminbankoj.

La kostoj por starigo kaj funkciigado de termina sciobanko dependas de la grado de komplekseco. La sciobanko enhavu i.a. indikojn pri konceptrilatoj, kiuj permesas pli fidinde precizigi la samsignifecon inter malsamlingvaj terminoj, trovi nekonitajn terminojn kaj rekoni sinonimecon kaj homonimecon. Tiaj sciobankoj ankoraŭ devas esti uzataj de trejnitaj fakuloj.

Se oni komparas scion al granda stokejo kun multaj ĉambroj kun bretaroj sur kiuj staras kestoj plenaj de eroj de iuj produktoj, la dokumentada lingvo reprezentas la ordon de la ĉambroj, bretaroj kaj kestoj, dum la terminologio reprezentas la ordon interne de la kestoj. Dum evoluas novaj modeloj kaj produktoj, pli granda ŝanĝo okazas interne de la kestoj, ol inter la kestoj, bretaroj kaj ĉambroj kaj lastakonsekvence en la tuta stokejo.

La malnova gvidostilo "direktado per nescio" tro facile fariĝas direktado fare de nescio. En informadministrado tia evoluo havus altgrade nedezirindajn sekvojn.

Terminologia Esperanto-Centro

Efforts for Terminological Standardization in the Planned Language

Wera Blanke

Terminologia Esperanto-Centro
Otto-Nagel-Straße 110
Postfach 113-05
DDR-1141 Berlin

It is not the aim of this paper to outline the special suitability of the planned language Esperanto for automatic processing of language data – other authors have already done this.

Schubert (1988: 205), for instance, mentions three reasons why the software firm BSO chose Esperanto for its "Distributed Language Translation" project as intermediate language for the semiautomatic multilingual translation. After some (not particularly essential) modifications of its grammar in order to increase its unambiguity it was in his opinion better suited for this purpose than all three kinds of possible competitors:

Esperanto lämpar sig för mellanspråksfunktionen i ett datoröversättningssystem bättre än

1. **folkspråk**, eftersom mellanspråket måste vara syntaktiskt oambiguöst, och folkspråken är på språktecknets formsida för oregelbundna;
2. **formella symbolsystem**: Eftersom mellanspråket som enda förbindelselänk mellan utgångs- och målspråk måste återge textens fullständiga innehåll med alla nyanser, är konstgjorda system genom själva sin beskaffenhet otillräckliga [...];

3. **andra planspråk** (volapük, ido, novial, interlingua m fl) eftersom mellanspråket måste äga ett **autonomt** semantiskt system som är oberoende av utgångs- och målspråken. Ett sådant system, som gör ett konstgjort och i början referensspråksberoende system till ett självständigt mänskligt språk, kan inte skapas, utan det kan bara uppstå genom långvarigt oreflekterat bruk av språket i en tillräckligt stor språkgemenskap. Av alla planspråksprojekt har bara esperanto genomgått denna utveckling fullständigt [...].

('For the function of an intermediate language in a machine translation system Esperanto is better suited than

1. **ethnic languages**, because the intermediate language must be syntactically unambiguous and ethnic languages are on the form side of the linguistic sign too irregular for this;
2. **formal symbol systems**: Since the intermediate language as the only link between the source and the target languages needs to render the full content of the text with all its nuances, artificial symbol systems are inherently insufficient [...];
3. **other planned languages** (Volapük, Ido, Novial, Interlingua etc.) since the intermediate languages needs to possess an **autonomous** semantic system which is independent from the source and target languages. Such a system, which turns an artificial and in the beginning reference language-dependent system into a human language of its own right, cannot be made. It can only come about through long-standing unreflected use of the language in a sufficiently large language community. Of all projects of planned languages, only Esperanto has undergone this development completely [...].')

These are obviously qualities which are relevant also for information retrieval and documentation; Esperanto is accordingly well-suited for this purpose; its significance for artificial intelligence is as yet little explored.

In spite of all these advantages, one chief disadvantage impedes its universal use as international language in these fields: the insufficiently developed vocabulary of technical terms. The now existing about 200 – 300 technical dictionaries (see Haferkorn 1962, Ockey 1982) do not meet the demand in quantity and, to some extent, in quality required for these purposes.

In the following I shall try to outline a few reasons for this shortcoming, as well as initiatives designed to remedy it.

1. Some problems in the development of terminologies in Esperanto

1.1. Reciprocal dependence of specialized literature and terminology

In ethnic languages – at least in the so-called big ones, used worldwide in science and technology – specialized dictionaries are usually by-products of specialized literature. New terms usually come about through the spontaneous naming of new products, materials and processes (as so-called shop-terms) or as their translations in other languages as a result of taking over or describing the products, materials and processes. No country can afford not to produce such information literature simply because of a lack of local terms.

The planned language does not know this economic pressure. Though Esperanto is increasingly used in technical language and the number of lectures, articles, books and conferences dealing with scientific subjects is rapidly increasing all this is still stimulated and supported by the enthusiasm of those who have realized the **potential** advantage of a neutral homogeneous means of information. The qualitative improvement which would result in a **general** interest in this new means of information and, subsequently, general efforts to perfect it from a terminological point of view as well, has not yet developed. We are therefore confronted with, among other things, the following vicious circle, stated simply: there does not exist sufficient specialized literature from which to extract reliable terminologies, and it cannot be developed to the desired extent because of the lack of these very terminologies. The self-evident result is that the attractiveness for specialists remains limited for the time being.

1.2. Synonymity through natural development

Since the authors of scientific-technical literature in Esperanto belong to different language groups regarding their mother tongue and often live geographically isolated from their planned-language colleagues, we should not be surprised if they find different solutions when translating technical terms from ethnic languages. In addition, technical dictionaries, if they exist, are not always available to those who need them. This situation may arise for reasons linked to differences in currency, for instance. As in ethnic languages, therefore, equivalent expressions develop which rather obstruct than promote technical communication.

Since the number of Esperanto colleagues in the world is not yet excessively large, the situation is especially suitable for working out a common solution. This is, however, not always sufficiently exploited.

1.3. Non-congruence of ethno-language definitions

Since technical inventions and scientific discoveries which are initially named in Esperanto are not usual at this moment we have to conclude that Esperanto terms are, in general, translations of ethnic terms. It would therefore pay to scrutinize this initial material.

Since internationality is also an important criterion concerning the technical development of the planned language, it seems reasonable to base it, if possible, on multilingual rather than monolingual dictionaries. How thing may be in practice I should like to indicate with an example.

The terminology commission of the railwaymen's International Esperanto Federation (with branches in 19 countries) has for years been working on an Esperanto version of a six-language dictionary published by the International Railway Union (UIC) which, therefore, may be considered authentic material. It has one decisive shortcoming, however: it does not contain any definitions – "die Schwierigkeit liegt darin, daß im Eisenbahnwesen die Definitionen der Fachtermini in den einzelnen Ländern zu einem beträchtlichen Teil voneinander abweichen" (Hoffmann 1981: 2).

Similar things can probably also be found in other technical fields.

1.4. Unsystematic presentation

The lack of conformity of the content of technical terms which makes their homogeneous definition more difficult if not impossible also partly explains another shortcoming of many technical dictionaries in national languages: their lack of systematization. Terminologies are frequently presented in alphabetical order which makes the survey and the orientation in the structure of any one technical field additionally difficult. If such lists of technical terms are simply "translated" in the same alphabetical order (as is often done, unfortunately), inaccuracies and "false friends" will almost inevitably result. Chiefly, however, an essential advantage of the planned language which bears special weight for automatic data processing would be lost: its regularity. In combinations with systematic groupings and appropriate classifications, this regularity would make possible an exact expression of meaning to an extent only rarely possible in ethnic languages.

1.5. Specialization and integration

According to Hornung (1981: 1), the qualitative drawbacks of a great number of terms such as inexact and unsystematic definitions, the lack of systematic motivation in the selection of names, ambiguity, synonymy and others are being further intensified by the fact "daß zwei Prozesse, die ständig zunehmende Spezialisierung der Disziplinen in sich und ihre Verflechtung untereinander, gleichzeitig ablaufen, wobei letztere zur Herausbildung von Mischterminologien führt. Die Kurzfristigkeit, in der die sprachliche Bewältigung der genannten Erscheinungen erfolgen muß, stellt eine Selbstregulierung der terminologischen Wortschätze, ähnlich wie sie in den allgemeinsprachlichen erfolgt, immer mehr in Frage". Hornung therefore comes to the conclusion that it is required "die für eine Überführung in eine Plansprache vorgesehenen Termini vorher nach der Methodologie der Terminologienormierung zu standardisieren".

Though this reasoning is, no doubt, correct, its realization, however, is hardly possible in view of the present economic and personnel situation of the only really functioning planned language.

Therefore, in order to get useful terminological solutions despite the very limited resources of the Esperanto community, it would be important to base them on ethno-lingual materials which are systematically classified and defined, elaborated by international bodies, authorized and regularly brought up to date. So are most of the terminological standards of relevant international organizations, chiefly the International Standardizing Organization (ISO) and the International Electrotechnical Commission (IEC).

2. International terminological standardization – an historical excursus

2.1. ISA and ISO

Without standardization in science and technology, the 20th century industrial revolution would be hardly imaginable. Three phases can be determined in the process of standardization: object standardization, standardization of terms and terminological systems, and standardization of terminological principles.

The rapid industrialization at the beginning of this century required clear rules for the standardized production of machine parts and other (semi-finished) products (**Sach-Normung**, "object standardization"). But it soon became evident that the standardization of objects (and processes) was not possible without simultaneous agreement on their names. Terminological standardization ("Terminologie-Normung", also called **terminologische Einzelnomung**) was the result. This, however, leads "zu mangelhaften Ergebnissen, solange sie nicht durch einheitliche Grundsätze geleitet wird. Es ist verständlich, daß sich diese Erkenntnis erst durchsetzen konnte, nachdem man 10 bis 20 Jahre lang Einzelnormung ohne kodifizierte Grundsätze betrieben hatte" (Spiegel 1985: 641). This codification is called **terminologische Grundsatznormung**, i.e. "standardization of terminological principles".

Object standardization and standardization of terms in most countries began during or soon after World War One. They were (and are being) organized by national, usually governmental standards bodies, 17 of which formed the International Federation of the National Standardizing Associations (ISA) in 1928. World War Two interrupted their cooperation. When the federation was reconstructed in 1946 it became the International Standardizing Organization (ISO) with a membership of 74 national standards bodies by 1982. Spiegel writes (1985: 639): "Jede der nationalen Normungsorganisationen verfügt in den großen Ländern über hunderte von hauptamtlichen Mitarbeitern und über viele tausende von ehrenamtlichen Sachverständigen. Diese Mitarbeiter teilen sich auf 100 oder mehr Normenausschüsse auf", which in addition to object standardizing in their specialized fields are also occupied with the relevant terminological standardization.

International terminology standardization is organized the same as the national one: the major international umbrella organizations of the national standards bodies, ISO and IEC, have international Technical Committees (TC) which work, at the same time, on object and terminology standardization. Under the ISO, 180 such TCs are dealing with many different disciplines (only electrical engineering in its widest meaning is dealt with by the IEC).

The ISO/TC number 37 (now called "Terminology – Principles and Coordination") differs from the other TCs by being exclusively occupied with elaborating, standardizing and bringing up to date principles which are to be applied uniformly in the terminological standardization of the individual disciplines.

2.2. Pioneers of principle standardization: Wüster and Drezen

In 1936, the ISA set up this special committee for terminology and terminological lexicography. This had become possible due to two men, Eugen Wüster, Austria, and Ėrnest Karlovič Drezen of the Soviet Union. Wüster's international renown as the founder of the General Theory of Terminology (GTT), the significance of his doctor's thesis in 1931 which is still considered an important standard work (Wüster 1931), and the key function of Infoterm, his last foundation, in international terminological work today, to name but a few of his lasting contributions, make it unnecessary to say more about the terminologist Wüster. But E. K. Drezen has also gone down in the history of terminology standardization. He was one of the five translators who put Wüster's standard work into Russian. Like Wüster he was an engineer. As an expert in terminology, which in the multi-nation state Soviet Union was of special importance, the All-Union Committee for Standardization (VKS) appointed him in 1934 as the head of its newly founded terminology commission. In the same year, he submitted to the ISA conference in Stockholm a report on the problem of the internationalization of scientific and technical terminology (Drezen 1935). In this report which "bleibt bis heute ein Klassiker der Terminologie-Wissenschaft" (Warner 1983: 82), he made two proposals which were carried unanimously and implemented, though in different ways. He proposed to:

1) establish a key to terminology which, with the aid of internationally comprehensible roots of words, is to make possible the development of an international terminology,

2) set up an international commission dealing with this and similar tasks.

It is a well-known fact that Wüster above all strove for the continual work of the TC 37, that he had a decisive part in the first version of each of its seven principle recommendations and carried on and developed the idea of a key to terminology for tens of years, so that Infoterm today owns a manuscript filling 20 "Bene" files which is waiting to be used (Nedobity 1982: 306-313).

Less well known, probably, is a fact which may be of interest in the frame of this paper, namely that both Wüster and Drezen were also planned language specialists, interlinguists and Esperantologists who through numerous studies decisively helped to develop these still young fields of science. At the respective ages of 15 and 17, they learned Esperanto and later also other planned languages and were engaged in the thorough study of their theoretical backgrounds. At age 18 Wüster wrote an eight volume Esperanto-German *Enciklopedia Vortaro* ('Encyclopedic Vocabulary'). In this large-scale lexicon, the first four volumes of which were published in Leipzig in 1923, he established "Esperantologic Principles" which he could just as well have called "Terminological Principles" (Wüster 1923). This early and intensive preoccupation with questions relating to language planning in planned languages could not influence his choice of profession since he was obliged to take over his father's factory, but without any doubt decisively influenced his choice of subject for his doctor's thesis and all resulting developments.

The questions facing us now are:

1) whether and to what extent these impulses which clearly played a part in the development of the international terminology standardization in its present form, influenced the development of the planned language Esperanto and, in particular, the development of its terminology, and

2) if they did not, why not.

The answer to the first question is that there were initial positive reactions but that they did not suffice, for instance, to make Esperanto speaking specialists, scientists and technologists so clearly aware of Wüster's results and conclusions or of the Principle Recommendations of ISO/TC 37 that rational homogeneous terminology work could have been done on this basis to prove the existing suitability of Esperanto as a terminological language.

In answer to question two, it can be said that the reasons for this inadequate development can be found not in the language itself but rather in the reality of its relatively short (hundred-year) history. From the 1887 project, a slender booklet containing a basic vocabulary of 900 roots (despite two world wars and other serious setbacks), a language has developed functioning in all practical spheres, including everyday communication in bilingual families. The Esperanto-speaking community speaks, writes, reads, maintains correspondence – but it has not yet become sufficiently aware of the possibilities and the necessity of conscious language planning, of the rational use of the systematic nature of its idiom. In other words: the metalevel is not sufficiently developed. There are hardly any professional interlinguists, there are no trained terminologists working for Esperanto, and there is no organization able to guide the systematic development of the terminology comparable, perhaps, to the national standards bodies with their hundreds of staff members. Most of the activities listed below are on an honorary basis.

3. TEC – Terminological Esperanto-Centre

3.1. Aims and structure

On 24 July 1987 the UEA Committee, the supreme body of the Universal Esperanto Association, agreed on the foundation of an Esperanto terminology centre with the following aims:

A. Improvement and unification of the terminology work through
   a) study of the international terminology standardization, publication and adaptation of its results to the requirements of Esperanto ("research and teaching");
   b) organization of international discussions, both within and between disciplines, about terminology proposals;
   c) organization of the standardizing procedure;
   d) publication of standards, particularly terminological ones, and their regular revision.

B. Reprezentation of the planned language Esperanto to national and international bodies concerned with terminology and standards and cooperation with these bodies to mutual advantage.

The main idea is to get together a team of as many and as competent Esperantists as possible knowledgeable in different fields and languages and representatives of all important Esperanto institutions, all national and all specialist Esperanto-associations. That is, an organization capable of granting authority to the terminological work of specialists. These experts will be joined in terminographic committees of preferably 3 to 10 persons from different language regions and mentored by both a linguist and a terminologist. Ruled by general principles in accordance with those of the ISO they should discuss concepts, definitions and terminologies in their fields of investigation and propose standards. These in their turn have to go through a complicated procedure of approval by the above mentioned boards also according to international patterns. This procedure should ensure a degree of quality and reliability of the resulting technical vocabularies which is comparable to terminological achievements of national standards bodies.

3.2. Implementation so far

These proposals found approval because they obviously meet a growing demand. Up to now more than 100 persons from 25 countries have promised cooperation. The official TEC headquarters is in Rotterdam, the secretariat in Budapest, the network of representatives is being organized from Berlin (GDR). Most of the real work now is done by the standardizing section centred in Prague. Some proposals for standards have already been submitted, for instance a paper on "Standardization principles – arrangement, composition, approval procedures" (TEC PRI 006350) presently going through the procedure of its own approval, and a first terminological standard – "aeronautics generally" (TEC TER 629700/01, 2nd proposal). One of the most important projects running is a basic standard "technology generally" as well as other projects in accordance with interests of GATT (General Agreement on Tariff and Trade). Priority is granted to basic vocabularies for trade and economics, commercial law, computer science, politics, and culture. Groups of experts have started to work on their own on terminology projects for astronomy, casting, chemistry, computer science, dentistry, electro-acoustics, forestry, fur industry, geodesy, hydraulics and others.

A considerable number of lectures and periodicals have dealt with the problem. A first course on terminology was organized by the Czech Esperanto Association in 1986 with experts from four countries participating. More instructions are planned, as for instance a seminar for organizers of terminology work.

3.3. Pekoteko (Per-komputora Termino-kolekto)

Another initiative independent of TEC may help to considerably promote the terminological discussion, as mentioned in 3.1./A.b. The system Pekoteko is based on the use of microcomputers with IBM-compatible hardware and WordPerfect, Lettrix and Termex software. More detailed information may be obtained from R. Eichholz (1987) soon to be published by Infoterm (cf. also Eichholz 1988).

It remains to be hoped that Esperanto terminology will be developed at least so far in the near future that even today's sceptics may convince themselves of its potential usefulness. It is to be hoped that this will also make clear the advantage of paying more attention to its promotion and lead to funds which are a fraction of the size of those granted without hesitation to work on terminology in national languages. Surely this would benefit not only Esperantists.

References

Blanke, Detlev (1985): *Internationale Plansprachen – eine Einführung.* Berlin: Akademie-Verlag

Blanke, Wera (1986): Multlingva mondo kaj fakvorta normigado. In: *Esperanto* 79, pp. 207-208

Blanke, Wera (1987): Plánovojazykové korene medzinárodnej terminologickej normalizácie a jej vplyv na esperanto // Planlingvaj radikoj de internacia terminologia normigo kaj ties re-efiko sur Esperanton. In: *Problemy Interlingvistiky.* Stanislav Košecký (ed.). Bratislava: Jazykovedný ústav L. Štura Slovenskej akadémie vied, Slovenský esperantský zväz, Český esperantský svaz, pp. 130-139

Drezen, Ernest (1935): *Pri problemo de internaciigo de science-teknika terminaro – historio, nuna stato kaj perspektivoj.* Moskvo: Standardizacija i racionalizacija / Amsterdamo: EKRELO

Eichholz, Rüdiger (1987): Microcomputers, tools for efficient terminological work. (Manuscript, to be published by Infoterm).

Eichholz, Rüdiger (1988): The creation of technical terms in Esperanto. In: *Terminology and knowledge engineering. Supplement* (Proceedings. International Conference on Terminology and Knowledge Engineering, Trier 1987). Hans Czap / Christian Galinski (eds.). Frankfurt/M.: Indeks, pp. 93-97

Galinski, Christian (1982): Standardization in terminology – an overview. In: *Infoterm Series* 7, pp. 186-226.

Haferkorn, Rudolf (1962): Sciencaj, teknikaj kaj ceteraj fakvortaroj en Esperanto. [With a bibliographic index]. In: *Scienca Revuo* 12, pp. 111-123

Hoffmann, Heinz (1981): Wie bildet man Fachtermini des Eisenbahnwesens in Esperanto? Summary of a paper, read at "Interlinguistik-Seminar" in Ahrenshoop/GDR (manuscript)

Hornung, Wilhelm (1982): Zur Übernahme von Termini natürlicher Fachsprachen in eine Plansprache. Summary of a paper, read at "Interlinguistik-Seminar" in Ahrenshoop/GDR (manuscript)

Terminologies for the Eighties. (1982) = Infoterm Series 7. Wolfgang Nedobity (ed.). München: K.G. Saur Verlag KG

ISO (1982): *Verzeichnis der Standards der Internationalen Organisation für Standardisierung, Stand 1.1.82.*
ASMW (ed.). Berlin: Verlag für Standardisierung

Nedobity, Wolfgang (1982): Key to international terminology.
In: *Infoterm Series* 7, pp. 306-313

Ockey, Edward (1982): A bibliography of Esperanto dictionaries.
Banstead: Longvida (manuscript)

Schubert, Klaus (1988): Att knyta Nordens språk till ett mångspråkigt datoröversättningssystem.
In: *Nordiske Datalingvistikdage og symposium for datamatstøttet leksikografi og terminologi 1987, Proceedings.* = Lambda 7. [København:] Institut for Datalingvistik, Handelshøjskolen i København, pp. 204-216

Spiegel, Heinz-Rudi (1985): Aufgaben, Probleme und Organisation der Terminologienormierung.
In: *Die Neueren Sprachen* [84: 6], pp. 636-651

Warner, Alfred (1983): La internacia asimilado de science-teknika terminologio.
Supplement to Drezen (1935), reprint, Saarbrücken: Iltis, pp. 82-90

Wüster, Eugen (1923): *Enciklopedia Vortaro Esperanta-Germana.*
Leipzig: Ferd. Hirt & Sohn

Wüster, Eugen (1931): *Internationale Sprachnormung in der Technik – besonders in der Elektrotechnik.*
Berlin: VDI-Verlag

Wera Blanke

Terminologia Esperanto-Centro
Klopodoj pri terminologia normigo en la planlingvo

Resumo

Kvankam Esperanto pro sia reguleca strukturo speciale taŭgas por aŭtomata prilaborado, tiun celon malhelpas la kvante kaj kvalite ne kontentiga terminaro. Pludaŭro de libera evoluo neeviteble kaŭzos konfuzantan sinonimecon.

Malgraŭ la gravaj impulsoj, kiujn ricevis la internacia terminologi-normiga movado el planlingvaj radikoj fare de siaj pioniroj Wüster kaj Drezen, la Esperanto-komunumo ĝis nun ne utiligis en sufiĉa grado ties spertojn kaj rezultojn. Tion parte klarigas objektivaj faktoroj: la ne-esto de ekonomia premo, la manko de profesieco kaj organiziteco, la foresto de ŝtata aŭ interŝtata subvenciado k.a.

Terminologia Esperanto-Centro (TEC), fondita 87-07-24, estas provo, malgraŭ tiuj mankoj realigi jenajn celojn:

1. Plibonigo kaj unuecigo de terminologia laboro.
  1.1. Studado de internacia terminologia normigo, adaptado de ĝiaj rezultoj al la bezonoj de Esperanto kaj diskonigo de rilataj scioj (esploro kaj instruo).
  1.2. Organizado de internaciaj, fakaj kaj interfakaj diskutoj pri terminar-proponoj.
  1.3. Organizado de normiga procedo.
  1.4. Eldonado de normaj dokumentoj, precipe terminaraj, kaj ilia reviziado.

2. Reprezentado de Esperanto en naciaj kaj internaciaj terminologiaj kaj normigaj institucioj kaj kunlaboro kun ili je reciproka utilo.

La baza ideo estas strukturita kolektivo el fake kaj lingve kompetentaj esperantistoj, inkluzive reprezentantoj de ĉiuj gravaj Esperanto-institucioj, la fakaj kaj la landaj asocioj, kiu havu la necesan aŭtoritaton por doni norman karakteron al la terminaroj proponitaj de fakaj specialistoj. Tiuj estos kunigitaj en terminografiaj komisionoj, kie 3-10 fakuloj el laŭeble diversaj lingvo-regionoj, konsilataj de terminologo kaj lingvisto, diskutos pri nocio-sistemoj, difinoj kaj terminaroj de siaj fakoj. Tiujn diskutojn povos konsiderinde akceli la projekto "Pekoteko", kun kiu TEC kunlaboros.

Inter la terminaraj projektoj prioritaton havos: tekniko ĝenerale, komerc-ekonomiko, komerc-juro, informadiko, politiko kaj kulturo.

Universal Applicability of Dependency Grammar

Dietrich M. Weidmann

Postfach 639
CH-8201 Schaffhausen
Switzerland

1. Introduction

Among modern linguists at least two different schools exist. These I call here the Chomsky school and the Tesnière school. When we speak about dependency grammar, we think normally only about the school of Tesnière (1959) and his followers (especially valency grammar). But in a larger sense, dependency grammar includes Chomsky's (1981) structuralism as well. Both valency grammar and Chomsky's structuralism postulate an underlying representation which is universal and a surface structure which is specific for every language. Chomsky postulates a system of rules to generate any sentence and another system of transformation rules which make it possible to construct sentences with different surface structures which have the same meaning. However, neither the structuralism of Chomsky nor valency grammar can really explain the relation between the universal deep structure and the specific surface structure. If we try to apply these theories for example to an ergative language, they become completely useless. Terms like subject and object are here suddenly inadequate.

For example (Basque; quoted from Comrie 1978: 329ff.):

Martin	*ethorri*	*da.*	'Martin came'	
Martin	came	Aux		
Martinek	*haurra*	*igorri*	*du.*	'Martin sent the child'
Martin Erg.	child	sent	Aux	

The idea of syntactic tree structures in a dependency grammar system is still very fascinating, although neither the valency grammar nor generative transformational grammar are universal. It has been recognized that there exist some universal rules in the surface structure and some kind of universality in the deep structure. But the way to generate a surface structure from an underlying one seems to be different from language to language, limited only by the fact that the number of possibilities of realisation is finite.

It is a fact that languages are different and sometimes even incompatible. But even in cases of "untranslatable sentences", it is always possible to explain the meaning. The problem is that no item of any language has its full meaning in isolation. Only in context can any one sentence can be fully understood. The same English sentence articulated by different people may have a totally different meaning and would have to be translated in a totally different way. But if we are dealing with machine translation, we are concerned not with these problematic cases, but rather with the other 90%, which consists of relatively clear sentences.

In looking for universals, however, it was necessary to develop a modified theory of dependency grammar which I call Kernel, Pilot, Guest member grammar or just KPG-grammar. The theory of KPG-grammar is a further developed and improved version of the concept which was presented by Claude Gacond, the director of the Esperanto Cultural Centre of La Chaux-de-Fonds, Switzerland, on the occasion of a training seminar for Esperanto-teachers in November 1986. Claude Gacond on this occasion introduced the terms of *kerno, mastro* and *gasto*, which he had heard from a Chinese Esperantologist. Unfortunately no paper exists on this subject. A part of the seminar discussions has been recorded and the magnetic tapes are in the archives of the Esperanto Cultural Centre and of the CDELI (Centro de Dokumentado kaj Esploro pri la Lingvo Internacia, Bibliothèque de la ville, 33 rue de Progrès, CH-2301 La Chaux-de-Fonds, Switzerland). Because this work is based mainly on the oral statements of Gacond, the origin of the expressions *kerno, mastro* and *gasto* is not yet known. The Chinese friend of Gacond told him that those expressions were very common in some East Asian schools. This is, however, not of importance for the following theory. For us it is important that this concept be applicable not only for Esperanto and Chinese but, with the necessary prudence, for every other language. It was a challenge to transform Gacond's concept into a useful theory of grammar, creating an easily understandable terminology. It is important to note that some expressions already have other meanings in common linguistic theory. For this reason, the expressions used for the KPG-grammer will be defined below.

2. The relation of the KPG-grammar to the language model

We may treat language as a model universe which can be represented by the following pattern:

On the level Unit of Meaning, Text and higher there are only a few differences of structure between different languages (that means for a translation it is usually not necessary to rearrange the order of sentences). For this reason the KPG-grammar is restricted to the levels lower than Sentence. The most important terms of KPG-grammar are: Unit of Meaning, Pilot member, Kernel member and Guest member. More specifically, this essay will treat the problems at the level of Unit of Meaning. On the word and morpheme levels, there are probably only very few rules which are universal; for that reason research on the deeper levels has to be specific for every language.

3. Sentence

The exact definition of sentence is for the KPG-grammar of only secondary importance. Significant for the theory is that a sentence contains at least one Unit of Meaning. For the KPG-grammar we can operate with the following definition of sentence (this definition describes only the boundary between sentence and word, i.e. what the minimum for a sentence is. The maximum limit, i.e. between sentence and Thought Cluster is not investigated here):

A sentence is an item of language, which consists of at least one Unit of Meaning, can stand alone and contains information. The following items are sentences in this sense:

Au!
Liebling!
He is rich.
He says nothing.
Er sagt, dass er Zeit habe, und ich glaube ihm das gerne.
Er hat nur das Geld, welches er geliehen hat.

4. Unit of Meaning

A Unit of Meaning is the smallest unit of communication. A Unit of Meaning consists of exactly one piece of information about a situation, position, movement, relation, action, change modification etc.

The centre of a Unit of Meaning is the Kernel member. Any further members may be linked to the kernel member. These further members can be Pilot member and Guest members. To refer to this link, I shall use the Esperanto-term *ligita* in the discussion of KPG-grammar.

The members of a Unit of Meaning may for their part consist of or contain subordinated Units of Meaning. We speak here of Complex Units of Meaning. There may even exist Units of Meaning which are subordinated to subordinate Units, and so on. We accordingly speak about Units of Meaning of a specific degree of subordination, such as 3d degree, according to the number of subordinating steps. The patterns in section IX represent the blueprints of the units of meaning graphically.

5. Kernel member

The Kernel member forms the centre of a Unit of Meaning. The Kernel member includes the part of the Unit of Meaning which expresses the action, modification, situation etc. In normal transitive sentences, the Kernel member corresponds to the conjugated verb.

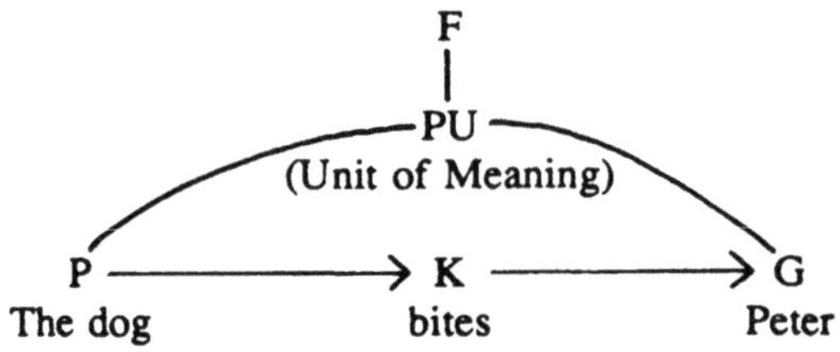

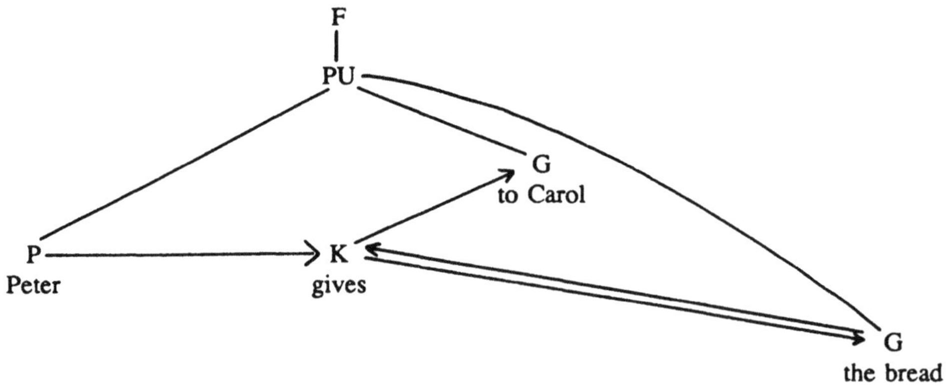

The essential novelty of this theory is that the Kernel member is not directly dependent on the PU (Unit of Meaning), but it is the link-member between the actants, if there is more than one, and gives information about the relation between them; it gives the information about the actant, if there is only one; it gives information about the general situation (for example when a natural phenomenon is being described), if there is no actant.

Very often the Kernel member consists only of the conjugated verb. But there are also much more complex types of Kernel members. The noun phrase of the predicate of copulas like *to be* is a part of the Kernel member. For example:

(English) *The boy* **is good.**
(Russian) *Mal'čik* **charošij.**
(Esperanto) *La knabo* **bonas** / *La knabo* **estas bona.**

A Unit of Meaning may also consist of only one element which is the Kernel member. For example:

(Esperanto) **Pluvas.**

6. Pilot member

In nominative-accusative languages, the Pilot member is normally identical with the subject. In ergative languages the pilot member is normally in the absolutive case. The Pilot member is in most languages that member of the sentence which is unmarked. We can find agreement in a lot of languages between Pilot and Kernel members in number, person and noun-class. But there are also languages which have congruity between the first Guest member and the verb or even double congruity (Pilot and first Guest member have to be marked at the verb.) E.g.: (Swahili)

Peter	*a-*	*na-*	*mw-*	*penda*	*malajka*
Peter	Subj.3.Pers.Sing.	Pres.	Obj.3.Pers.Sing.	love	baby

Peter anamwpenda malajka 'Peter loves the baby'

In certain languages, it is possible to form sentences without a pilot member. E.g.:

(German) *Mir ist übel.*

7. Guest member

The guest members are all the other members of a Unit of Meaning. A Unit of Meaning has only one Kernel and one Pilot member. In most languages it is possible for a Unit of Meaning to have more than one Guest member (s. example from Jabem in the next chapter).

Guest members are always marked as such. They can be marked by case or function affixes, by function words, or by special position.

8. Universality of the KPG-model

The model of Units of Meaning consisting of kernel, pilot and Guest members is universal. But Complexity of Units of Meaning and the relation between underlying representation and surface structure are specific for every language. In the International Language (Esperanto), for instance, it is possible to build very complex Units of Meaning with the help of the causative-suffix *-ig-* (Weidmann 1988).

There are languages which cannot describe complex ideas with one Unit of Meaning. Such languages have other devices to perform this function. Such a device is the verbal serialisation of Jabem an Austronesian language which is spoken in New Guinea (Dempwolff 1939: 81-82, par. 81c).

The sentence 'The missionary gives me the taro' in Jabem must be divided into two Units of Meaning, because in Jabem a verb can have only two actants; this sentence must be formed in the following way:

Binsi	*ke'ke'ng*	*mo*	*e'nde'ng*	*ae'.*
Missionary	acts on	taro	aims at	I.

One property of this verb series is that the Guest member of the first Unit of Meaning is always the Pilot member of the next one.

Theoretically there could exist an absolutely analytic language in which every component of an event has to be described by a separate Unit of meaning. However, every language community has created complex verbs for events which can be often observed, but the more different culture and customs of peoples are, the more different may be the events for which complex verbs have been created. Most European languages, for example, have a verb with the meaning 'give', which consists of the components: (1) taking an object, (2) moving this object towards a person, (3) making this person the new "owner" of the object. (The components may be defined more exactly, but the principle is represented by this example). In the above mentioned Jabem, there is no verb 'give'. The event accordingly has to be divided into two Units of meaning. In order to produce a successful translation by computer with the help of an intermediate language, it is necessary to divide the events into such small components that neither the output nor the input language contains a word which cannot be composed by these elements. It is not necessary to provide an absolutely exact componential analysis, it is only necessary to find the largest common divisor.

Practical experience suggests that the International Language has all the linguistic material which is necessary to divide every event into components. Sometimes it might result in a stylistically unusual form, but every text would be grammatically correct and understandable.

9. The structure of the members

The members of a Unit of Meaning can be constructed in a lot of different ways. Every language has its own methods to mark the function of the different members. Such methods are case inflection, marking verbs with personal and temporal affixes, functional words, word order.

Very complex languages like the International Language use all those methods together. A member may consist of only one word, but it may also be a whole complex which can be subdivided into Units of Meaning (which may in turn be subdivided).

The KPG makes a fundamental distinction between two types of members:

a) **Members consisting of a simple member heart**
  - without member attribute: *Peter comes.*
  - with member attributes:
    The man who works a lot never has enough money.

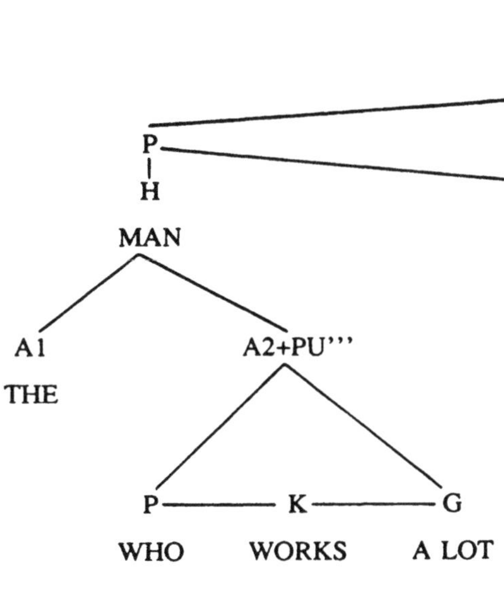

b) **Members consisting of a Unit of Meaning**
For example: *He says that he does not have time.*

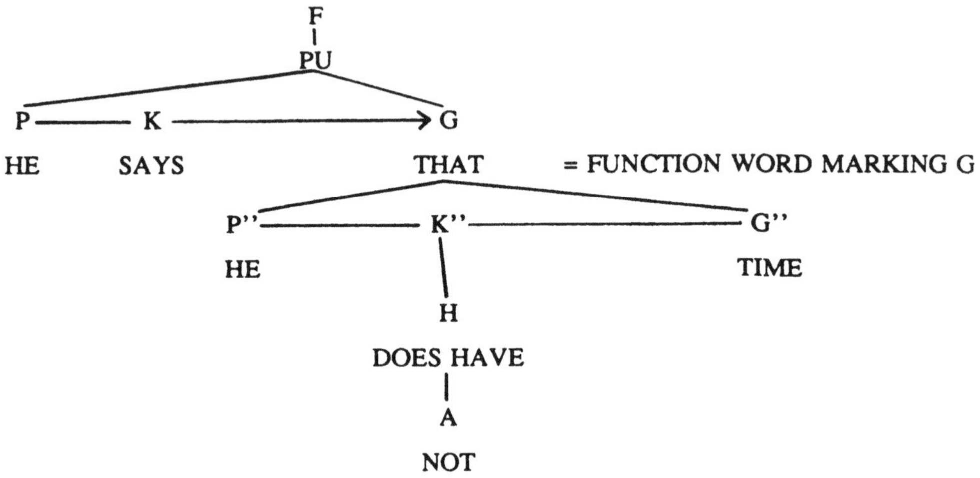

10. Blueprints for sentences

With the methods illustrated in the above patterns, it is now possible to construct a blueprint for every sentence. The KPG normally uses the following symbols:

F = sentence, PU = Unit of Meaning, K = Kernel member, P = Pilot member, G = Guest member, mk/H = member Heart, ma/A = member Attribute.

References

Chomsky, Noam (1981): *Lectures on government and binding.* Dordrecht: Foris

Comrie, Bernard (1978): Ergativity. In: *Syntactic Typology.* Winfried P. Lehmann (ed.). [Sussex]: The Harvester Press, p. 329ff.

Dempwolff, Otto (1939): *Grammatik der Jabem-Sprache auf Neuguinea.* = Hansische Universität, Abhandlungen auf dem Gebiet der Auslandkunde 50. Hamburg: Friederichsen, De Gruyter & Co.

Gacond, Claude (1986/87): [Several speeches about the verbal system of the International Language, Kultura Centro Esperantista, La Chaux-de-Fonds.] (A part of the speeches has been registered on tape, not published).

Helbig, Gerhard / Joachim Buscha (1984): *Deutsche Grammatik.* Leipzig: Enzyklopädie, 8th rev. ed.

Tarvainen, Kalevi (1981): *Einführung in die Dependenzgrammatik.* Tübingen: Niemeyer

Tesnière, Lucien (1959): *Éléments de syntaxe structurale.* Paris: Klincksieck

Weidmann, Dietrich M. (1987): Ueberlegungen zu den Satzbauplänen der deutschen Sprache. Seminararbeit. Zürich: Universität, unpublished

Weidmann, Dietrich M. (1988): *Das Kausativ und das Antikausativ in der gemischten Plansprache Esperanto.* Lizentiatsarbeit an der philosophischen Fakultät I der Universität Zürich. Schaffhausen: Weidmann's Mondo-Servo

Dietrich M. Weidmann

Universala aplikebleco de dependogramatiko

Resumo

En la KPG-gramatiko oni distingas tri principe malsamajn frazmembrojn (membrojn de pensunuoj), kiuj verŝajne universalas: kernmembro, pilotmembro kaj gastmembro. Pilot- kaj gastmembroj entenas unuojn, ecojn, objektojn aŭ personojn, kiujn la kernmembroj interrilatigas. Ekzistas kernmembro sen aliaj membroj, tio priskribas okazaĵon. Se la kernmembro staras kun nur unu membro, tiam la kernmembro priskribas la rolon de la alia membro. la diversaj roloj de gast- kaj pilotmembroj priskribeblas per la profundaj kazoj (Helbig/Buscha 1984: 535sekv.). Bedaŭrinde ne ekzistas leĝoj laŭ kiuj al certa profunda kazo korespondus certa klaso de gastmembroj (Weidmann 1987). Necesas klarigi por ĉiu unuopa kernmembro, kiuj membroj per ĝi rilatigataj korespondas al kiu profunda kazo.

Ĉar en la frazo Petro estas viro / Petro viras *ekzistas nur unu persono (nome* Petro*), viro ne povas esti sendependa membro sed nur la rolo de Petro, do parto de la verbo. Tial la KPG konsideras* esti viro *kiel kernmembron (kio ankaŭ estas pravigita de la sinonimeco de* esti viro *kun* viri*).*

Per la KPG eblas same bone priskribi nominativ-akuzativajn lingvojn kiel ergativajn lingvojn. Ĝi ankaŭ precipe taŭgas por klarigi kaŭzativon kaj antikaŭzativon (Weidmann 1988).

Translating to and from Swedish by SWETRA – a Multilanguage Translation System

Bengt Sigurd

Lunds universitet
Institutionen för lingvistik
Helgonabacken 12
S-223 62 Lund
Sweden

lingvist@seldc51.bitnet

The project SWETRA (Swedish Computer Translation Research Group at the Department of Linguistics and Phonetics, University of Lund, Sweden) is supported by HSFR (Swedish Council for Research in the Humanities and Social Sciences). SWETRA uses a special type of Generalized Phrase Structure Grammar, called Referent Grammar (RG), and the work consists very much in writing program modules for Swedish and selected languages, deciding on formats and experimenting with different implementations (see references). Substantial fragments of Swedish and English grammars have been described and implemented, which makes it possible to translate typical sentences between the two languages (see print-out of demo session below). Presently the lexicon only includes about 500 sample word forms. Inflectional forms are to be derived from these base forms using implicational morphological rules (developed by M. Eeg-Olofsson). Fragments of French, Polish,

Russian (B. Gawronska-Werngren), Georgian (K. Vamling) and Irish (S. Dooley Collberg) have also been implemented in order to find out how typologically different languages can be described by RG and which problems appear when translating between different pairs of languages using the "universal" functional representations derived by RG and additional transfer rules which adjust the functional representations when needed.

Referent grammar

Referent grammar (abbreviated RG) has been developed as a tool for analyzing, generating and translating sentences and texts (Sigurd 1987, 1988a,b). Referent grammar can be written directly in the formalism called Definite Clause Grammar (DCG), supported by most Prolog versions (see Clocksin/Mellish 1981). This formalism is very convenient for linguists, as it resembles ordinary generative phrase structure rules. RG rules, however, deviate from ordinary phrase structure rules by stating which functional representation, given to the left of the arrow, corresponds to the string of categories and words to the right of the arrow, or, looked at from a generating point of view, which string of categories and words corresponds to a certain functional representation. DCG may contain conditions (within curly brackets), e.g. for agreement, and one may have any number of arguments (slots) to the left of the arrow for storing information about mode, focused constituent, etc.

Referent grammar is a kind of Generalized Phrase Structure Grammar (GPSG; see Gazdar 1982; Gazdar et al. 1985) and certain slots in the rules are used in such a way that movement transformations are not needed. Nor are empty (null, zero) constituents needed in RG. Instead, RG uses labels for the different categories which lack a constituent (defective categories). This approach seems to have practical and pedagogic advantages as well.

Currently the RG programs are implemented and run on Vax and PC computers. The PC prolog developed by Arity is used for the PC versions.

Referent grammar adopts the distinction between word and phrase class representation (o-representation; *o* for Swedish *ord* 'word') and functional representation (f-representation). These two levels have long been identified, but neither old nor modern grammatical research has agreed on the concepts and terminology to be used on the two levels. When a grammar is to be implemented in a computer program, it is, however, necessary to establish a systematic terminology and format, which allow consistent and exhaustive treatment of all or most sentences. This section will present some of the decisions which have to be made and discuss some of the problems involved.

Functional representations should serve as an interface to semantics and logic. In spite of the lack of good definitions of subject, predicate, object etc. these concepts recur in all grammatical theories and descriptions of languages. This indicates a reasonable universality and that it should be possible to use normalized functional representations as an intermediate (meta)language in automatic translation between languages, if the grammatical and lexical meanings are also given in a standard format.

The normalized format for the f-representation of a sentence used by RG includes: subject (subj), particle adverb (padv), predicate (pred), dative object (dobj), accusative object (obj), 2 sentence adverbials (sadvl), 3 other adverbials (advl). Although infinitely recursive repetitions of constituents are theoretically interesting, constraining the number of constituents has great computational advantages. RG assumes that most sentences can be mapped on the maximum list of functional categories given above. The categories are always presented in the order given above in the functional representations. If a constituent is missing, an empty list, [], is found at its place in the print-outs (see Appendix).

The meanings of the grammatical and lexical units are given in RG in an English-oriented language (machinese), but when such details are irrelevant in the presentation here, the ordinary words are used in the representations as well as other simplifications. The English-oriented semantic representations are very useful in the automatic translation projects, but the lack of corresponding words and ambiguity of some English words may cause problems (to be solved by transfer rules).

A functional representation of *The boy ate an ice-cream slowly* and the Swedish equivalent *Pojken åt en glass sakta* would be:

s(subj(1:boy,sg,def),pred(eat,past),obj(2:ice-cream,sg,indef),advl(slowly))

In this formula, s = sentence, subj = subject, sg = singular, def = definite, pred = predicate, past = past tense, obj = object, indef = indefinite, advl = adverbial. The successive numbers before the colon (:) denote nominal referents. Thus, since the boy is the first referent mentioned, it gets the number 1, ice-cream, the number 2. These referents in the functional representations are a characteristic feature of RG and the reason for its name. Some referents can be identified (the numbers set to the same value) in the discourse as will be shown below.

Assuming that the next sentence is *The little girl saw him* (Swedish *Den lilla flickan såg honom*), we can give it the following functional representation:

s(subj(3:girl,sg,def,little),pred(see,past),obj(1:pro))

This representation indicates that the girl is the third nominal referent, but that the object can be identified with the boy previously mentioned. The words after the colon indicate how the referent is denoted in this particular sentence. The referents are seen as cognitive objects recurring in the discourse (discourse referents) and the sentences evoke these referents in different ways by their words. As is well known, these referents are often introduced by indefinite noun phrases, but evoked or alluded to later by definite noun phrases or pronouns.

A relative clause is a part within a noun phrase which adds further information about the referent and helps to identify it. This is shown in the following f-representation of a subsequent sentence in the text: *The boy, whom the girl saw, came* (Swedish: *Pojken, som flickan såg, kom*):

s(subj(1:boy,sg,def,s(subj(3:girl,sg,def),pred(saw),obj(1))),pred(came))

This representation puts the relative clause beside the other information about the referent 1, and shows that the object of the girl's seeing is the referent 1. RG does not say that one particular word is the antecedent or correlate of the relative clause but the referent, a cognitive object to be connected with the whole noun phrase. This approach seems to have many advantages.

Note that *whom* (*som*), the relative pronoun (marker) does not appear in the functional representation. Similarly, subjunctions such as *that* (Swedish *att*) and the infinitive marker *to* (Swedish *att*) will not be seen in the functional representations of RG. A subsequent sentence: *Yesterday a dog bit her* (Swedish: *Igår bet en hund henne*) would have the following f-representation:

s(subj(4:dog,sg,indef),pred(bit),obj(3:pro),advl(yesterday))

Referent grammar also records the mode of the sentence and the focused (topicalized) constituent. In the last sentence, the constituent *yesterday* (*igår*) can be stored as the focused constituent as it appears initially. The sentence *A dog bit her yesterday* (*En hund bet henne igår*) would not have *yesterday* in focus, but have the same f-representation, where "surface" word order does not show. Note that Swedish inverts the word order when a constituent other than the subject begins the sentence.

If the functional representations of the successive sentences of a text are stored in a data base, it should be possible to retrieve all information gathered about a certain referent, e.g. about the girl (referent number 3) in our sample text above. It should also be possible to generate a new text on the basis of the information about the referents stored, e.g the following based on the facts gathered about the girl: *There was a little girl. She saw a boy and was bitten by a dog yesterday.* High quality translation needs such a possibility to keep track of the referents of the text in order to make appropriate use of pronouns and definite forms.

Word and phrase class representation (o-representations) in RG

Referent grammar adopts traditional word and phrase categories, but uses defective categories in addition. The idea of using defective categories in RG stems from Gazdar (1982), who carries on ideas from Ajdukiewicz (1935), who conceived of categorial grammar. In RG, a category (phrase) is said to be defective if it lacks a constituent. Normally, a prepositional phrase (pp) has both a preposition and a noun as e.g. *at the boat*, and the *at* in *What are you looking at?* can therefore be said to represent a defective prepositional phrase (object defective prepositional phrase: odpp). Naturally, *what* is identified as the missing constituent.

In the Swedish sentence *Flickan trodde pojken att hunden bet* 'The girl the boy thought that the dog bit' the clause '(that) the dog bit' is defective as the transitive verb *bet* does not have its object. The girl (*flickan*) is naturally identified as the object, which – in TG terms – has been moved to the front. RG does not try to locate the missing constituent in the surface string of words by placing a trace (null, zero, empty) constituent there. RG accepts what is found, but places the constituents in the functional roles required in the corresponding f-representation. This seems to be a clear advantage made possible by having two representations.

The Swedish sentence *Honom bet hunden* 'Him the dog bit' is naturally assumed to have the (simplified) functional representation:

s(subj(hunden),pred(bet),obj(honom))

The RG analysis would also state that *honom* is in focus and that it is a declarative sentence. The word and phrase class analysis of RG would state that *honom* is an object noun phrase (npo) and that the two words *bet* and *hunden* together represent an object defective sentence (odsent). This particular object defective sentence consists of a transitive verb (vt) followed by a subject noun phrase (nps). If we use *sent* as the name of the root we can write the (simplified) o- and f-representations as follows:

o-representation: sent(npo(honom),odsent(vt(bet),nps(hunden)))
f-representation: s(subj(hunden),pred(bet),obj(honom))

We may look at the o-representation from below (corresponding to a bottom-up parsing process) and say that it shows that if we identify *honom* as an npo, followed by the transitive verb (vt) *bet* followed by the nps *hunden*, then we can identify a sentence "sent", where the first constituent is an npo and the second is an odsent. Looked upon from above (as a top-down process) we may say that a sent may consist of (be rewritten as) an npo followed by an odsent. An odsent may consist of a vt followed by an nps. The word *honom* may be an npo, *bet* may be a vt and *hunden* may be an nps. It is convenient to use the categories "nps" = subject noun phrase and "npo" = object noun phrase in Swedish, although the formal difference only shows up in pronouns (*honom* is npo, *han* is nps) in modern Swedish.

The sentence *Vem bet hunden?* 'Whom did the dog bite?' can be analyzed accordingly taking *vem* as an npo (or rather npqo = object question nominal) and *bet hunden* as an object defective sentence (odsent). The o-representation would be:

sent(npqo(vem),odsent(vt(bet),nps(hunden)))

and the corresponding f-representation:

s(subj(hunden),pred(bet),obj(vem))

We note that English must have *do*-support in such questions. The Swedish sentence: *Vem bet hunden?* allows a second interpretation, as *vem* can also be an nps. In that case, the o-representation will be:

sent(npqs(vem),sdsent(vt(bet),npo(hunden)))

and the f-representation:

s(subj(vem),pred(bet),obj(hunden))

This interpretation is, however, pragmatically odd, as dogs bite more than they are bitten. The advantages of having two representations should be obvious by now and we will proceed to show how they are related by the rewriting rules with no need for transformational rules and traces.

Rewriting rules in RG

The grammatical rules of RG are traditional rewriting rules describing how the category to the left of the arrow may be rewritten as the categories to the right of the arrow, or inversely, how the categories to the right of the arrow may be combined to form the category to the left of the arrow.

The grammatical rules of RG look like ordinary phrase structure rules. However, the rules do not only state which categories to the right of the arrow can make up the category to the left of the arrow but also state what the functional representation will be. The RG rules derive the f-representation when applied to a certain sentence and, inversely, the rules derive the phrases and (eventually) words, which correspond to a certain f-representation.

The rules are written in the Prolog formalism called Definite Clause Grammar (DCG). Such rules can be interpreted directly by the computer and they can be used both for analysis (parsing) and synthesis (generation). To illustrate, we show below some (simplified) rules which can treat sentences such as: *Honom bet hunden* 'Him the dog bit' and *Igår kom hunden* 'Yesterday the dog came'. The rules do not include referent numbers – how they are introduced will be shown later. Capital letters denote variables, which are bound only within the same line (rule). This means that e.g. an X does not denote the same variable in all places in the program. The sign "_" denotes an anonymous variable in the slot (DCG is described in Clocksin/Mellish 1981 and various papers).

```
sent(d,_,X,F) → npo(X),odsent(_,_,X,F).
sent(d,_,X,F) → adv(X),adsent(_,_,X,F).
odsent(_,_,X,s(subj(Y),pred(Z),obj(X))) → vt(Z),nps(Y).
adsent(_,_,X,s(subj(Y),pred(Z),advl(X))) → vi(Z),nps(Y).
nps(hunden) → [hunden].
npo(honom) → [honom].
vt(bet) → [bet].
vi(kom) → [kom].
adv(igår) → [igår].
```

The first rule states that a sentence may be declarative (have the value "d" in the first slot, as the first argument of "sent"), have an npo (X) as the focused constituent in the third slot and have the functional representation F, if there is an npo (X) as the first member of the sentence and the rest of the sentence is an object defective sentence (odsent) with the functional representation F (in the last slot). In order to find out what an object defective sentence requires we have to look at the third rule. It says that it requires a transitive verb (vt) followed by a subject noun phrase (nps). If we find those we may establish a functional representation where the nps is the subject, the transitive verb is the predicate, but the object is not found to the right of the arrow. The value of this missing object constituent X has to be found by finding the value of the X in the third slot. Going back to the first rule it is seen that the value in the third slot (X) of odsent has to be the same as the value of the preceding npo (X). As a result of these requirements the functional representation (F) of the odsent will be supplemented by the value of the object and inserted into sent.

The rules illustrated do not derive any o-representations. The application of the rules involving an adverb followed by an adverb defective sentence work in the same way. It is to be noted that RG extends the "defective approach" to cover adverbs, although an adverb is not a constituent which is obligatory in the same sense as the object of a transitive verb. The third slot is normally used for the missing constituent. The second slot is in reserve.

More technically, if the program (set of rules) is loaded, the parsing of the sentence *honom bet hunden* is brought about by writing the following to the computer:

```
sent(M,_,P,F,[honom,bet,hunden],[ ]).
```

The computer will then return the solutions (values) for M,P,F: M = d, P = honom, F = s(subj(hunden),pred(bet),object(honom)). Inversely, one may write:

```
sent(d,_,igår,s(subj(hunden),pred(kom),adverb(igår)),X,[ ])
```

which will cause the program to return:

X = *Igår kom hunden*

The two square brackets, [], mark the empty list and we say that here it means that no words should be left over. Prolog is a declarative language and the rules state requirements, relations, implications, etc. How the rules are applied, how the searching is carried out and how the solutions are reached may be seen by calling the built-in predicates "spy" and "trace", but unless this is done nothing is shown but the result.

We will not go into further details here, but only mention that apparently rules of the type suggested make it possible to handle all the phenomena to be handled: word order, agreement, unbounded dependencies, optional constituents, word inflection, word derivation, etc. There are substantial RG programs for Swedish and English to support this statement. But these modules (about twenty pages each, excluding the lexical rules) will not be presented here.

Noun phrases and relative clauses

Typical Swedish noun phrases are: *den snälle pojken* 'the nice boy', *den snälla flickan* 'the nice girl', *en liten flicka i ett fönster* 'a little girl in a window', *det lilla barnet som hunden bet* 'the little child that the dog bit', *mannen vilken hunden sprang till* 'the man whom the dog ran to'. We can identify the word classes: articles, adjectives, prepositions, relative markers, etc. We note that there is agreement within the Swedish noun phrase defined on the basis of definiteness, number, gender (in southern Sweden also sex). The basic rule for noun phrases is the following:

np(R,nom(A,B,C)) → nph(R,A),ppa(R,B),relcl(R,C).

This rule states that a noun phrase may consist of a noun phrase head (nph), followed by an attributive prepositional phrase (ppa) followed by a relative clause (we do not discuss cases of several prepositional phrases and relative clauses here). The rule says that the value (functional representation) of the nph (A), the value of the ppa (B) and the value of the relcl (C) are to be inserted after "nom" (= name).. The rule also says that the referent (R) with its features (see below) recurs in the three constituents of the np. This makes it possible to select the proper relative marker and control agreement in the relative clause in Swedish. The noun phrases *huset vilket var stort* 'the house which was big' and *stugan vilken var stor* 'the cottage which was big' differ in inflectional forms because *huset* 'the house' is neuter (gender) and *stugan* 'the cottage' non-neuter (reale). Further details of agreement will be presented in the next section.

The relative clauses will be considered as clauses lacking a constituent – corresponding to the antecedent or correlate in traditional grammar (cf Sigurd 1988a,b). We will distinguish different types of clauses depending on the functional role of the missing constituent. Languages may have different forms of the relative marker depending on the functional role of the missing constituent and on the grammatical features of the noun phrase head (the referent). The noun phrase *pojken som sprang* 'the boy who ran' is analyzed as an nph (*pojken*) followed by *som*, a subject relative marker ("rels"), followed by a subject defective subordinate clause ("sdsunt"). The noun phrase *pojken som hunden bet* 'the boy whom the dog bit' is analyzed as an nph followed by *som* now an object relative marker followed by an object defective subordinate sentence ("odsunt"). We note that English can make a distinction between the two types of relative markers (*who/whom*). Swedish uses the same form of the relative marker (*som*), but it is an interesting fact that the subject relative marker cannot be deleted, while the object relative marker can.

The noun phrase head (nph), the enriched referent and agreement

Common noun phrases such as *en snäll flicka* 'a nice girl', *den snälla flickan* 'the nice girl', *ett snällt barn* 'a nice child', *de snälla barnen* 'the nice children' can be covered by the following main rule with sample lexical rules ({} include conditions):

```
nph(r(R,A,D,N,S,G,_),h(A,B)) → art(X),a(Y),n(Z),
  {lex(X,D,art,D,N,S,G,_,_,_),
   lex(Y,B,a,D,N,S,G,_,_,_),
   lex(Z,A,n,D,N,S,G,_,_,_)}.

lex(en,indef,art,indef,sg,_,re,_,_,_). /* indef article sg reale */
lex(ett,indef,art,indef,sg,_,ne,_,_,_) /* indef article sg neuter */
lex(den,def,art,def,sg,_,re,_,_,_). /* def article sg reale */
lex(de,def,art,def,pl,_,_,_,_,_). /* def article pl */
lex(snäll,nice,a,indef,sg,_,re,_,_,_). /* snäll indef sg reale */
lex(snällt,nice,a,indef,sg,_,ne,_,_,_). /* snäll indef sg neuter */
lex(snälla,nice,a,indef,pl,_,_,_,_,_). /* snäll indef pl */
lex(snälla,nice,a,def,_,_,_,_,_,_). /*snäll def */
lex(flicka,m(girl,sg),n,indef,sg,fe,re,_,_,_).
lex(flickan,m(girl,sg),n,def,sg,fe,re,_,_,_).
lex(flickor,m(girl,pl),n,indef,pl,fe,re,_,_,_).
lex(pojke,m(boy,sg),n,indef,sg,ma,re,_,_,_).
lex(barnet,m(child,sg),n,def,sg,_,ne,_,_,_).
```

The abbreviations should be easy to interpret, e.g. "ma" = male, "fe" = female, "ne" = neuter, "re" = reale (non-neuter). The rules constrain the possible combinations of words and handle agreement, since e.g. only words with a specific feature such as "def", "sg" (or the anonymous feature) can cooccur.

The noun phrase head will also get a number as a value of the variable R. We may identify this R with the R mentioned in earlier rules and then talk about the referent presented now as an enriched referent. When this enriched referent is inserted as the missing constituent, it is possible to make constituents within a defective sentence, e.g. a relative clause, agree as required.

Auxiliaries, infinitives and participles

Infinitives and participles are considered in RG as "minor" sentences lacking tense and one or several constituents. This accords well with the traditional view, and the rules may be designed to insert the missing constituents as required. The sentence *Pojken skall komma* 'The boy shall come' may be given the following o-representation:

sent(nps(pojken),sdsent(mod(skall),isent(komma)))

corresponding to the following (simplified) f-representation:

s(subj(pojken),pred(skall),obj(s(pojken),pred(komma)))

We use "isent" = infinitival sentence, "mod" = modal auxiliary. We consider the infinitive sentence as an object in the functional representation, which is natural considering that we may ask: *Vad skall pojken?* and get the answer:*komma* 'come'.

Participial constructions are analyzed accordingly assuming that participial minor sentences can get missing constituents from the matrix sentence. The sentence: *Pojken har kommit* 'The boy has come' may be assigned the following f-representation:

s(subj(pojken),pred(har),obj(s(subj(pojken),pred(kommit))))

if we insert the subject of the matrix sentence as the subject in the participial sentence. Participial sentences may take infinitives as their object and our approach allows the handling of long strings of verbs inserting missing constituents at will, e.g. sentences such as: *Pojken måste ha önskat äta* 'The boy must have wanted to eat', where the subject should recur as the subject of all the verbs down to *äta*. RG rules can achieve that.

Other languages

The functional representations of the "same" sentence in different languages are or can be made to be the same in most cases. The differences between languages appear as "local" differences in the words for different meanings, in the word order, in the use of different cases and in the requirements of agreement. There are, however, differences between languages which cause difficult problems – and may be unsolvable for the computer. We will discuss some of the problems involved.

French would say *J'ai faim* corresponding to Swedish *Jag är hungrig* and English *I am hungry*. There is a fundamental difference between French and the other languages here, as French uses a construction which may be characterized as 'have' + noun, while Swedish and English use 'be' + adjective. It is true that the two ways of rendering the same meaning can be related. One may write a rule which transfers the functional representation of the Swedish and English sentences into a functional representation with a 'have' expression and the proper denominalization of the adjective. It is not clear how many rules of this sort are needed and how general they are even for the language pair Swedish-English.

When translating into English *do*-support causes a well-known problem. Certain questions and most clauses with *not* need *do*-support. The use of the term *do*-support is slightly misleading. It is not only a question of "support", since English actually requires a basically different construction involving a finite auxiliary (*do*) followed by an infinitive (a defective minor sentence). This could be handled by general transfer rules which change one type of functional representation into another. SWETRA, however, takes the traditional approach assigning the same functional representation to Swedish and English sentences including the negation.

Most Samoan sentences begin in a tense particle followed by an inflexible (infinite) verb form. Then come the subject and the objects. Thus, *John came* can be rendered by *Sa alu Ione* in Samoan, where *sa* indicates past tense and *alu* means 'come'. Although Samoan uses a basically different construction, such sentences can be given the same functional representation as in English by deriving the tense from the particle and inserting it after the verb meaning as is done in the functional representation of the coresponding English (and Swedish) sentence. It is not clear how far such "normalization" of functional representations can be carried.

The use of definite articles varies between languages. Georgian is an example of a language where there are no articles. When translating from Swedish into Georgian the Swedish information about definiteness cannot be transferred in a simple way. It may influence the word order, but the word order rules are very subtle. When translating from Georgian into Swedish, it is necessary to decide whether noun phrases are to be definite or indefinite. Seemingly, this can only be made by keeping track of the referents of the noun phrases. If e.g. a submarine has been mentioned before, it must be called *ubåten* 'the submarine' in Swedish. Bad translations of Russian novels are often characterized by inadequate handling of definiteness.

A demo session (Appendix)

We will show some of the results of using the RG programs for Swedish and English developed by SWETRA and comment on the results (print-outs). These examples are run on a PC and they take only seconds.

The first example in the print-out shows stages in the translation of the sentence *Windscale börjar släppa ut plutonium* into English. The predicate "setrans(X)" means "translate X from Swedish into English". The f-representation of the Swedish sentence is not printed before the English module tries to find an equivalent f-representation and finally a corresponding English sentence. Note that the Swedish f-representation includes complex referent expressions, where the numbers are arbitrary numbers of the referents, and the values in four slots are grammatical features. Many empty constituents (above all adverbials) occur in the f-representations.

The translation of *Barnen i Windscale sprang inte ut igår* shows that the English module can handle *do*-support properly. When one of the sentence adverbials is "nix" (the semantic representation of *not*) the proper form of *do* is inserted. The translation of the English sentence *Children were sick* into Swedish shows how the Swedish module can handle agreement in Swedish using the proper plural form *sjuka*.

Appendix

A demo session with SWETRA

```
?- setrans([windscale,boerjar,slaeppa,ut,plutonium,.]).
s(subj(np(r(_03D5,windscale,def,sg,_03E5,ne,_03ED),nom(h(windscale,def,[]),[],[],
[]))),pred(m(begin,pres)),obj(s(subj(np(r(_03D5,windscale,def,sg,_03E5,ne,_03ED),
nom(h(windscale,def,[]),[],[],[]))),padv(out),pred(let),obj(np(r(_1209,plutonium,indef,
sg,_1219,ne,_1221),nom(h(plutonium,indef,[]),[],[],[]))),advl([]),advl([]))),sadvl([]),
advl([]),advl([]),advl([]))
[windscale,begins,to,let,out,plutonium,.]

yes
?- setrans([barnen,i,windscale,sprang,inte,ut,igaar,.]).
s(subj(np(r(_03F9,m(child,pl),def,pl,_0409,_040D,_0411),nom(h(m(child,pl),def,
_0421,_425),[],pp(in,np(r(_09F1,windscale,def,sg,_0A01,ne,_0A09),
nom(h(windscale,def,[]),[],[],[]))),[]))),padv(out),pred(m(run,past)),sadvl([]),
sadvl(nix),advl([]),advl([]),advl(adv(_1545,nom(yesterday))))
[the,children,in,windscale,did,not,run,out,yesterday,.]

yes
?- estrans(children,were,sick,.]).
s(subj(np(r(_03E1,m(child,pl),_03E9,pl,_03F1,_03F5,_03F9),nom(h(child,pl),_03E9,
[],[],[],[],[]))),pred(m(be,past)),cobj(sick),sadvl([]),sadvl([]),advl([]),advl([]),
advl([]))
[barn,var,sjuka,.]

yes
?-
```

References

Ajdukiewicz, K. (1935): Die syntaktische Konnexität.
In: *Studia Philosophica* 1, pp.1-27

Chomsky, N. (1981): *Lectures on Government and Binding.*
Dordrecht: Foris

Clocksin, W. F. / C. S. Mellish (1981): *Programming in Prolog.*
Berlin: Springer

Dooley Collberg, S. (1988): Preliminaries to a referent-grammatical analysis of Modern Irish relative clauses.
In: *Working Papers* (Lund: Dept. of Linguistics and Phonetics) 33

Gawronska-Werngren, B. (1988): A referent grammatical analysis of relative clauses in Polish.
In: *Studia Linguistica* 42[1] (to appear)

Gazdar, G. (1982): Phrase structure grammar.
In: *The nature of syntactic representation.* P. Jacobson / G. Pullum (eds.).
Dordrecht: Reidel

Gazdar, G. / E. Klein / G. Pullum / I. Sag (1985): *Generalized Phrase Structure Grammar.*
Oxford: Basil Blackwell

Sigurd, B. (1987): Referent grammar (RG). A generalized phrase structure grammar with built-in referents.
In: *Studia Linguistica* 41 [2], pp. 115-135

Sigurd, B. (1988a): A referent grammatical analysis of relative clauses.
In: *Acta Linguistica Hafniensia* (to appear)

Sigurd, B. (1988b): Using referent grammar (RG) in computer analysis, generation and translation of sentences.
In: *Nordic Journal of Linguistics* (to appear)

Bengt Sigurd

Tradukado el kaj al la sveda per la multlingva traduksistemo SWETRA

Resumo

La projekto SWETRA funkcias ĉe la Instituto pri Lingvistiko kaj Fonetiko de la Universitato de Lund en Svedujo. Ĝi aplikas adaptitan version de Ĝenerala Sintagmostrukturgramatiko (GPSG), nomatan Referencgramatiko (RG). Ĝiajn regulojn eblas skribi senpere en DCG (Gramatiko de Difinitaj Propozicioj), kiu funkcias en Prolog.

Referencgramatiko distingas inter reprezentaĵo de vort- kaj sintagmoklasoj (o-reprezentaĵo) kaj funkcia (f-) reprezentaĵo. Ĉi-lastaj servas kiel interfaco inter semantiko kaj logiko. La f-reprezentaĵo baziĝas sur sufiĉe universale validaj normaj funkcikategorioj, tiel ke devus ebli uzi ĝin kiel interan (meta)lingvon en perkomputila tradukado.

La signifon de gramatikaj kaj leksikaj unuoj oni en RG indikas per angladevenaj glosoj (t.n. "maŝineca lingvaĵo"), sed kie detaloj ne gravas, ĉi tiu artikolo anstataŭe enhavas normalajn anglajn vortojn. En la reprezentaĵo aperas ĉe substantivkarakteraj vortoj cifero antaŭ duobla punkto, kiu identigas samreferencajn vortojn.

Por la o-reprezentaĵo RG uzas la tradiciajn kategoriojn kaj krome nekompletajn kategoriojn laŭ la ideoj evoluigitaj de Ajdukiewicz (1935) kaj Gazdar (1982). Kategorio estas nekompleta kiam el ĝi forestas konstituanto. En frazo kiel What are you looking at? *la* at *estas nomata nekompleta prepozicia sintagmo, kaj* what *estas identigata kiel la mankanta konstituanto. Ĉi tiu mekanismo funkcias i.a. por la identigo de la korelato de rilativaj pronomoj.*

RG uzas anstataŭigajn regulojn laŭ la kutima modelo. La RG-programaro povas esti uzata por transformi frazon en f-reprezentaĵon kaj inverse (parsi kaj generi).

En substantivaj sintagmoj kaj rilativaj propozicioj DCG-ecaj kondiĉoj povas esti uzataj por zorgi pri akordo kaj formrego pri gramatikaj trajtoj.

La sintaksaj ŝanĝoj bezonataj por traduki inter malsamstrukturaj lingvoj estas realigataj per intera paŝo al RG-reprezentaĵo. En SWETRA oni eksperimentas pri tia tradukado inter la sveda kaj la angla, la franca, la pola, la kartvela kaj la samoa.

La aldonaĵo montras SWETRA-tradukon el la sveda al la angla kaj inverse.

Hungarian – a Special Challenge to Machine Translation?

Gábor Prószéky

OPKM – National Educational Library
Pf. 49
H-1363 Budapest
Hungary

1. Historical overview: Hungarian and MT

Approximately a quarter century ago the question whether Hungarian is a real challenge to machine translation or not was also an issue. It was not a theoretical but a practical question, because at that time a Hungarian-Russian experiment, one of the first East-European machine translation projects, was being prepared with Igor' Mel'čuk as one of its leaders. Hungarian was chosen as a language presenting many of the special difficulties met with in a number of languages. As a consequence of this research on Hungarian Mel'čuk came to formulate his notion of an interlingua. The problems of Hungarian word order compelled the abandonment of a direct word-by-word approach which might be feasible for MT systems with non-agglutinative source languages (Hutchins 1986: 138f.). The main problem was that up to that time no descriptions that could be handled by computers had been elaborated for Hungarian. As a first step in writing the needed formal syntax for Hungarian, some members of the MT research group developed (1) an abstract parsing algorithm called the Dömölki-filter and (2) a morphological analyzer that functioned quite well, but the elaboration of the syntactic module – in spite of Varga's good ideas – was broken by the ALPAC-report or, strictly speaking, by the influence of the ALPAC-report. That is the skeleton of the story of an old fashioned unsuccessful direct machine translation project of the sixties, the only one to date in the history of Hungarian computational linguistics.

Since the sixties, there has not been any project using Hungarian as source or target language. Several kinds of morphological analyzing and generating programs have been developed since then, because all the possible systems – whether MT-oriented or not – have been thought to need them. Syntactic methods that are relevant from a computational point of view were also lacking in the seventies. The theoretical linguists dealing with Hungarian have been working in Chomskyan frameworks (standard theory, extended standard theory, trace theory, government-and-binding theory) or Montagovian models. Some of their results would have been applicable (with modifications, of course) in natural language processing systems, but such a system did not then exist.

The interlingual approach to machine translation expects the existence of an interlingua, the transfer method must rely on the target language in order to identify the optimal way and "depth" of the source language formalization. Suppose that the source language is Hungarian. Both methods of machine translation have modules that must occur in the target-language-independent part of the analysis of Hungarian. There is, for instance, a typical order of stem and case morphemes in a Hungarian word, but the suffixation of pronouns is somewhat different. In order to handle this phenomenon generally, one has to reorder the morphemes of the suffixed pronouns in a way which is independent of the existence of a target language or interlingua.

The generalization of the order of morphemes cannot be aim-independent. This aim, a category system and a syntax adequate to it, have been elaborated and are introduced in this paper in order to overcome the challenge to machine translation caused by the application independent descriptions of Hungarian.

2. Some important grammatical phenomena of Hungarian

In this paper I would like to point out that Hungarian and other agglutinative languages, like Finnish, Estonian, Japanese, Turkish etc. cannot be always analyzed in the same way as the Indo-European languages. In the following, I should like to sketch a method that can be useful for the computational processing of Hungarian and its "structural relatives". This type of language, except Japanese and perhaps Finnish, has no well-worked out set of computational grammars, but nowadays, at a time of revival of MT systems, it seems to be important to fill the gap. For instance, grammatical roles like subject or object are often expressed by suffixes in Hungarian sentences. Wordforms consequently consist not only of a stem and several items of other syntactic information contained in grammatical morphemes (e.g. personal suffix, possessive suffix etc.) but also the **relationships** among these morphemes. This idea of morpheme-word relations is analogous to Tesnière's concept of word-sentence relations.

To build a grammar for Hungarian, it is not convenient to use the definition of word as a sequence of letters between two spaces, but it would be better to define a word as an element of the output of a **morphological analyzer**. This will form the minimal syntactic unit in our study. With regard to its internal structure this unit can be a word in the usual sense or a morpheme sequence, but at least one morpheme.

Each Hungarian noun can, for example, occur in nearly 1000 wordforms as a stem, because the majority of the Indo-European prepositions and possessive determiners are expressed by suffixes (it would be too much to store them in the dictionary!), thus we have one more reason to use morphological segmentation as the first phase of parsing.

Let us look at an example. The Hungarian sentence

> *Beszélhetek a könyvemről.*
> 'speak-can-I the book-my-about'
> 'I can speak about my book.'

without morphological analysis would give a structure where the word forms as they stand could not be found in the dictionary:

Dependency based structure **Constituency based structure**

beszélhetek
|
könyvemről
|
a

or

To receive a rather adequate structure, similar to those in usual descriptions of other languages we have to pass the sentence through the morphological analyzer and build the dependency tree from its output:

> *beszél- -het- -ek a könyv- -em- -ről*

where the morphemes with "-" express their need for a link on the left, the right or on both sides, these are the output of the morphological analyzer. Now the trees will be similar to that of, for example, English:

Dependency based structure and Constituency based structure

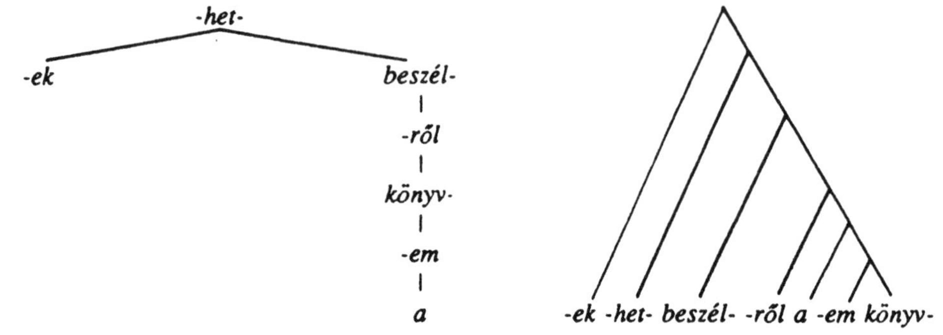

Finite endings follow the verbs directly. There are two parallel endings series for the definite and indefinite verbal conjugations in Hungarian:

Meaning	Definite x = 'it'			Indefinite x = 'something'		
I see x	*lát-*		*-om*	*lát-*		*-ok*
I saw x	*lát-*	*-t-*	*-am*	*lát-*	*-t-*	*-am*
I would see x	*lát-*	*-ná*	*-m*	*lát-*	*-n-*	*-ék*

The role of the object is rather explicit in the 2nd person, singular:

lát- **-l-** *-ak*
'see-you-I'
'I see you'

Personal endings mark the possessive relation between two nominal elements:

ház- **-am**
'house-my'
'my house'

ház- **-aitok**
'house-s-your'
'your houses'

In the possessive sentences there can be a facultative element, a facultative "argument": a nominal element or a pronoun that is coreferent with the personal ending, e.g.

Péter *ház- -a*
'Peter house-of-him'
'the house of Peter'

Péter- **-nek** *a ház- -a*
'Peter-DAT the house-of-him'
'the house of Peter'

(az) **én** *ház- -am*
'(the) I house-of-mine'

Possessive endings (*-é,-éi*) stand for a noun phrase whose referent is possessed by the referent of the nominal element directly before them:

barát- -om- **-é-** *-ban*
'friend my that in'
'in that of my friend'

barát- -aim- **-éi-** *-val*
'friend- -s my those with'
'with those of my friends'

Participle endings (*-ó, -tt, -andó* etc.) follow a verbal stem to form an adjective-like element. Complements and adjuncts depend on the verbal part of a participle:

a szobá- -ban könyv- -et olvas- **-ó** *fiú*
'the room-in book-ACC read-ing boy'
'the boy reading a book in the room'

Case morphemes are a closed subset of the suffixes, but the close "relatives", the postpositions are autonomous words. All the heads of nominal phrases are followed directly by case endings (the nominative case ending is Ø). Case morphemes and postpositions play the same role in Hungarian as prepositions in the Indo-European languages.

Another phenomenon which requires the splitting of words is the eventual shift of certain verbal endings:

Meg akarlak érteni.
'PERF want-you-I understand-INF'
'I want to understand you.'

The ending *-lak* of the auxiliary expresses at the same time the subject and the object of the main verb *megért* "understand" that forms a discontinuous constituent:

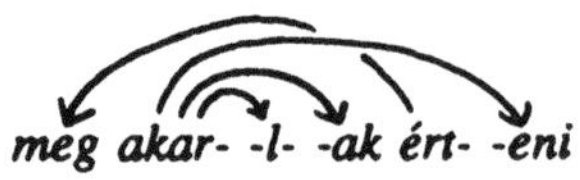

The above sentence presents us with a further problem, the verbal prefix. The morphological analyzer provides us with the possibility of identifying the verb *megért* by both its forms *meg* ... *ért* or *ért* ... *meg*. This approach enables the homogeneous treatment of the accusative, locative, etc. cases, e.g.,

látom a házat

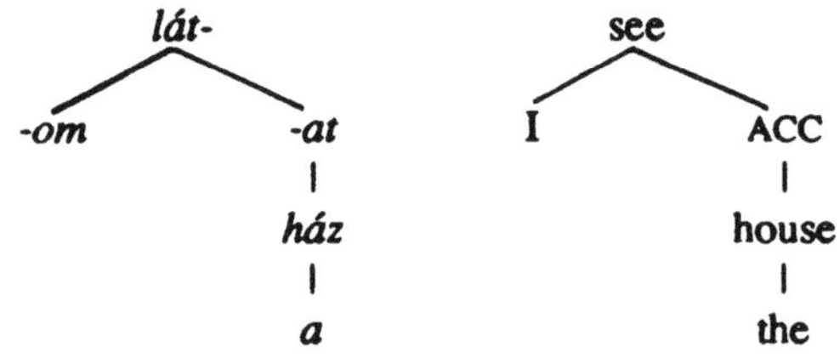

a házban laksz

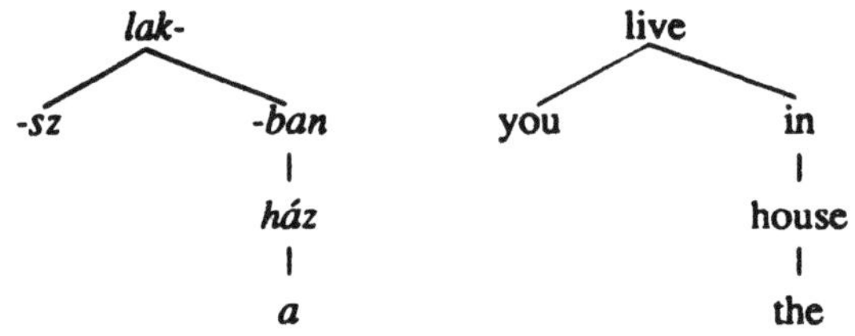

az asztal alatt ül

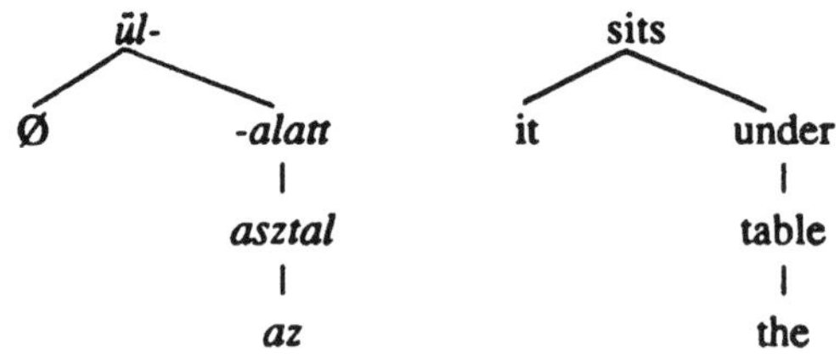

3. The nature of syntactic relations in Hungarian

The **basic pattern** of a Hungarian sentence is as follows:

((__CAS)* (V NFIN)* ADV*)* V FIN ((__CAS)* (V NFIN)* ADV*)*

The case endings and postpositions (marked here as CAS) and the endings of the verb (NFIN, FIN) are obliged to immediately follow their dependents, that is, the nominal phrase and the verbal stem, respectively. Bound morphemes used to identify the syntactic relations form a closed class. What is interesting is that Hungarian verbal stems also form a closed class (Kálmán/Prószéky 1985: 39). New verbs can be formed always by derivational suffixes.

Some syntactic relators are **Ø-morphemes** in Hungarian, like the copula, the finite ending in the 3rd person singular, and the nominative, the genitive and the predicative cases.

The **word order** is not as free as is generally claimed. What is free is the phrase order, but there are important rules controlling their sequence. The phrase order has strong interrelations with the sentence prosody and the informational structure of the sentence. Thus, the same relation can express several shades of information depending on the order of the elements it governs.

There are some lexical, morphological, syntactic and semantic **constraints** that can help us to recognize the correct relation. Lexical constraints can occur in the case of collocations and idioms. Morphological constraints are always positional, but syntactic constraints can be positional (___ *terül el,* ___ *is*), model-dependent (in ___*re fest,* "___" must be an ADJ) or referential (in ___*nek eszébe jutott,* where "___" and "*é*" in *eszébe* are coreferential. Semantic constraints are not Hungarian-specific phenomena. the subject of *eszik,* for example, 'to eat' has to be a person and that of the *zabál* 'to feed' has to be an animal.

4. The morpheme classes

The first part of our description must be the **classification** of the minimal units, in our case, morphemes. Members of the same class are characterized by similar morpho-syntactic relational patterns. The stems are classified by the usual category names, but the use of such category names for bound morphemes as well is new (the sign ^{0} serves to distinguish them). We aim in this way to conserve the advantages of the agglutinative nature of the language and at the same time to follow the use of word classes as a descriptive device for Indo-European languages.

The Hungarian Morpheme Classes			
Abbr.	**Subclasses**	**Poss. feat.**	**Examples**
+v	1-valency verb	+1	*él, ...*
	2-valency verb	+2	*lakik, ...*
	3-valency verb	+3	*ad, ...*
	4-valency verb	+4	*mond, ...*
	nominative slot	(nom)	*él (valaki), ...*
	accusative slot	(acc)	*ad (valamit), ...*
	dative slot	(dat)	*ad (valakinek), ...*
	infinitive slot	(inf)	*szándékozik (tenni), ...*
	adverbial slot	(adv)	*él (valahol), ...*
	copula	+cop	*van, vol-, marad, ...*
	auxiliary	+aux	*kell, akar, fog, ...*
	auxiliary^0	+aux^0	*-tat-, -het-, ...*
+n	noun		*liba, kacsa, ...*
	proper noun	+prop	*MTA, Magyarország, ...*
	verbal noun^0	+ver^0	*-ás, -és*
	measure name	+meas	*kg, méter, ...*
	adjectival noun	+adj	*orvos, ifjú, ...*
	pronoun	+pro	
	- personal	+pers	*én, te, maga, ...*
	- general	+q	*mindenki, minden, ...*
	- demonstrative	+dem	*ez, az*
	- question	+wh	*ki, mi, ...*
	- relative	+rel	*aki, ami, ...*
	- negative	+neg	*senki, semmi, ...*
	- indefinite	+ind	*valaki, akárki, ...*
	finite ending^0	+fin^0	*-om, -unk, ...*
	possessive ending^0	+poss^0	*-é, -éi*
	personal ending^0	+pers^0	*-m, -d, -ja, -eink, ...*
+adj	adjective		*zöld, nagy, ...*
	proadjective	+pro	
	- demonstrative	+dem	*ilyen, ekkora, ...*
	- question	+wh	*milyen, melyik, ...*
	- relative	+rel	*amilyen, amekkora, ...*
	- negative	+neg	*semmilyen, ...*
	- indefinite	+ind	*valamilyen, ...*
	i-ending^0	+i^0	*-i*
	s-ending^0	+s^0	*-s, -os, -es, -ös*
	u-ending^0	+u^0	*-ú, -ű, -jú, -jű*
	participle^0	+part^0	
	- continuous^0	+cont^0	*-ó, -ő*
	- perfect^0	+perf^0	*-t, -tt, -ott, -ett, -ött*
	- future^0	+fut^0	*-andó, -endő*
	hato-ending^0	+hato^0	*-ható, -hető*
	empty adjective	+emp	*való, történő, ...*
	ik-ending^0	+ik^0	*-ik*
	ordinal number^0	+ord^0	*-odik, -ödik, ...*
	positional adj.	+pst	*alsó, középső, ...*
	quantifier	+q	*minden, néhány, ...*

Abbr.	Subclasses	Poss. feat.	Examples
+num	numeral		*három, ezer, ...*
	fractional	+fra	*-ad, -ed, -od, -öd*
	pronumeral	+pro	
	- general	+q	*minden, mindannyi, ...*
	- demonstrative	+dem	*ennyi, annyi*
	- question	+wh	*mennyi, hány*
	- relative	+rel	*amennyi, ahány*
	- negative	+neg	*semennyi, sehány, ...*
	- indefinite	+ind	*valahány, bármennyi, ...*
+adv	adverb		*tegnap, otthon, ...*
	degree	+deg	*nagyon, alig, ...*
	modifier	+mod	*nem, csak, talán, is, ...*
	proadverb	+pro	
	- general	+q	*mindenhol, ...*
	- demonstrative	+dem	*ímhol, itt, ...*
	- question	+wh	*hol, merre, hová, ...*
	- relative	+rel	*ahol, amerre, ahová, ...*
	- negative	+neg	*sehol, semerre, ...*
	- indefinite	+ind	*valahol, bármerre, ...*
	postposition	+postp	*után, alatt, mögé, ...*
	adverbial ending^0	+adv^0	*-an, -lag, -ül, ...*
	case ending^0	+cas^0	*-nak, -ból, -ra, -t, ...*
	infinitive^0	+inf^0	*-ni, -ani, -eni, ...*
	gerund^0	+ger^0	*-va, -ve, -ván, -vén*
+vpv	verbal prefix^0		*ki-, alá-, haza-, ...*
+art	article		
	definite	+def	*a, az*
	indefinite	+idf	*egy*
	demonstrative	+dem	*ez, e, az*
+con	conjunction		*és, vagy, ...*
	propositional	+prop	*azonban, csakhogy, ...*
+sbj	subjunction		*hogy*
+int	interjection		*igen, bizony, óh, jaj, ...*

The feature structure of our sample sentence

Beszél- -het- -ek a könyv- -em- -ről.

will look like this:

[+v+2][+v+aux^0][+n+fin][+art+def][+n][+n+pro+pers][+adv+cas]

5. Classification of the relations

After some generalization we can say that the following kinds of morpheme-relations can be distinguished in Hungarian:

(1) morphologically **marked** syntactic relations,

(2) morphologically **unmarked** syntactic relations,

(3) relations between proper names, relations between the elements of idioms or relations between interjections and their matrix sentences, that is relations with **no structure**, at least, on this level of processing.

Class (1) is easy to handle, if we have a morphological segmentation process such as the one mentioned above. In the following we use an

relation as a typical morphological dependency pattern, where y and X^0 are the morphologically decomposed parts of the same word form and X is a kind of adverbial. In a constituency approach one would say that

is a typical morphological $\bar{X}$ pattern.

Our sample sentence has the morphological dependency patterns as follows:

[+v+2]	[+v+aux^0]	[+n+fin]	[+art+def]	[+n]	[+n+pro+pers]	[+adv+cas]
beszél-	*-het-*	*-ek*	*a*	*könyv-*	*-em-*	*-ről*

Some morpho-syntactic relations can be identified uniquely on the basis of the order of the morphemes that play the roles of the head and the dependents, but some not, as it is shown below:

	Marked relations	Unmarked relations
Adjacency-based relations	tense determiner	appositive attributive numerals
	modifier	possessive
Not adjacency-based relations	conjunctive object relative subject	conjunctive object relative subject
	adverbial dative infinitive	adverbial adjunct linking adjunct predicative

The common problem in connection with the unmarked phenomena listed above is how to identify them. Syntactically, all of them form a source of ambiguity and if two or more of them occur in a sentence at the same time, the number of the possible combinations can be quite large.

The only solution seems to be a **heuristic approach**, but it will produce all the syntactically possible combinations of the subtrees identified with the help of the marked relations. Thus, if this solution is chosen, we need a source language based semantic/pragmatic disambiguation process that can select the only possible structure from the set of all the syntactically possible sentences if translating from Hungarian. Translating into Hungarian is relatively simple, at least from the viewpoint of disambiguation of the phenomena above. But in a MT system that does not use an interlingua it is too expensive. For instance, the DLT system offers a disambiguation processor, the SWESIL, with a help of which the above sketched ideas about parsing Hungarian can be maintained.

6. Present connections between Hungarian and MT

The structures that can be handled sequentially will be parsed first and then the possible combinations of them will be made by a second step based on our valency-oriented description. On the basis of the above mentioned facts, we can summarize our proposals as follows:

(1) This system is suitable for the syntactic scheme of DLT proposed by Schubert (1987: 28ff.).

(2) There is a system that can pick out the most likely solution on a semantic/pragmatic basis: it is SWESIL, a subsystem of DLT (Papegaaij 1986: 75ff.)

The above-mentioned considerations took a prominent part in the decision to make Hungarian one of the languages whose syntax has begun to be elaborated in the DLT-framework (Prószéky/Koutny/Wacha 1988).

References

Hutchins, William John (1986): *Machine Translation: Past, Present, Future.* Chichester: Horwood / New York etc.: Wiley

Kálmán, László / Gábor Prószéky (1985): FMR Grammar. In: *Working Papers of the Institute of Linguistics of the Hungarian Academy of Sciences* [1], pp. 31-41

Papegaaij, B. C. (1986): *Word expert semantics. An interlingual knowledge-based approach.* V. Sadler / A. P. M. Witkam (eds.). Dordrecht/Riverton: Foris

Prószéky, Gábor / Ilona Koutny / Balázs Wacha (1988): A dependency syntax of Hungarian (for use in DLT). Unpublished report. Utrecht: BSO/Research

Schubert, Klaus (1987): *Metataxis. Contrastive dependency syntax for machine translation.* Dordrecht/Providence: Foris

Gábor Prószéky

La hungara – ĉu speciala defio al perkomputila tradukado?

Resumo

Jam antaŭ kvaronjarcento la hungara ekrolis en perkomputila tradukado. Unu el la plej fruaj en orienta Eŭropo estis la hungara-rusa projekto gvidata de Mel'čuk. La morfemstrukturo kaj la vortordo de la hungara necesigis rezignon pri la ĝistiama vortopa tradukmetodo. El tiu klopodo evoluis la ideo de interlingvo. De kiam efikis projekthaltige ankaŭ en Hungarujo la ALPAC-raporto, ne plu ekzistas komputila tradukprojekto kun la hungara, sed ja unuopaj tekstprilaboraj programoj, ekz. por parsado kaj por morfologia analizo.

Ne eblas analizi aglutinan lingvon same kiel la hindeŭropajn. Mi analizas la morfemstrukturon de hungaraj vortoj iom laŭ la maniero, kiun Tesnière aplikas al vortoj en frazo, do dependosintakse. Eblas konstrui dependoarbon kiu rilatigas la funkciajn kaj enhavajn morfemojn (do ne kompletajn vortojn) en frazo. Por tiu celo necesas plivastigi la nocion de vortspecoj, enkondukante morfemspecojn. Morfemoj povas esti portantoj de trajtoj.

Klasinte la morfemojn, oni povas etikedi la sintaksajn rilatojn inter ili. Laŭ la identigaj karakterizaĵoj oni povas distingi rilatojn identigitajn per apudeco kaj per morfemoj kaj rilatojn kun aŭ sen markita identigilo.

La montrata sistemo taŭgas por la dependosintaksa sistemo (metatakso) de la komputila traduksistemo DLT. Ĝi tiel donas aliron ankaŭ al ties semantika-pragmatika vortekspertsistemo SWESIL, kiu realigas enhavrilatan elekton el sintakse eblaj tradukalternativoj. Hungara dependosintakso laŭ la DLT-modelo estas ellaborita.

Learning from Translation Mistakes

Claude Piron

Université de Genève
Faculté de psychologie et des sciences de l'éducation
25 chemin des Rannaux
CH-1296 Coppet
Switzerland

As a former translator and reviser of translations, I find it very difficult to believe that a data processing system is really able to do the same job as a human translator. This is probably due to my lack of knowledge and understanding of how computers work. But whatever my incompetence in that field, I hope the examples I will draw from my experience in translation units will give you an interesting insight into some of the most frustrating problems encountered when transferring ideas from one language to another.

When taking part in the selection of candidates for translator jobs, I have often been amazed by the fact that a number of candidates with a perfect knowledge of both the source and the target languages and an impressive mastery of the relevant field could be very poor translators indeed. Why is that? One of the human factors is the lack of modesty. The translator's personality and intelligence interfere with the very humble task he has to perform. Instead of putting aside his own ideas, fantasies and style to blindly follow the author's, he embelishes, adds or transforms. This kind of problem, I suppose, cannot arise with a machine translator, although, being something of an

Asimov fan, I may have my doubts: if machine translation is actually working, it must come close to the capabilities of Asimov's robots.

Anyway, besides humility, candidates must possess two other qualities that may be difficult to develop in machines, however sophisticated: judgment and flexibility.

Judgment

By judgment I mean the ability to solve a problem through wide knowledge of the background, through awareness that a problem exists and by taking into account the various levels of context.

Wide knowledge of the background

Let's take the phrase *to table a bill.* The translator must know that if the original is in British English, it means 'to submit a bill – i.e. a text proposed to become law – to the country's legislative body', in French *déposer un projet de loi* [in Esperanto, *submeti leĝprojekton*], but that if the author followed American usage, he meant 'to shelve', i.e. 'to adjourn indefinitely the discussion of the text', in French *ajourner* sine die *l'examen du projet de loi* [in Esperanto *arkivigi la leĝprojekton*].

Here is another example. The word *heure* in French can mean 'hour' as well as 'o'clock'. To be able to translate correctly the French phrase *une messe de neuf heures*, you have to know that a Catholic mass lasting nine hours is extremely improbable, so that the translation is 'a nine o'clock mass', and not "a nine hour mass". Since the linguistic structure is exactly the same in *un voyage de neuf heures*, which means 'a nine hour journey', only knowledge of the average duration of a mass can help the translator decide.

Awareness that a problem exists

When you become a professional translator, the chief development that occurs during your first three or four years is that you become aware of problems that you had no idea could exist. If you are transferred to another organization, the whole process will start anew for a few years because the new field implies new problems that are just as hidden as those in your former job. Some of the public in this room may know that in the history of international communication there was an organization called *International Auxiliary Language Association.* Well, if you ask people how they understand that title, you will realize that, for a number of them, it means 'international association dealing with an auxiliary language', whereas for others it means 'an association studying the question of an international auxiliary language'. The interesting point lies not so much in the ambiguity as in the fact that most people are not aware of it. When exposed to the phrase, they immediately understand it in a certain way and they are not at all conscious of the possibility that the very same words are susceptible of another interpretation and that their intuitive understanding does not necessarily coincide with what the author had in mind.

Similarly, most junior translators simply do not imagine that the words *Soviet expert* usually designate, not a Soviet citizen, but a Westerner specializing in studying developments in the USSR.

Taking into account the various levels of context

The English word *repression* has two conventional translations in French. In politics, the French equivalent is *répression* [in Esperanto *subpremo*], whereas in psychology, it is *refoulement* [*repuŝo*]. You might believe at first glance that translating it correctly is simply a matter of knowing to what field your text belongs. If it deals with politics, you use one translation, if with psychology another. Reality is not that simple. Your author may use the psychological sense within a broad political context. For instance, in an article dealing with the Stalin era, you may have a sentence beginning with *Repression by the population of its spontaneous critical reactions led to...* In this case, although the text deals with politics, the sentence deals with psychology. The narrow context is at variance with the broad context.

I recently revised a text which had me wondering how a computer would deal with the various meanings of the word *case*. It was about packaging. In a section on wooden cases, it said: *Other reasons for water removal important in specific cases are: (1) to avoid gaps between boards in sheathed cases; (2) to (...).* A human translator's judgment leads him to a correct understanding of the first *case* as a synonym of 'occurrence' and of the second as 'a kind of big box', but how will a computer know? If the text includes such phrases as *A case can be made for plastic boxes* or *the importer complained about the poor quality of the cases. When the case was settled in court (...).* Knowing the broad context does not help to choose the right translation if there is no mechanical means to determine that the author switched, in a narrow context, to a different meaning of the word.

Flexibility

Besides judgment, the other quality I mentioned as indispensable to make an acceptable translator is flexibility. This refers to the gymnastics aspect of translation work. Mastering the specialized field and the two relevant languages is not enough, you have to master the art of constantly jumping from one into the other and back. Languages are more than intellectual structures. They are universes. Each language has a certain atmosphere, a style of its own, that differentiates it from all others. If you compare such English expressions as *software* and, on a road sign, *soft shoulder* with their French equivalents, you realize that there is a very definite switch in the approach to communication. The French translations are respectively *logiciel* and *accotements non stabilisés*. The English phrases are concrete, metaphorical, made up, with a touch of humor, from words used in everyday speech, although this does not contribute to better comprehension: knowing the meaning of *soft* and of *shoulder* does not help you to understand what a *soft shoulder* is. In French, the same meanings are conveyed by abstract and descriptive terms, which do not belong to everyday usage. You don't understand them either, but for a different reason: because they are based on morphemes that are so intellectual, sophisticated, and unusual, that most foreigners have to look up the words in dictionaries.

The difficulty lies in the fact that this difference in approach has to be taken into account at the level, not only of words (a good dictionary may often solve that problem), but of sentences. Consider the sentence *Private education is in no way under the jurisdiction of the government*. It includes mostly English words of French origin, but common etymology does not imply a common way of expressing one's thoughts. In this case, a good French rendering would be *L'enseignement libre ne relve en rien de l'Etat*. You will realize the importance of those differences in the approach to communication if you take the French sentence as the original and translate it literally into English. The result would be *Free teaching does not depend in any way on the State*, which means something quite different, especially to an American.

In order to translate properly, you have to **feel** when and how to switch from one atmosphere to another. No human beginner, in translation work, knows how to do that, and I wonder how a machine will detect the need to do it, unless its memory is so huge that it includes all the practical problems that translators have had to solve for decades, with an appropriate solution. For instance, when new translators arrive in the World Health Organization and have to translate the phrase *blood sugar concentration*, practically all of them use an expression like *concentration de sucre dans le sang*. This is what it means, but this is not how the concept is expressed in French, in which you have to replace those three English words with a single one: *glycémie*.

Similarly, knowing that the French equivalent of *software* is *logiciel* does not help you to translate it by *didacticiel* when it refers to a teaching aid, which is the word you should normally use in that particular case. French uses narrower semantic fields, and this is something you have to bear in mind constantly.

The problem is that with languages, you never know how you know what you know. (Sorry, I am being self-centered. **I** never know, but perhaps, with your experience in the computerized analysis of languages, **you** know.) If, in a text dealing with economic matters, I meet the phrase *the life expectancy of those capital goods*, I know – because I **feel** – that I have to translate it by *la longévité des équipements*. I also know that when that same text mentions *the consumers' life expectancy*, I'll have to say, in French, *espérance de vie*, because the author for a while deals with a demographic concept which is included in his economic reasoning. But how do I know I know? I don't know. This ability to adjust to the various approaches to reality or fantasy embodied in the different languages, linked to an ability to pass constantly back and forth, is what I call flexibility. This is the quality which is the most difficult to find when you recruit translators.

We can now approach the same field from a different angle, asking ourselves the question: what are the problems built-in in languages that make judgment and flexibility so important in translation work? They relate to the grammar and the semantics of both the source and the target languages.

Grammar

The more a language uses precise and clear-cut grammatical devices to express the relationships among words and, within a given word, its constitutive concepts, the easier the task for the translator. The worst source languages for translators are thus English and Chinese. A Chinese sentence like *ta shi qunian shengde xiaohair* can mean both 'he (or she) is a child who was born last year' and 'it was last year that she gave birth to a child'.

In English similar ambiguities are constant. In *International Labor Organization*, the word *international* modifies *organization*, as shown in the official French wording: *Organisation internationale du Travail.* But in another UN specialized agency, the *International Civil Aviation Organization*, the word *international* modifies *aviation*, not with *organization*, as shown, again, by the French version: *Organisation de l'aviation civile internationale* (and not *Organisation internationale de l'aviation civile*). This is legally and politically important, because it means that the organization is competent only for flights that cross national boundaries. It is not an international organization that deals with all problems of non-military flying. However, since the linguistic structure is similar in both cases, no text analysis can help the translator; he has no linguistic means to decide which is which. He has to refer to the constitution of the relevant organization.

The problem is complicated by the fact that most English texts on which a translator works were not written by native English speakers, who might be more able to express themselves without ambiguity. Let us consider the following sentence: *He could not agree with the amendments to the draft resolution proposed by the delegation of India.* The draft translation read: *Il ne pouvait accepter les amendements au projet de résolution proposé par la délégation indienne.* I am not able to judge if the English is correct or not, but, as a reviser, I had to check the facts, so that I know that the translator, who had understood that the text submitted by India was the draft resolution, was mistaken. Actually, it was the amendments. In French, you would have *proposé* if it modifies *draft resolution* and *proposés* if it modifies *amendments*. Similarly, in Esperanto you would have *proponita* or *proponitaj* according to what refers to what.

I wonder how a computer solves similar problems. I have been told that it detects the possible ambiguities and asks the author what he means. I wish it good luck. All translators know that authors are usually unavailable. Much translation work is done at night, because a report or a project produced during the afternoon session has to be on the desks of the participants to the conference in the various working languages on the following morning. They are not allowed to wake up authors to ask them what they meant.

Or the author is far away and difficult to get in touch with. When I was a reviser in WHO, I had to deal with a scientific report produced by an Australian physician. He mentioned a disease which had broken out in a *Japanese prisoner of war camp*. We decided to write to Australia to know if the disease affected American soldiers who were prisoners of the Japanese or Japanese caught by the Americans. When the reply arrived, it stated that the author had been dead for a few years.

Many mistakes made by professional translators result from this impossibility, in English, to assign an adjective to its noun through grammatical means. When a translator rendered *Basic oral health survey methods* by *Méthodologie des enquêtes fondamentales sur l'état de santé bucco-dentaire*, he was mistaken in relating the word *basic* to *survey*, whereas it actually relates to *methods*, but he should be forgiven, because only familiarity with the subject enables the reader to understand what refers to what. The correct translation was *Méthodologie fondamentale applicable aux enquêtes sur l'état de santé bucco-dentaire*.

My wife teaches translation to American students who come to Geneva for one year. A standard translation task she gives them includes the subtitle *Short breathing exercises*. Every year, half her class understands 'exercises in short breathing', whereas the real meaning is 'short exercises in deep breathing'. The fact that native speakers of English so consistently make the same mistake, although the context provides all the necessary clues, keeps me wondering. Does a computer have a better judgment than humans? Can a machine discern, compare and evaluate clues?

The fact that, in English, the endings *-s, -ed* and *-ing* have several grammatical functions often complicates matters. In the sentence *He was sorting out food rations and chewing gum*, it is impossible to know if the concerned individual was chewing gum while sorting out food rations, or if he was sorting out two kinds of supplies: food, and chewing gum.

Semantics

Problems caused by semantics are particularly difficult for human translators. They are of two kinds: (1) the problem is not apparent; (2) the problem is readily seen, but the solution either requires good judgment or does not exist.

An example of the first category is provided by the phrase *malaria therapy*. Since *malaria* is a well known disease, and *therapy* means 'treatment', a translator not trained in medical matters will think that it means 'treatment of malaria'. But the semantic field of *therapy* is not identical with that of *treatment*, although this is not apparent if you simply consult a dictionary (Webster's defines *therapy* as 'treatment of a disease'). It would be too long to explain here the differences, but the fact is that *malaria therapy* should be rendered, not by *traitement du paludisme* [*kuracado de malario*], but by *impaludation thérapeutique* or *paludothérapie* [*permalaria kuracado*], because it means that the malaria parasite is injected into the blood to elicit a febrile reaction designed to cure the attacked disease, which is not malaria. In other words, it means 'treatment **by** malaria' and not 'treatment **of** malaria'.

In the French version, published by Albin Michel, of Hammond Innes' novel *Levkas Man*, one of the characters complains about *les jungles concrètes* in which an enormous population has to live. This does not make sense for the French reader. Since some of you understand Esperanto, I can explain the misunderstanding better using that language. *Jungles concrètes* means *konkretaj ĝangaloj*. What the author meant by *concrete jungles* was *jungles de béton, betonaj ĝangaloj*, i.e. high-rise housing developments made of concrete. This is a case in which the translator was not aware of the existence of a semantic problem, namely that *concrete* has two completely unrelated meanings: a building material, and the opposite of 'abstract'.

An example of a semantic problem requiring good judgment – and, with all my prejudices, I fail to imagine how a computer can exercise that kind of judgment – is the word *develop*. It has such a wide semantic field that it is often a real nightmare for translators. It can mean 'setting up', 'creating', 'designing', 'establishing' and thus refer to something that did not exist before. It can mean 'intensifying', 'accelerating', 'extending', 'amplifying', and thus express the concept 'making larger', which implies that the thing being developed has been concretely in existence for some time. But it can also mean 'tapping the resources', 'exploiting', in other words 'making use of something that has been having a latent or potential existence'. In all other languages, the translation will vary according to the meaning, i.e. to that particular segment the author had in view within the very wide semantic field covered by the word. To know how to translate *to develop such or such an industry*, you have to know if the said industry already exists or not in the area your text is covering. In most cases, the text itself gives no clue on that matter. Only the translator's general culture or his ability to do appropriate research can lead him to the right translation.

Such a simple word as *more* can pose problems, because its semantic area covers both the concepts of quantity and of qualitative degree. What does *more accurate information* mean? Does it mean 'a larger amount of accurate information' or 'information that has greater accuracy'?

A word like *tape* is just as tricky. If it refers to sound recording, you translate it into French as *bande* or *cassette* (provided you know which kind of recorder was used). But if it refers to the gluing material, as in *Scotch tape*, you have to render it by *ruban adhésif*, since in that particular case, the French word *bande* evokes the bandaging of a wound.

Often, a problem arises – without being always apparent – because a word has a special semantic value in the particular milieu in which the author works; in that case, an underlying concept is frequently unexpressed, since the author addresses persons working in the same field and used to the same kind of compact expressions. In the sentence *WHO helped control programs in 20 countries*, only knowing that in WHO parlance *control program* means 'a program to fight a disease and put it under control' may make the translator suspect that the author meant 'WHO granted its assistance to help fight the relevant disease in 20 countries'. The junior translator who understood it as meaning 'it helped to control the programs' was grammatically justified, since in English the verb *to help* can be construed without the particle *to* in the following verb and, in such a sentence, nothing enables you to know if *control* is used as a noun or as a verb.

However, most of the difficulties that human translators meet relate to the different ways in which various languages cut up reality into differentiated semantic blocks. I use the word *block* on purpose, because very often reality is continuous, as well as concepts, whereas language is discontinuous. *Blue* and *green* are what I call 'semantic blocks', whereas in the spectrum there is perfect continuity. Very often, a concept that exists in a language has no translation in another, because peoples cut up the continuum in different sizes and from different angles.

In a number of cases, it does not matter. The fact that for the only French word *crier* English has to choose among *shout, scream, screech, squall, shriek, squeal, yell, bawl, roar, call out*, etc., does not pose serious problems in practice.

But how can you translate *cute* into another language? The concept simply does not exist in most. Conversely, the French word *frileux* has no equivalent in English, so that a simple French sentence like *il est frileux* cannot be properly translated. Still, you can say *he feels the cold terribly* or *he is very sensitive to cold.* Although those are poor renderings, they are acceptable. What resists translation most is the adverbial form: *frileusement.* How can you translate *il ramena frileusement la couverture sur ses genoux*? You have to say something like *He put the blanket back onto his knees with the kind of shivering movement typical of people particularly sensitive to cold.* To those of you who might think that this is literary translation, something outside your field of research, I have to emphasize that descriptions of attitudes and behavior are an integral part of medical and psychological case presentations, so that the above sentence should not be considered unusual in a translator's practice.

An enormous number of words, many of them appearing constantly in ordinary texts, present us with similar difficulties. Such words as *commodity, consolidation, core, crop, disposal, to duck, emphasis, estate, evidence, feature, flow, forward, format, insight, issue, joint, junior, kit, maintain, matching, predicament, procurement* and hundreds of others are quite easy to understand, but no French word has the same semantic field, so that their translation is always a headache. Dictionaries don't help, because they give you a few translations that never coincide with the concept as actually used in a text; in most cases the translations they suggest do not fit with the given context.

Another case in point is provided by the many words that refer to the organization of life. You cannot translate *Swiss Government* by *Gouvernement suisse*, because the French word *gouvernement* has a much narrower meaning than the English one.

(Interestingly, although the semantic extension of both words does not coincide exactly, you can translate it into Esperanto by *svisa registaro*, because the Esperanto concept is wide enough). In French, you have to say *le Conseil fédéral* or *la Confédération suisse* according to the precise meaning. The French *gouvernement* designates what in English is often named *cabinet*. The English word *government* is one of the frustrating ones. You may render it by *l'Etat, les pouvoirs publics, les autorités, le régime* or similar words, evaluating in each case what is closest to the English meaning, and you have to bear in mind that at times it should be *sciences politiques* (for instance in the sentence *she majored in government*, in which the verb *major* is another headache, because American studies are organized in quite a different way from studies in French speaking countries).

The Russian word *dispanserizacija* illustrates a similar problem. It designates a whole conception of public health services that has no equivalent in Western countries. If you want your reader to understand your translation, you should, rather than translate it (it would be easy enough to say *dispensarisation*), explain what it means.

Conclusion

As you see, each one of the problems I mentioned makes the translators' task very arduous indeed. Problems caused by ambiguities, unexpressed but implied meanings, and semantic values without equivalent in the target language require a lot of thinking, a special knowledge of the field and a certain amount of research – as for instance when you have to find out if an industry being *developed* already exists or not, or if secretary Tan Buting is a male or a female, which, in many languages, will govern the correct form of the adjectives and even the translation of *secretary* (*Sekretär*? *Sekretärin*?). Such problems take up 80 to 90% of a professional translator's time. "A translator is essentially a detective", one of my Spanish colleagues in WHO used to say, and it is true. He has to make a lot of phone calls, to go from one library to another (not so much to find a technical term as to understand how a process unfolds or to find basic data that are understood, and thus unexpressed, among specialists) and to tap all his resources in deduction. I do hope that computers will free the poor slaves from those unrewarding tasks, but I confess that, with my incompetence in data processing, I am at a loss to imagine how they will proceed.

Claude Piron

Lerni de tradukeraroj

Resumo

Kiel kunjuĝanto pri kandidatoj por tradukistaj postenoj mi ofte miris, ke homoj kun perfekta kono de ambaŭ lingvoj kaj impona scipovo pri la koncerna faktereno povas esti sufiĉe malkapablaj tradukantoj. Laŭ mi tradukisto devas posedi du esencajn kvalitojn kiujn doni al tradukmaŝinoj povas esti malfacile: juĝkapablon kaj flekseblecon.

Juĝkapablo necesas ĉefe en la formo de ampleksa scio pri la faktereno kaj konscio pri la ekzisto de komprenaj kaj tradukaj problemoj. Necesas krome kapabli rekoni, kiam aŭtoro interne de teksto el difinita faktereno subite uzas terminojn en signifo el alia tereno.

Fleksebleco ĉefe estas la nemalhavebla kapablo kvazaŭ gimnastike salti tien kaj reen inter la du universoj reprezentataj de la du lingvoj. Ekzemple en la angla terminoj ofte estas kunmetitaj el ĉiutagaj morfemoj, sen ke la sumo de iliaj signifoj donus ajnan indikon pri la signifo de la tuto. El tiaj kombinaĵoj malfacilas traduki ekzemple al la franca, kie similterenaj terminoj ofte konsistas el multe pli precizaj, sed kompense tre erudiciaj kaj maloftaj morfemoj.

Ofte necesas per scio pri la fako konjekti pri tio, kion vualas la manko de neambiguaj sintaksaj rilatiloj, ekz-e en anglaj esprimoj. Necesas ankaŭ bone koni la lingvouzon en la koncerna organizaĵo, kaj ne ĉiam eblas fidi, ke la aŭtoro de la teksto verkis aŭ eldiris ĝin en sia gepatra lingvo.

80 aŭ 90% de sia tempo profesia tradukisto pasigas per detektiva laboro: klopodante eltrovi ĉu iu priparolata industrio jam ekzistis aŭ ne, de kio povas dependi la traduko de develop *('starigi' aŭ 'kreskigi'), esplorante ĉu iu "sekretario" estas viro aŭ virino, de kio povas dependi la traduko de la profesiindiko samkiel la sintaksa formo de adjektivoj ktp., kaj serĉante bazajn informojn pri iuj industriaj aŭ medicinaj procesoj, kiuj estas subkomprenitaj en teksto direktita al fakuloj. Estus dezirinde ke la komputilo liberigu la tradukistojn de tiuj sklavotaskoj, sed kiel komputoscienca laiko mi tute ne povas imagi kiel ĝi tion faru.*

On Some Results of the Conference

Petr Sgall

Charles University
Department of Applied Mathematics
Malostranské nám 25
CS-118 00 Praha 1
Czechoslovakia

Although our short conference has witnessed no spectacular achievement in the Machine Translation research, it has clearly shown that MT keeps growing both in width and in depth. The variety of topics and approaches discussed at the meeting is characteristic of the new situation in the research, which displays more and more detailed analyses, subtly articulated systems, as well as more distinctions in methods and attitudes. This also facilitates a more articulated discussion.

1. Binary translation versus the intermediate language

One of the salient questions open for discussion concerns the difference between **binary** translation (with a transfer procedure, or direct) and that using an **intermediate** language. It was confirmed by Hutchins' contribution to this conference that an intermediary position is possible here, working with different variants of an intermediate language, namely with interface structures, each of which might be suitable for a group of closely cognate languages. This approach, based on the experience of the research by Vauquois, Boitet and others in G.E.T.A. and corroborated by that of Eurotra, does not substantially reduce the number of the necessary transfers, but reduces their complexity.

Speaking about the use of **Esperanto** (adapted) as an intermediate language, Schubert is correct (in his paper presented here) that this language is sufficiently expressive. Although it does not contain all technical terms of different domains, it contains an efficient system of word formation which makes it possible to add new terms and other lexical units whenever needed. Some of the arguments against the use of a single intermediate language, formulated by Boitet and others, perhaps are not generally valid: the difficulties concerning e.g. E. *wall* to be translated either by G. *Mauer* or *Wand*, or the boundaries of paraphrases, style, etc. (cf. also Tsujii's example of E. *Who is he?*, where the personal pronoun differs from its counterparts in Japanese and other languages) are only partly diminished in binary translation. A multilingual translation system in any case has to cope with the great number of lexical meanings, with more or less subtle stylistic differences, and so on.

It belongs to the urgent tasks to start a systematic linguistic inquiry into such discrepancies between languages. It is possible that its results will support the idea of multiple interface structures, especially if many cases of such structural differences are found as the dual number, a specific resultative tense (such as the English perfect), or another opposition which either gets lost in the intermediate language or burdens its structure without being relevant for most target languages.

Also Boitet's more subtle classification into source and target interface structure would then be useful. Conceptual systems for these structures do not yet really exist (in this respect Esperanto has a great advantage), but, as Harris recalled during the conference they should be discussed and developed. The representations of sentences in interface structures may well have the shape of multilevel labelled trees or of similar graphs (which, due to the interplay of coordination with other syntactic relations, perhaps should be theoretically characterized as having more than two dimensions, but for which such properties as projectivity make it possible to be more or less directly linearized).

In Tsujii's classification of approaches to intermediate language, the interface structures belong to systems specific for groups of language. While in natural language understanding it is necessary to proceed through linguistic (literal) meaning to the deeper layers of cognitive content (cf. the classical dichotomy known since De Saussure, Hjelmslev and Coseriu, and more recent approaches concerned with metaphor, inferencing, frames and scripts), the interface structures may come close to the disambiguated underlying structures (i.e. to the representations of literal meaning), in which individual languages differ much less than in their outer shapes.

Discussions on questions of intermediate languages still have much in common with those taking place at the beginning of the 1960's, when they were a source of hope that effective international cooperation would be feasible. However, no such concentration has been achieved, and MT research has remained scattered, the development of its methods being restricted by external obstacles. Only seldom was it possible to use a group's own longterm experience to an amendation of the methods used. Perhaps the single major exception can be seen in the research by G.E.T.A., which has been of major significance also for the work of other groups and deserves our full support.

2. The linguistic method

Issues of **linguistic method** have been discussed at our conference, first of all those concerning **syntax**. I am convinced that especially the attention devoted to **dependency** grammar is of crucial importance. This approach, based on the motion of valency (first systematically elaborated by Tesnière) and on the central position of the verb in the sentence, usually works with deep syntactic relations underlying those of surface subject, object, etc., i.e. with notions similar to Fillmore's deep cases or to the more recent $\bar{X}$ theory and theta grids, and makes the use of constituents superfluous. It seems that all the constituency based approaches miss an important generalization, since they connect the basic syntactic structure directly with word order, although the latter (corresponding more immediately to the topic-focus dichotomy) should not be preferred to prepositions, endings and other means expressing the syntactic structure. Constituency is perhaps the only idea Chomsky took over from Bloomfieldian linguistics, without checking for available alternatives.

In MT research, dependency always has been used (in some cases in a combination with constituency, in others without it), as is known from the writings of Nagao and others in Japan, from the werk of G.E.T.A., Eurotra, and now especially from the DLT project, initiated and carried out by Witkam, Schubert, Maxwell and others. In Prague, a dependency based parser for English was formulated by Kirschner (1982; 1988)[1], and a detailed elaboration of the linguistic issues of a dependency based description can be found in Sgall, Hajičová and Panevová (1986).

In accordance with what was stated in Weidmann's contribution, the dependency approach can be characterized as universally applicable, although the sentence structure itself is not fully identical in different languages (not even in its underlying layer). The main advantages of dependency syntax can be seen in the following three points:

(i) the trees or other graphs representing sentence structure are much more economical than P-markers or similar trees based on constituency (no non-terminal nodes are necessary in the dependency representations, also specific nodes corresponding to function words can be dispensed with);

(ii) dependency grammar can be formulated as fully lexically driven, i.e. containing few general rules or principles and many lexical valency frames or grids (now see also Schubert 1987);

(iii) all semantically relevant information gained from the sentence can be included in terminal representations of sentences.

Several arguments used against dependency syntax have been shown to be fallacious: initially the very equivalence of dependency grammars and of context-free phrase structure grammars in generative power was understood by some linguists as corroborating the view that dependency should not be studied, although this equivalence makes a linguistically qualified choice necessary; later, the equivalence was characterized as too weak, since it was not realized that according to the Prague School's definition dependency grammar is connected with no specific restrictions on nonterminal symbols in its derivations[2].

Although the differences between the approaches to syntax are important from the viewpoints of economy and modularity of systems of MT, it is in any case necessary to analyze and describe many questions of interlingual correspondences, including large amounts of idiosyncratic cases, so that – as Dong observed in his contribution – the basis of the syntactic framework is not always crucial for the quality of a MT system.

Also in what concerns **semantics**, several more or less recent approaches have been discussed during the conference. Semantics has been understood here first of all as concerning an interface between language structure and logic. In this sense, Sigurd presented some of the main features of his referent grammar; Kosaka's operator trees play a similar role. A specific level of the patterning of (linguistic, literary) meaning should be handled by means suitable also for agglutinative languages, the problems of which were characterized here by Prószéky, and for ergative languages. To this aim, it appears as necessary to use formal means that are neutral to the differences between function words, word other, affixes and alternations as expressing grammatical oppositions, and to work with kinds of complementation underlying the surface syntactic relations; furthermore, it is necessary to include the topic-focus articulation into the representation of the meaning of the sentence, as is done in the Prague School's tectogrammatical representations[3]. While in Japanese the functioning of certain sentence parts as parts of the topic is more or less directly rendered by the morpheme *wa* (their values as Actor, Addressee, Objective, Locative, etc., has to be determined by a more complex analysis), in most European languages the difference between topic and focus is only partially determined by a combination of word order, intonation patterns and other means. Since this difference is relevant for the scopes of negation and quantifiers, as well as for other semantico-pragmatic aspects of linguistic meaning, it is important for an adequate translation to transfer the topic-focus articulation of the source sentence to its target equivalent.

A level of linguistic meaning is also important as a basis for a division of labour between empirical linguistic research and intensional (Montaguian or other) semantics. It is then necessary to have criteria for determining linguistic meaning (one of them, concerning synonymy, was discussed in Chapter 1 of Sgall/Hajičová/Panevová 1986). One of the urgent problems concerning the choice or design of an intermediate language (perhaps with its variants, or dialects, i.e. interface structures) is the determination of the repertoire of semantico-pragmatic oppositions, categories and their values to be included in such a language. In any case, disambiguation (which in binary translation can be restricted to those cases in which the target language does not share the ambiguities of the source language) appears to be necessary for a multilingual translation system.

3. Human and artificial intelligence

Among the other parameters important for a classification and evaluation of MT systems, there is, first of all, the amount and kind of **human** activities required by the system. While post-editing appears to be necessary for most systems, also pre-editing (i.e. a controlled, standardized input language) was discussed here by Hutchins, and so was interaction in a kind of human-assisted translation, esp. by Schubert; also possibilities of interaction during editing, known from Melby, deserve further attention. It seems that the dichotomy of MT versus machine assisted translation will soon give place to a gamut of different kinds and degrees of interaction, including translator's working stations with text-editing systems and various lexical devices. Among the latter, the terminological data banks were characterized here by Galinski, who presented starting points for their classification and duly warned us against 'management by ignorance', which might have broader consequences. A specific type of lexical data bank was discussed in Blanke's account of the Terminological Esperanto Centre.

Furthermore, different kinds and degrees of methods of **artificial intelligence** as included in MT systems were discussed. The use of semantic markers in the lexicon and of small sets of rules of natural-language interfacing is generally accepted. More efficiency will be gained when large terminological data banks (see Galinski's paper), and perhaps also knowledge bases for specific domains (as discussed by Kosaka) are applied within MT systems.

Methods of AI are necessary for the patterning of the **discourse** in order to be appropriately handled in MT (see the papers by Hauenschild and by Tsujii); it might be added that understanding of discourse as a whole can only be achieved through a suitable analysis of the individual sentences, the description of which should be conceived in such a way as to characterize them also from the viewpoint of context (by means of their topic-focus articulation).

MT systems are either based on large **lexicons** or include detailed **grammatical** procedures. Some of the systems characterized here by Oubine, as well as the Systran systems, belong to the former kind; the latter kind is instantiated by most other systems (including such successful ones as Météo, and, in the Soviet Union, those by Kulagina and by Apresjan). While the former systems are aimed at quickly finding customers, the latter kind pursues the aim of a high-quality translation (although in most cases post-editing is understood as necessary). For an evaluation of the results of translation we need criteria, some aspects of which were analyzed here by Guzmán de Rojas.

4. Prospects

Learning from translation mistakes (which were amply illustrated by Piron) is one of the main sources of hope for the future of MT, especially if it can take place on a large scale, on the basis of functioning systems (with different kinds of human-machine interaction). Then only will it be possible to find out which kinds of mistakes reoccur so often that they have to be solved as thoroughly as possible at any price, even when this means to complicate the system heavily. Other mistakes perhaps will be so rare that an economical system might better tolerate them (e.g. leaving them to be amended by a post-editor). This standpoint may be interpreted as assuming that a practically applicable system of MT is a necessary condition to reach such a system. However, the circle perhaps is not quite complete, since:

(i) different degrees of practical success (and of necessary interaction) can be distinguished,

(ii) the less expensive hardware now available makes large-scale experiments feasible,

(iii) not only experience, but also more knowledge of what has already been found can be gained if researchers in MT pay more attention to the others' writings.

Moreover, if MT is not successful as a whole, then the Babylonian confusion of language ca still be overcome, if all of us learn Esperanto, which can be recommended in any case.

Notes

1. I would like to thank Dr. Kirschner for having helped me to collect the results of our conference as completely as was possible.

2. The recent form of the definition was presented by Petkevič (in press).

3. As for a computational procedure for determining topic and focus, see Hajičová and Sgall (1985).

References

Hajičová, Eva / Petr Sgall (1985): Towards an automatic identification of topic and focus. In: *Second conference of the European Chapter of the Association of Computational Linguistics* (Geneva 1985). s.l.: Association of Computational Linguistics, pp. 263-267

Kirschner, Zdeněk (1982): *A dependency-based analysis of English for the purpose of Machine Translation.* Prague: Faculty of Mathematics and Physics, Charles University.

Kirschner, Zdeněk (1987): *APAC 3-2: An English-to-Czech Machine Translation system.* Prague, Faculty of Mathematics and Physics, Charles University.

Schubert, Klaus (1987): *Metataxis.* Dordrecht/Providence: Foris Publications.

Sgall, Petr / Eva Hajičová / J. Panevová (1986): *The meaning of the sentence in its semantic and pragmatic aspects.* Dordrecht: Reidel / Prague: Academia.

Petr Sgall

Pri kelkaj rezultoj de la konferenco

Resumo

La faktereno perkomputila tradukado evoluis al pli grandaj larĝeco kaj profundeco. La konferenco traktis la jenajn esencajn temojn.

Vigle diskutita demando estas la alternativo inter lingvopara aŭ interlingva tradukado. Eblas ankaŭ kompromisaj solvoj, variantaj laŭ la speco de la interstrukturo. Malgraŭ la neceso pluevolui sur termina tereno, Esperanto havas la esprimivon bezonatan por roli kiel interlingvo. La argumentoj kontraŭ la uzo de unusola interlingvo kaj por lingvofamiliopaj interlingvoj estas parte malĝustaj. Necesas tamen pli profunda kontrasta lingvokomparado, kiu povos influi la strukturigon de interstrukturoj. La diskuto pri interlingvoj multe similas tiun de la 60-aj jaroj. La internacia kunlaboro, tiam esperata, ĝis nun ne vere ekestis.

Inter la pritraktitaj lingvistikaj metodoj menciindas dependogramatiko. Ĝi havas universalajn kvalitojn, longe malprave preterviditajn en perkomputila tradukado, kiuj igas ĝin supera al konsistogramatikaj modeloj. Dependosintakso disponigas facilan aliron al la necesa semantika informo. Sur la semantika tereno oni ĉefe atentis la interfacon de lingvostrukturo al logiko. Necesas solvoj uzeblaj por tre malsamtipaj lingvoj, inkluzive de aglutinaj kaj ergativaj. Ili uzu ankaŭ la frazdividon en temaon kaj remaon.

La kunagado de homo kaj komputilo estis plia debattemo. Malambiguiga dialogo, dumtraduka interago kaj aliaj solvoj estis traktitaj, kaj oni konsideris la implicojn de la uzado de grandskalaj terminaj informbankoj en perkomputila tradukado. Ĉi-rilate rolas ankaŭ artefarita inteligento kaj ĝia apliko kaj al vastaj temterenoj kaj la mallarĝaj lingvofrakcioj.

Tekstnivela analizo nepras por perkomputila tradukado, kaj ĝi prezentas interesan agadterenon por artefarita inteligento. Necesas konsideri frazojn el la vidpunkto de ilia funkciado en kohera teksto.

Tre utilas lerni el la eraroj farataj dum tradukado. La progreson de la fakterenoj ankaŭ multe stimulus pli vasta atento al la publikaĵoj pri la spertoj de aliaj. Kaj se ĉi ĉio ne helpas – ni ĉiuj lernu Esperanton, kion oni ja ĉiukaze povas rekomendi.

Index

The index contains persons, languages and subjects. The names of companies, institutes, machine translation systems etc. are normally not spelled out here, but given in an abbreviated form if this is the form commonly encountered in the text. Many of the abbreviations are explained in the article by Hutchins, especially on pp. 22-52. Names of subsequent versions of systems, that differ only in a number, an extension or the like have been subsumed under the same entry word. The names of universities have in most cases been reduced to the name of the place plus the abbreviation "U.", e.g., "Lund U.".

Bei Fragen zur Produktsicherheit wenden Sie sich bitte an:
If you have any questions regarding product safety,
please contact:

Walter de Gruyter GmbH
Genthiner Straße 13
10785 Berlin
productsafety@degruyterbrill.com